Case Studies
in Public Management
and Administration

James C. Simeon

Captus Press

Case Studies in Public Management and Administration
Copyright © 2009 James C. Simeon and Captus Press Inc.

Captus Press Inc.
Units 14 & 15, 1600 Steeles Avenue West,
Concord, Ontario   L4K 4M2
Telephone: (416) 736–5537
Fax: (416) 736–5793
Email: Info@captus.com
Internet: www.captus.com

Library and Archives Canada Cataloguing in Publication

Simeon, James C.
      Case studies in public management and
administration / James C. Simeon.

ISBN 978-1-55322-196-8

1. Public administration.   2. Public administration — Case studies.   I. Title.

JF1351.S485 2009   351   C2009-902732-1

Canada We acknowledge the financial support of the Government of Canada through the Book Publishing Industry Development Program (BPIDP) for our publishing activities.

0 9 8 7 6 5 4 3 2 1
Printed in Canada

Contents

Contents

Preface

This collection of original case studies in public management and administration is rooted in the firm belief that case studies and the case study method are among the most effective instructional tools and techniques for all those who aspire to become not only proficient but superior public sector managers and administrators. It is also premised on the notion that case studies and the case study method build and develop students' skills and abilities in problem identification, analysis and problem solving and resolution. They also develop students' capabilities in strategic and tactical planning and execution, among a number of other essential skills and abilities. For scholars, researchers, and instructors case studies provide unique perspectives and insights in the public policy process and public administration in action. Case studies demonstrate how individual choice and group decision-making, within the dynamic of the managerial and administrative institutional setting and formal and informal rules and procedures, can affect public policy issues and outcomes.

For those who are new to the field of public management and administration, case studies and the case study method provide students with a real sense of what it is like to be employed as a manager or administrator in a public sector organization, such as the municipal, provincial or federal governments and the vast array of organizations in the not-for-profit sector. For those who have many years of experience working in this field, case studies and the case study method provide an opportunity to acquire new skill sets and to further develop and refine their management and administrative skills and abilities.

The problems that confront managers and administrators on a routine basis cover the gamut from personnel and performance management, to budgeting and financial management, and from strategic planning and execution to program implementation and evaluation. The case studies presented here try to cover the wide range of difficulties and challenges that managers and administrators typically face and are expected to confront and handle with relative ease. From a public policy or public interest perspective, these case studies demonstrate some of the enormous challenges that public organizations and institutions face in the formulation, adoption and implementation of public policies and programs.

Furthermore, the case studies presented here are also intended and expected to be interesting as well as challenging for students, irrespective of their background and experience in public management and administration. The case studies have been created to be educative, in the best sense of the term, by illustrating various essential principles in public policy and public administration, such as, accountability, responsibility, economy, effectiveness and efficiency, equity, transparency, integrity, responsiveness, sustainability, productivity, innovation, leadership, team work, representativeness, justice, and others.

The effort that the student puts into analyzing and developing solutions to the case studies presented in this volume will pay significant dividends in furthering their understanding and appreciation of the challenges that confront managers and administrators and, thus, better enable and prepare them for the rigours of a career in the public sector.

It is our hope that students and instructors alike will enjoy working on the issues, problems and dilemmas presented in these case studies and applying the case study instructional method that is presented in the introductory chapter of this book that is intended to help find "optimal constructive public interest solutions" to answering the questions posed for each case study.

Acknowledgements

This volume would not have been possible without the encouragement and support of a number of people. First, I should like to thank all of my colleagues over the years in various levels of government and within the broader non-profit sector who are the true inspirations for each of these case studies. Second, I should like to acknowledge the contribution of three anonymous reviewers who took the time and care to read the draft manuscript and to offer their observations, comments and suggestions for how this volume could be improved. I have tried to incorporate as many of their constructive comments, ideas and suggestions as possible in this current volume. Third, I should like to thank my colleague Tom Klassen and all of the graduate students in the Masters of Public Policy, Administration and Law (MPPAL) program at York University, who took our course in Public Management in the 2008–2009 academic year and who worked with the "pilot edition" of this book. In essence, they tested many of the case studies in the present volume. I should also like to thank other colleagues in the MPPAL program who gave me their encouragement and constructive feedback on the "pilot edition" of this book. In particular, I would like to acknowledge Ian Greene, Director of the MPPAL Program, for his ongoing support for this project.

I would be remiss if I did not thank Ros Woodhouse, Director of the Centre for Support of Teaching (CST), at York University, for introducing me to the vast academic research literature on teaching and learning and for suggesting a number of sources that I have tried to include in the introduction for this book. The staff and other faculty associated with the CST have provided a highly positive and supportive environment for experimenting with how case studies and the case study method can be used more effectively as instructional and learning tools.

Finally, I should also like to acknowledge Captus Press Inc. for their interest in this volume and for their support and encouragement at various stages of this project. They were a pleasure to work with. I would, however, like to thank, in particular, Randy Hoffman and, especially, Jason Wormald, for their advice and guidance on the production of this volume.

James C. Simeon, Assistant Professor
School of Public Policy and Administration
Atkinson Faculty of Liberal and Professional Studies,
Centre for Refugee Studies (CRS),
Faculty Associate, Centre for Support of Teaching (CST)
York University, Toronto, Canada
March 2009

Introduction

This book offers 30 original case studies in public management and administration that can be used as a basic text in college and university courses in public management and public administration. The case studies are also useful for in-house training and professional development programs for both new and experienced public sector managers, whether within government or not-for-profit organizations.

The case studies presented here are drawn from my many years of experience working in government, at both the federal and provincial levels, and the not-for-profit sector. The cases cover a broad range of issues that public sector managers and administrators often address in the workplace.

Like any profession, public management and administration requires initial training and ongoing professional development. Indeed, proficiency in any field or profession demands the acquisition of knowledge; learning a specialized set of skills; staying abreast of the latest innovations, discoveries, and developments in the field; and continuous practice. Like any other professional practice, public management and administration requires the continuous acquisition of specialized skills and abilities and ongoing professional development. Accordingly, the skills and abilities necessary to excel in public management and administration are acquired through dedicated effort and commitment over many years of study and practice. Typically, this is done through formal study in an institutional educational setting, learning "on-the-job" in a management and/or an administrative position in the public sector workplace, through personal reflection, self-assessment, and examination, or any combination of any of the above.

A number of years ago, Honeywell studied how its senior managers learned. They found that "managers learn to manage based on 50 percent on-[the-]job experience, 30 percent relationships, and 20 percent from formal training."[1] It is interesting to note that the Honeywell corporation found that only 20 percent of what the managers learned about management came from formal training and that 80 percent of what they learned about management came from other sources — principally, learning on-the-job.

A common maxim in management is that it is a skill that is best learned by doing. Generally, the traditional instructional methods of lecture, seminar, and tutorials do little to prepare public management and administration students for real-life management challenges. Junior managers in an organization can sometimes rely on their senior colleagues for guidance and advice. However, this may not always be possible or feasible. Even though managers will gain all the experience necessary from on-the-job training, learning by trial and error could prove to be disastrous for both the manager and the organization where they are employed. This explains, at least to some extent, why the case study method has emerged as the foremost viable instructional alternative for giving students an opportunity to develop their management and administration skills. In essence, the case study method provides the public management and administration student with an opportunity to explore real-life public management and administration issues in a risk-free, hands-on instructional setting.

Irrespective of the teaching and learning setting, case studies and the case study method are among the chief instructional tools employed for management and administrative training in the both the public and the private sector.

Many experts have expounded the value of case studies and the case study method for public management and administration education. For instance, Lloyd Brown-John has observed the ubiquity of the case study method in teaching public management and administration[2] and Sanford F. Borins has pointed out the value of case studies and the case study method for public management education and professional development.[3]

Common sense dedicates that for genuine learning to take place, the student must be engaged actively in the learning process. It follows that the

---

[1] Jacques Bourgault and Donald J. Savoie, "Managing at the Top," in *Governance in the Twenty-First Century: Revitalizing the Public Service*, eds. B. Guy Peters and Donald J. Savoie (Montreal & Kingston: McGill-Queen's University Press, 2000), p. 376.

[2] C. Lloyd Brown-John, "Book Review: Public Management and Administration: Case-Study Resource Book," by Petrus Brynard and Kallic Erasmus, van Schaik, Pretoria, 1995, *Public Administration and Development*, 17:5 (December 1997), p. 546.

[3] Sanford F. Borins, "Simulation, the case method, and case studies: their role in public management teaching and research," *Canadian Public Administration*, 33:2 (Summer 1990), pp. 214–228.

more engaged the student is in the learning process, the more learning will likely take place. Jo Barraket has argued that "constructivist understandings for the way in which knowledge is produced is that students are the key initiators and architects of their own learning and knowledge-making, rather than passive 'vessels' who receive the transmission of knowledge from 'expert' teachers."[4]

The case study method, by its very nature, is premised on an "active learning" approach. It demands the student's participation in the learning process. At the very core of any case study is the problem, difficulty or issue that the student must try to resolve and to find an appropriate, if not, optimal solution. Problem solving requires the use of higher-level skills, such as critical and creative thinking.[5] One of the principal values of case studies and the case study method of teaching is, then, that it requires students to practice and develop their higher-level thinking skills, that some have termed, "effective thinking."

When used properly and effectively, case studies can be a powerful way of engaging students in the learning process. Case studies have the potential to stimulate the student to reflect on their own experiences. Consequently, the case study method can become a truly "experiential learning system."

Defining Terms: Case Studies and the Case Study Method

It is always important to start with a clear definition of the key terms. One must be clear, of course, on what is meant by the terms "case study" and the "case study method" of instruction.

Broadly and simply defined, a case study is a description of a situation in which one or more persons made, influenced, or implemented a deci-

---

[4] J. Barraket, (2005) "Teaching Research Methods Using a Student-Centred Approach? Critical Reflections on Practice," in *Journal of University Teaching and Learning in Practice* Vol 2 (2), 65.

[5] This point has been made by many researchers, including, W. Gary Howard, who states: "The Socratic Method has impacted thinkers and instructors from Hegel, who moved through the negation to the negation of the negation, to Marx, who viewed history through dialectical materialism, to C.C. Langdell, who introduced case law as an innovative method to study law as a science, to present-day professors who use this method to compel students to distinguish the *ratio decidend* (rule of law) from *obiter dicta* (incidental comments) and defend their reasoning. As with Socrates, there is no single path in the development of ideas; the process is what is critical. In many disciplines today the Socratic Method of instruction continues to be a dominant method for developing critical thinking skills." See W. Gary Howard, "Socrates and Technology a New Millennium Conversation," *International Journal of Instructional Media*, 33 (2), (Spring, 2006), p. 197.

sion.[6] Marie Bittner has defined a case study as "a realistic application or demonstration of a theory or principle."[7] Josephine Ruggiero states that cases are "short, realistic, action-oriented, story-like accounts ... designed to raise issues" (Hutchings 1993, p. 14). The actor, or actors, in the case face a problem or conflict which requires a solution."[8]

H.J. Maltby and M.A. Andrusyszyn state that a "case is a description of a specific situation, incident, or issue which requires resolution. It puts the student in the position of the decision-maker."[9] They further point out, quoting M.C. Baetz and P.W. Beamish, that the purpose of a case study is

> not to learn authoritative answers to specific problems but to become skilled in the process of designing workable action plans through evaluation of the prevailing circumstances.[10]

The Association for Case Teaching defines the case study method as "a means of participatory and dialogical teaching and learning by group discussion of actual events."[11] This definition can include written cases, video cases, interactive cases, simulations, games, and field trips. It is important to stress that the case study method of teaching is participatory, discussion-focused, and uses actual events to illustrate general principles.[12] Indeed, one of the chief values of the case study method is that it uses real or hypothetical situations, circumstances, and problems to help students understand and practice resolving public management and administration issues, problems and situations. In the process, it also assists the student to become familiar with different approaches to decision-making.

Josephine Ruggiero notes that "cases can be used to *engage* students in active learning about the complexities of relationships, about the various di-

---

[6] Kenneth Kernaghan, *Canadian Cases in Public Administration*, (Toronto: Methuen Publications, 1977), p. 3.

[7] Marie Bittner, "The IRAC Method of Case Study Analysis: A Legal Model for the Social Studies," *The Social Studies*, Vol. 81, No.: 5, (Sept./Oct., 1990), p. 228.

[8] Josephine A. Ruggiero, "'Ah Ha' Learning: Using Cases and Case Studies to Teach Sociological Insights and Skills," *Sociological Practice: A Journal of Clinical and Applied Sociology*, Vol. 4, No. 2, (June 2002), p. 115.

[9] Hendricka. J. Maltby and Mary Anne Andrusyszyn, "The case study approach of teaching decision-making to post-diploma nurses," *Nurse Education Today*, (1990), 10, p. 416.

[10] Ibid. (As found in M. C. Baetz and P. W. Beamish, *Strategic Management: Canadian Cases*. Illinois: Irwin, 1987, p. 16.)

[11] David Dunne and Kim Brooks, *Teaching With Cases*, Green Guide No. 5, Society for Teaching and Higher Education, (Halifax, Nova Scotia: Dalhousie University Bookstore, 2004), p. 9.

[12] Yong S. Lee in "Public Management and Case Study Methods," *Teaching Political Science*, Vol. 11, No.: 1, (Fall, 1983), points out that, "In political science and public administration, the term *case study* generally has been associated with the study of a case or a group of cases contributing to empirical generalizations. Philip Selznick's *TVA and the Grassroots* (1949), Harold Stein's *Public Administration and Policy Development* (1952), and Edwin Bock's *Government Regulation of Business: A Case Book* (1965) represent the early examples of theory-oriented case studies." (p. 6)

mensions of a social situation, and about the diverse social, cultural, and other factors which may affect decision making."[13]

Kenneth Kernaghan elaborates further by pointing out that, "In combination with lectures and assigned readings, case study discussions can greatly enhance the understanding of public administration by enabling students to relate theory to practice and the abstract to the concrete."[14] He further notes that, "Case research involves both a type of literature (a case) and a pedagogical technique (the case method)."[15]

As a pedagogical technique, the case study method can be distinguished from such other teaching methods such as lectures, seminars, workshops, role-plays, programmed instruction, simulations, and so on.[16] Philip Camill argues that, "Together with lectures and labs, case studies assist students in acquiring content knowledge, process skills, and an understanding of the context and application of science to their daily lives."[17] What is stressed in the academic literature is that case studies and the case study method are valuable instructional methods in a teacher's pedagogical arsenal. The use of the case study method of instruction is considered most valuable when combined with other teaching methods.

The Prevalent Method of Instruction in the Professions

As noted, the predominant method of professional instruction in North America is the use of case studies and the case study method. "All professional schools," D.A. Gravin states, "face the same difficult challenge: how to prepare students for the world of practice. Time in the classroom must somehow translate directly into real-world activity: how to diagnose, decide, and act."[18]

> It is generally known that lawyers, physicians and managers rely on past cases in doing their work. When these practitioners review legal, medical or corporate cases it is primarily to search for precedents. Future practice

---

[13] Josephine A. Ruggiero, "'Ah Ha' Learning: Using Cases and Case Studies to Teach Sociological Insights and Skills," *Sociological Practice: A Journal of Clinical and Applied Sociology,* Vol. 4, No. 2, (June 2002), p. 115.

[14] Kenneth Kernaghan, *Canadian Cases in Public Administration,* (Toronto: Methuen Publications, 1977), p. 3.

[15] Ibid. To complicate matters even further, it is important to note that the terms "case study" and "case study method" are also used to describe a particular type of research methodology. See, for instance, Sue Dopson, "The potential of the case study method for organisational analysis," *Policy & Politics,* Vol. 31, No.: 2, 2003, pp. 217–226.

[16] Ibid., p. 5.

[17] Philip Camill, "Case Studies Add Value to a Diverse Teaching Portfolio in Science Courses," *Journal of College Science Teaching,* Vol. 36, No.: 2 (October 2006), p. 31.

[18] D. A. Garvin, "Making the Case: Professional Education in the World of Practice," *Harvard Magazine,* 106, Sept.–Oct. 1, (2003), p. 1.

is informed by a history of prior practice. It is widely acknowledged, within academe, that the case study method is essential for teaching lawyers, physicians and executives' professional analytical and diagnostic skills.[19]

Paul C. Cline and P. Tony Graham have emphasized this same point with respect to the legal profession.

> Traditionally, attorneys have used the case study method in both the study and the practice of law. They have found this approach to be the most relevant and practical means for practising their profession. The case study method consists of tracing decisions of the courts on the point of controversy.[20]

Josephine Ruggiero not only underscores this central point for the traditional professional fields but also broadens it to encompass other scholarly disciplines and professions, including, education.

> Cases are commonly used as a *central instructional method* in many other fields including education, administration, social work, medicine, nursing, and engineering (*Nilson* 1998; *Silverman and Welty* 1995). Miller (1987) adds law to this list. Nilson (1998, p. 120) also points out that cases have been used in teaching pastoral studies, engineering, philosophy (e.g., ethics courses), music history, biology, chemistry, and ecology.[21]

Case studies and the case method are not only widely accepted as a basic instructional tool for teaching, but also the predominant teaching and learning technique used across the professions and scholarly disciplines.[22]

Learning Theories Underlying Case Studies and the Case Study Method

Educational theorist John Dewey is quoted as stating that "...education is not an affair of 'telling' and being told, but an active and constructive pro-

---

[19] Joyce Huth Monro, "Mastering the Case Method," *Innovations in Education and Training International*, Vol. 34, No.: 2 (May, 1997), p. 84.

[20] Paul C. Cline and P. Tony Graham, "The Case Study Method: An Inquiry Approach for Law-Related Education," *The Social Studies*, Vol. 68, No.: 1, (Jan./Feb., 1977), p. 20.

[21] Josephine A. Ruggiero, "'Ah Ha' Learning: Using Cases and Case Studies to Teach Sociological Insights and Skills," *Sociological Practice: A Journal of Clinical and Applied Sociology*, Vol. 4, No. 2, (June 2002), p. 116.

[22] For the application of case studies for teaching science at the college level, see Katayoun Chamany, "Science and Social Justice: Making the Case for Case Studies," *Journal of College Science Teaching*, Vol. 36, No.: 2, (October 2006), pp. 54–59 and Herreid, Clyde Freeman, "Using Case Studies in Science — And Still Covering the Content," in Michaelsen, Larry K., Bauman Knight, Arletta, Dee Fink, L., eds., *Team-Based Learning: A Transformative Use of Small Groups in College Teaching*, (Sterling, VA: Stylus Publishing, LLC, 2002), pp. 105–114. For the application of the case study method to engineering see James E. Brady and Theodore T. Allen, "Case Study Based Instruction of DOE and SPC," *The American Statistician*, Vol. 56, No.: 4 (Nov. 2002), pp. 312–315.

cess" that requires "direct and continuous occupation with things."[23] However, if these "occupation with things" or experiences are to become "educational," the individual must have an opportunity to reflect on the experiences in order to transform them into knowledge. In fact, learning has been described as "the reconstruction of experience through critical reflection."[24]

It has often been noted that students do not learn by simply sitting in class listening to teachers or by memorizing prepackaged assignments and providing set responses to questions. For learning actually to take place, it is argued, students must talk about what they are learning, write about it, relate it to past experiences, and apply it to their daily lives.

The learning process can be guided, coached, and modelled by a teacher, but it is only through the involvement and active participation of the student that learning can actually take place. Case studies and the case study method are vehicles to ensure that students are engaged actively in their own learning. It follows, then, that "the greater the student's involvement [in their own learning] the more profound the learning."[25]

Teaching with case studies also allows students to learn analytical and judgmental skills. Benjamin Bloom has classified six educational goals: knowledge; comprehension; application; analysis; synthesis; and, evaluation.[26] Cases studies emphasize the analysis of information presented and the application of theories to real-world events. Students are expected to conduct their analyses of the facts and draw conclusions (synthesis), as well as to weigh the totality of the evidence and make choices (evaluation).[27]

The case study method is also acknowledged, generally, as an "active learning" approach. Beverly Cameron states that, "Active learning comprises many ideas, but basically it requires that students *participate* in the learning process. Active learning asks that students *use* content knowledge, not just acquire it."[28] When students analyze a case study they are attempting, in effect, to diagnose the problem, decide on an appropriate remedy, and prescribe a particular course of action to resolve the concern, difficulty or problem. In the process of learning, the student is being taught how to be a sound decision-maker and an effective problem solver.

---

[23] David Dunne and Kim Brooks, *Teaching With Cases*, Green Guide No. 5, Society for Teaching and Higher Education, (Halifax, Nova Scotia: Dalhousie University Bookstore, 2004), p. 33.

[24] Carolin Kerber, "Learning experientially through case studies? A conceptual analysis," *Teaching in Higher Education*, Vol. 6 (2), (2001) p. 218.

[25] Ibid., p. 217.

[26] Benjamin Bloom and the Taxonomy of Learning, http://oaks.nvg.org/taxonomy-bloom.html [Accessed June 12, 2009.]

[27] David Dunne and Kim Brooks, *Teaching With Cases,* Green Guide No. 5, Society for Teaching and Higher Education, (Halifax, Nova Scotia: Dalhousie University Bookstore, 2004), p. 35.

[28] Beverly J. Cameron, *Active Learning*, Green Guide No. 2, Society for Teaching and Learning in Higher Education, (Halifax: Dalhousie University Bookstore, 1999), p. 9.

Problem solving has been defined as the process that requires a person "to define or describe a problem, determine the desired outcome, select possible solutions, choose strategies, test trial solutions, evaluate the outcome, and revise these steps where necessary."[29]

It has also been argued that cases studies "challenge the learner and promote the development of insight and knowledge in a realistic situation"[30] and that they "encourage self growth through an understanding of personal value systems, feelings and perceptions, and their effect on the decision making process."[31]

Some researchers have included problem solving or decision making as part of the definition of effective thinking.[32] The very purpose of education, it has been said, is to teach a person to think. It follows, then, that in order to be an effective thinker one must be a proficient problem solver. Case studies provide opportunities for students to practice different problem solving and decision-making techniques. By their very nature, of course, case studies compel the student to be involved actively in his or her own learning process, something that, as already noted, is essential for learning to take place.[33]

This is precisely what case studies and the case study method offer the student as an instructional technique. It is a method of learning that promotes effective, whether critical or creative, thinking.

Creative thinking has been described as involving a combination of processes, including: problem finding, idea generation, planning, and preparation. The difference between critical and creative thinking has been summarized in the following way: "The creative aspect allows us to generate new ideas, possibilities, and options. The critical aspect allows us to try out, test, and evaluate these products."[34] Both creative and critical thinking are essential elements in the case study method of learning.

When students analyze a case, they define problems, clarify issues, weigh alternatives, and choose a course of action. These abilities comprise critical reflection. They require students to use strategic knowledge and theoretical knowledge in dissecting and reassembling a case.[35] In essence, the student is required to think critically and creatively in order to solve the problem(s) at the core of the case study.

---

[29] Ibid., p. 10.

[30] Hendrika J. Maltby and Mary Anne Andrusyszyn, "The case study approach of teaching decision-making to post-diploma nurses," *Nurse Education Today*, (1990), 10, p. 416. (As found in M. D. Beckman, D. L. Kurtz, L. E. Boone, *Foundations of Marketing, 4th Edition*. Toronto: Holt, Rinehart and Winston, 1987.)

[31] Ibid. (As found in I. B. Marquis and C. J. Huston, *Management Decision Making for Nurses: 101 Case Studies*. Philadelphia: Lippincott, 1987.)

[32] Beverly J. Cameron, *Active Learning*, Green Guide No. 2, Society for Teaching and Learning in Higher Education, (Halifax: Dalhousie University Bookstore, 1999), p. 10.

[33] Ibid., p. 9.

[34] Ibid., p. 11.

[35] Joyce Huth Monro, "Mastering the Case Method," *Innovations in Education and Training International*, Vol. 34, No.: 2, May, 1997, p. 89.

The Value of Case Studies and the Case Study Method as Pedagogical Tools

Case studies require students to become active learners and to develop discipline-specific skills. Moreover, case studies foster the student's ability to work effectively with others and to instill the confidence to think critically and to articulate their views.[36]

For law related education, Paul C. Cline and P. Tony Graham, state that,

> [a] beneficial by-product of briefing cases is the development of the ability to see the central issue in a complex situation and apply the relevant facts and principles in order to arrive at a solution.[37]

Case studies in public management and administration are a form of experiential learning where students are encouraged to play the role of a manager facing a challenging decision. They call for *inductive reasoning* in that their purpose is to derive general principles from a specific situation.[38]

Case studies can allow students to see how managerial and administrative concepts can be applied to public sector situations, and to evaluate the practical usefulness of these concepts.[39]

As already noted, cases studies can be a powerful way of engaging students. Because case studies are often based on real-world incidents or problems, they appeal to the practical focus of most public management and administration students. In addition, the process of solving a problem by placing oneself in a decision-maker's shoes can be much more engaging than an abstract lecture.[40]

If cases studies can be used to stimulate learners to reflect on their own experiences, and to become more effective in their independent learning, then the approach can be very powerful.[41]

The case study method also draws heavily on the findings of modern cognitive science: learning and retention improve markedly when students are motivated, when prior knowledge is activated by specific cues, and when new knowledge is linked to a specific context.[42]

Yong S. Lee points out that the case study method of instruction,

---

[36] David Dunne and Kim Brooks, *Teaching With Cases*, Green Guide No. 5, Society for Teaching and Higher Education, (Halifax, Nova Scotia: Dalhousie University Bookstore, 2004), p. 9.

[37] Paul C. Cline and P. Tony Graham, "The Case Study Method: An Inquiry Approach for Law-Related Education," *The Social Studies*, Vol. 68, No.: 1, (Jan./Feb., 1977), p. 21.

[38] David Dunne and Kim Brooks, *Teaching With Cases*, Green Guide No. 5, Society for Teaching and Higher Education, (Halifax, Nova Scotia: Dalhousie University Bookstore, 2004), p. 16.

[39] Ibid., p. 17.

[40] Ibid.

[41] Ibid., p. 33.

[42] D. A. Garvin, "Making the Case: Professional Education in the World of Practice," *Harvard Magazine*, 106, Sept.–Oct. 1, (2003), p. 13.

> ... offers several learning opportunities that are not usually tapped in traditional classroom instruction: (1) the opportunity to force the student to relate the textbook principles to a concrete situation and to make a *practical judgment*; (2) the opportunity to foster a kind of practical, analytical capability that is required in job situations; and (3) the opportunity to increase the student's "vocabulary of experience."[43]

R.J. Spiro and L.S. Shulman argue the same point when they state that the best way to learn the wisdom of practice and to develop cognitive flexibility is through experience with a variety of case studies.[44]

Comparative research studies have shown that students who had taken a case study class demonstrated a greater ability to apply concepts than students who had taken lecture classes.[45] In one study that followed a pre-test post-test design with a group of engineering students, who were randomly assigned to one of two instructional approaches, either the case method or the traditional lecture, found that the case study method enhanced certain cognitive processes such as problem-solving and critical thinking, as well as organizational skills and peer learning.[46]

Josephine Ruggiero argues that,

> [u]sing cases as a teaching-learning tool produces positive learning outcomes. Although much of the evidence on which this conclusion is based appears to be anecdotal, Williams *et al.* (1995, p. 411) report obtaining evidence of both a qualitative and a quantitative nature in support of the conclusion that using cases produced successful results in their classes. Their qualitative indicators included informal comments from students about their higher level of interest, sustained attention, and enthusiasm.[47]

James E. Brady and Theodore T. Allen have reported that students' end-of-quarter evaluations increased when the case study method was implemented in their statistics and engineering courses. They further note that the students "seem to identify with the case study 'stories' much better than the traditional lectures."[48]

[43] Yong S. Lee, "Public Management and Case Study Methods," *Teaching Political Science*, Vol. 11, No.: 1, (Fall, 1983), p. 7.

[44] David M. Irby, "Three Exemplary Models of Case-Based Teaching," *Academic Medicine*, Vol. 69, No.: 12, December 1994, p. 947. (See R. J. Spiro, et al. "Knowledge Acquisition for Application: Cognitive Flexibility and Transfer in Complex Content Domains," in *Executive Control Processes*. B. C. Britton, and S. Glynn, eds. (Hillsdale, New Jersey: Erlbaum, 1987), pp. 177–200, and L. S. Shulman, "Toward a Pedagogy of Cases," in *Case Methods in Teacher Education*, J. H. Shulman, ed., (New York: Teachers College Press, 1992), pp. 1–30.)

[45] Watson, C. E. (1975) "The case-study method and learning effectiveness," *College Student Journal*, Vol. 9 (2), pp. 109–116.

[46] G. Halpin, J. Good, P.K. Raju, & C. Sankar, C. (2000) "Creative methods to evaluate case study instruction: Can problem-solving skills be measured?" paper presented at the meeting of the American Educational Research Association (AERA), New Orleans, LA, 24 April.

[47] Josephine A. Ruggiero, "'Ah Ha' Learning: Using Cases and Case Studies to Teach Sociological Insights and Skills," *Sociological Practice: A Journal of Clinical and Applied Sociology*, Vol. 4, No. 2, (June 2002), p. 117.

[48] James E. Brady and Theodore T. Allen, "Case Study Based Instruction of DOE and SPC," *The American Statistician*, Vol. 56, No.: 4 (Nov. 2002), p. 315.

The use of the case study method in post-secondary teaching, if appropriately facilitated, involves students in genuine experiential learning, which fosters logical reasoning as well as creative thinking, and ultimately greater self-direction in learning.[49] It also has been noted frequently that the ability to self-direct one's life and learning is to recognize an important pre-requisite for lifelong education.[50]

D.R. Garrison discusses the important link between critical thinking and self-directed learning, arguing that insight and intuition are part of critical thinking, which is needed for self-directed learning to take place. This idea is shared also by S. Brookfield, who considers the ability to envision alternatives, which is a key feature of creativity, to be an essential component of critical thinking.[51]

In summary, in order to solve a case study, students have to use their logical reasoning skills as well as their intuitive and creative skills. Furthermore, in analyzing the case study they transform their experience, by means of both internal reflection and active experimentation. Moreover, case studies and the case study method have been found to be an effective way to engage students in active and experiential learning.[52]

The pedagogy of the case study method is "active learning" at its best. It teaches key concepts in more lively and active ways.[53] Carol Chetkovich and David L. Kirp make the point that the "pedagogical argument for the case method as a teaching strategy is straightforward and persuasive: It grounds teaching in real situations characterized by complexity and ambiguity, it links analysis and action, and it engages the students, requiring their active participation in the learning process."[54]

H.J. Maltby and M.A. Andrusyszyn further add that because of the active role that students must take in the learning process it is "expected that students will transfer the process of decision-making from case studies to clinical practice with greater ease than if they had received the information solely in lecture format."[55]

---

[49] Ibid.

[50] Carolin Kerber, "Learning experientially through case studies? A conceptual analysis," *Teaching in Higher Education*, Vol. 6 (2), (2001) p. 225.

[51] Ibid. (See Garrison, D. R. (1992) "Critical thinking and self-directed learning in adult education: an analysis of responsibility and control issues," *Adult Education Quarterly*, 42, pp. 136–148 and Garrison, D. R. (1997) "Self-directed learning: toward a comprehensive model," *Adult Education Quarterly*, Vol. 48 (1), pp. 18–34, and Brookfield, S. (1987) *Developing Critical Thinkers*. San Francisco, CA, Jossey-Bass and Brookfield, S. (1995) *Becoming a Critically Reflective Teacher*. (San Francisco, CA, Jossey-Bass.)

[52] Ibid., p. 224.

[53] Ibid.

[54] Carol Chetkovich and David L. Kirp, "Cases and controversies: How novitiates are trained to be masters of the public policy universe," *Journal of Policy Analysis and Management*, Vol. 20, No.: 2, (Spring, 2001), p. 284.

[55] Hendrika J. Maltby and Mary Anne Andrusyszyn, "The case study approach of teaching decision-making to post-diploma nurses," *Nurse Education Today*, (1990), 10, p. 418. (As found

Analyzing Case Studies

Good cases studies have been described as "just plain interesting."[56] It has been noted that a good case study should not only be genuinely interesting but also "pertinent, be somewhat controversial or at least be open to a difference of opinion, and present events and objective facts from several members of the group."[57] Further, the students analyzing a case study, it is emphasized, should not be given more information than what the person in the situation actually had when the incident or event took place.

A.R. Dooley and W. Skinner have observed that there is a significant variation in the use of the case method by instructors. They state that this indicates that there is "almost an infinite array of alternative approaches to utilizing this method of instruction."[58] Indeed, it has been said that there is no single "case study method," even within disciplines; different instructors use case studies in different ways.[59]

For instance, the case method has been employed to frame conversations between mentors and novices, as stimulants to reflection, as techniques to enrich field experiences, as tools for professional evaluation, or to orient individuals to particular ways of thinking. Case methods have been used for small and large group discussions, role playing exercises, written analysis, or in group or team based discussions.[60]

Essentially, the task of the student who is analyzing a case study is to identify the underlying problem and its symptoms and causes, and then to consider alternative remedies and solutions. The ultimate task is to use one's theoretical knowledge in the field and apply it to the "real life" situation and by doing so, hopefully, find the optimal solution for the identified difficulties, problems or issues.[61]

R. Knoop developed what he has called a "pragmatic problem-solving model" that students can use when analyzing case studies. R. Knoop contends that his model provides the needed guidance and direction for groups of students or learners to be able to work effectively with case studies.

---

in J. Johnson and J. Purvis, "Case Studies: An Alternative Learning/Teaching Method in Nursing," *Journal of Nursing Education*, 26, (1987), pp. 118–120.)

[56] P. Hutchings, *Using Cases To Improve College Teaching: A Guide to More Reflective Practice.* (Washington, D.C.: American Association of Higher Education, 1993), p. 4.

[57] Ernest W. Brewer, *13 Proven Ways to Get Your Message Across: The Essential Reference for Teachers, Trainers, Presenters, and Speakers.* (Thousand Oaks, California: Corwin Press Inc., 1997), p. 43.

[58] R. Dooley and W. Skinner, "Casing casemethod methods," *The Academy of Management Review*, Vol. 2, (2), (1997), p. 277.

[59] David Dunne and Kim Brooks, *Teaching With Cases*, Green Guide No. 5, Society for Teaching and Higher Education, (Halifax, Nova Scotia: Dalhousie University Bookstore, 2004), p. 9.

[60] Katherine K. Merseth, "Cases, Case Methods, and the Professional Development of Educators," *ERIC Digests*, ED401272, ERIC Clearinghouse on Teaching and Teacher Education, Washington, D.C., 1994-11-00, pp. 1–2.

[61] Carolin Kerber, "Learning experientially through case studies? A conceptual analysis," *Teaching in Higher Education*, 2001, 6 (2), p. 222. (See R. Knoop. (1984) *Case Studies in Education.* (St Catharines, Ont., Praise Publishing.)

R. Knoop's model distinguishes five steps:

Step 1:   Identifying the problem.
Step 2:   Distinguishing the problem from its underlying causes and overt symptoms.
Step 3:   Generating alternative problem-solving strategies.
Step 4:   Evaluating each alternative; selecting the best strategy.
Step 5:   Developing a plan for implementing the preferred strategy.[62]

Students should follow these five steps when analyzing case studies.[63] To maximize the learning experience with case studies, instructors should divide their classes into study groups or teams. The study groups or teams should meet to analyze the assigned case studies prior to their class.

It is important to underscore the value of establishing study groups or teams to enhance student learning. For instance, Katie Coulthard points out that,

> Studies reveal that students who work in small groups tend to learn more of what is being taught, retain it longer and are more satisfied with their courses than when they cover the same content in other instructional formats.[64]

Those who have used study groups or teams have found that it not only improves students' grades but also has a positive social benefit by increasing students' sense of community. For example, Femida Handy conducted an experiment on the use of small working groups in two half courses she taught on mathematics methods for economists. She found that the class that worked in small groups had better grades than the class that used the traditional lecture format. In addition, Femida Handy found that students who worked in the small groups enjoyed, overwhelmingly, the experience that the increased social interaction provided by the small breakout groups.[65]

There is a real value in using study groups or teams when using the case study method of instruction. Instructors are encouraged to break-up

---

[62] Ibid., p. 222-223.

[63] Marie Bittner has advocated the IRAC method for analyzing case studies. IRAC is the acronym for Issues, Rule, Analysis, and Conclusion. See Marie Bittner, "The IRAC Method of Case Study Analysis: A Legal Model for the Social Studies," *The Social Studies*, Vol. 81, No.: 5, (Sept./Oct., 1990), pp. 227–230. Marie Bittner advocates the use of the IRAC method, at least in part, because it provides students with a "frame of reference when dealing with a particular issue" (p. 230). Her general point about the need to provide students with guidance and a "frame of reference" for analyzing case studies needs to be emphasized.

[64] Katie Coulthard, "Study Group Guide for Instructors and Teaching Assistants," in Janice Newton, Jerry Ginsburg, Jan Rehner, Pat Rogers, Susan Sbrizzi, and John Spencer, eds. *Voices from the Classroom: Reflections on Teaching and Learning in Higher Education*, (Toronto: Centre for Support of Teaching, York University, and Garamond Press, 2001), p. 215.

[65] Femida Handy, "Small is Beautiful: Using Small Groups to Enhance Student Learning," in Janice Newton, Jerry Ginsburg, Jan Rehner, Pat Rogers, Susan Sbrizzi, and John Spencer, *Voices from the Classroom: Reflections on Teaching and Learning in Higher Education*, (Toronto: Centre for Support of Teaching, York University, and Garamond Press, 2001), pp. 227–230.

their classes in to study groups or teams of no more than six students.[66] It is also suggested that the study groups or teams be formed randomly, because it avoids the bias of friends getting together, which is unlikely to form a disciplined or rigorous group as a consequence, or the best students getting together, which leaves poor groups who struggle.[67] Ideally, these study groups or teams will meet on a regular basis to analyze and to discuss the weekly case study assignment.

When the class meets to discuss the assigned cases the members of each of the study groups or teams should be ready to participate in the general class discussion that will be led and facilitated by the instructor. The instructor will then call on individuals and the respective study groups or teams to provide their solution(s) to the assigned case study. The instructor will also lead the class discussion through an analysis of the case study by following Knoop's "pragmatic problem-solving model" and each of its five steps in analyzing the case study.

By utilizing this model, students will have had an opportunity to analyze the case study on an individual basis, within their study group or team, and on a class basis. The opportunity to analyze the case study at these three inter-related levels will not only enhance the student's learning experience but also reinforce it.

In following this five-step framework of analysis, inherent in the "pragmatic problem solving model," it is suggested that the students should first take the time to read the case study several times in an "undirected" manner. At this point, students should not be thinking about the questions that are being asked or the method of analysis. Rather, students should be familiarizing themselves with the facts of the case study. Students will find it helpful to make notes on the salient points as they read the case study. Only after the student has read the case study several times, should he/she then read the questions assigned at the end of the case study. Students should then reread the case study and record information that is directly pertinent to answering the questions asked.

When students are reading and analyzing a case study it is important for them to try to distinguish the most important and relevant information pertaining to the central issue(s) of concern or problem(s) from the rest of the information presented in the case study. Issue or problem identification in case study analysis is often an acquired skill that improves with practice. (Steps 1 and 2 in the framework of analysis.)

Students should avoid making broad generalities or presenting superficial solutions when attempting to find the "best course of action" in their resolution of case studies. It is important for students to try to generate a number of possible problem-solving strategies in order to be able to select the "best course of action." It is critical for students to keep in mind that there are usually a number of possible solutions and, more often than not,

---

[66] Susan Wilcox, Christopher Knapper, Mark Weisberg, *Teaching More Students: Assessing More Students* (Instructional Development Centre, Queen's University at Kingston, Canada, January 1997), p. 25.
[67] Ibid.

no "one right or correct solution" to the central issue(s) of concern or problem(s). (Steps 3 and 4 in the framework of analysis.)

Students should not resort to using the argument or excuse that the case study assigned does not provide sufficient information in order to generate alternative problem-solving strategies or solutions.[68] This is precisely the situation in the real world. It is rare, indeed, for public managers and administrators to have the time and/or other resources necessary to try to obtain or to generate the information or data that may be necessary to find, ultimately, the ideal, or as it were, "the best course of action." Accordingly, as in the real world, the expectation is that a decision will have to be made in an attempt to find the preferred strategy(ies) for resolving the central issue(s) of concern or problem(s) that the case study presents.

No decision is complete without developing a plan for implementing the "best course of action." If one cannot devise a plan for implementing the "best course of action" then, by definition, it cannot be a "preferred strategy." In fact, the "best course of action" is invariably tempered by its practical feasibility in resolving the central issue(s) of concern or problem(s) that need to be addressed in the case study. (Step 5 in the framework of analysis.)

A key activity in analyzing case studies is for students to try to match public management and administration principles, concepts and theories to the information provided in the case studies. Students should avoid the temptation of attempting to generate solutions that are based on their intuition or "common sense" *per se,* as opposed to the sound application of public management and administration theory.[69] The application of the principles, concepts and theories of public administration should be integral to the analysis of case studies and not an afterthought.

Conclusion

Case studies and the case study method are proven instructional tools for providing superior public management and administration education. This helps to explain why the case study method is the preferred instructional tool for professional schools, irrespective of the discipline.

The pedagogical value of the case study method as an active experiential learning technique that can develop the analytical and judgmental skills of students has been demonstrated in a number of comparative studies of teaching and learning techniques. As previously noted, the higher order skills that students can develop when analyzing case studies aids in fostering "effective thinking" skills that are crucial to developing greater self-direction in learning. The capacity for self-direction in learning is considered to be

---

[68] Randy Hoffman, "The Purpose of Case Problems and How to Analyze Them," in *Organizational Behaviour: Canadian Cases and Exercises.* Edited by Randy Hoffman and Fred Rueper, (North York, Ontario: Captus Press, McGraw-Hill Ryerson Limited, 1991), p. 7.

[69] Ibid., p. 5.

an important prerequisite for promoting the value of life-long education, a key necessity for everyone in modern society.

The "pragmatic problem-solving model" presented here for analyzing case studies provides teachers and students with a simple five-step method for trying to resolve the central problem(s) or issue(s) at the core of the case study. To optimize student learning through the use of case studies, it is suggested that instructors should divide their class into study groups or teams. The study groups or teams should meet to analyze the assigned case study prior to the class period, following which the instructor will lead the entire class in a detailed analysis of the case study.

A key component in any case study analysis is the application of relevant principles, concepts and theories of public management and administration. The theoretical basis and rationale on which proposed resolutions to the central issue(s) of concern or problem(s) or the presentation of the "best course of action" must be the foundational elements to any quality case study analysis. The rationale and arguments in favour of adopting case studies and the case study method for courses or professional development and training programmes is, then, overwhelming. Comparative research studies have demonstrated the utility of the use of case studies as an instructional technique. The use of case studies is also supported by th latest learning and pedagogical theories. Is it any wonder, then, that it has emerged as the predominant method of instruction in the professions? This book of 30 original new case studies in public management and administration help to fill the constant demand for more case studies for the discipline as well as the profession and for the purposes of ongoing training, professional development, and for academic certificate and degree programmes at the undergraduate and graduate levels.

We are constantly striving to improve this new collection of case studies in public management and administration and, therefore, we welcome and value your comments and suggestions on the case studies presented in this volume, whether they be from instructors or students. Your feedback will help us to further our goal to improve our case studies through the comments and suggestions that we receive from those who have studied and analyzed these case studies for educational purposes. We will make every effort to try to incorporate your comments and suggestions in future editions of this volume.

Please send your comments and suggestions to:

James C. Simeon, Ph.D.
Assistant Professor

School of Public Policy and Administration,
Atkinson Faculty of Liberal and Professional Studies, Centre for Refugee Studies (CRS), Faculty Associate, Centre for Support of Teaching (CST)
York University
4700 Keele Street, N809 Ross Building
Toronto, Ontario, Canada, M3J 1P3

Tel: 416 736-2100 (33460)
Fax: 416 736-5382
Email: jcsimeon@yorku.ca

Cases

A Person of
Influence

Terrence Weston had been with the Ministry of Attorney General for less than a year yet it seemed that he already knew everyone in the ministry. Prior to entering the public service he had been a businessman in the private sector, primarily in the marketing and accounting fields. He had also held a number of mid-level management positions in medium- to small-size businesses. Before coming to the Ministry of the Attorney General (MAG) he had had his own small bookkeeping business and had also been heavily involved in politics at all levels of government. His forte, in this field, seemed to be fundraising.

Weston reported to Stan Waters, director of the human resources branch in the Corporate Services Division of MAG. When Weston was hired he came highly recommended by the assistant deputy attorney general of the division. Waters found Weston's strengths to be in the areas of accounting, were he seemed to be good at tabulating and manipulating numbers, and in human resource management. However, his weaknesses were in report writing and research and analysis. Further, he seemed to lack any facility or understanding of the law. Although this was not surprising, given his background in business accounting, it was obviously troubling since he was now employed in the Ministry of the Attorney General.

Shortly after Weston's arrival at the human resources branch, Waters had learned that Weston already knew a number of the employees in the division and throughout the ministry. This was evident during Weston's initial orientation and training period for new employees. However, it became more evident once he settled into his new responsibilities in the branch. Waters would see Weston spending a great deal of his time chatting with the same employees in his office.

Weston was a big man in every sense of the word. He was tall, overweight, and he liked to talk loudly, so that he could be easily heard by all those within his immediate area. He was particularly fond of telling humourous stories and he loved being the centre of attention. He also liked to talk about himself. It was not long before Waters and his other colleagues got to know a great deal about Weston's background, hobbies and personal interests.

Weston was also a great "name dropper." When he was talking with someone or with a group of people, he would mention that he knew a high-profile person in the community. He told Waters that he had been actively involved in politics for over 30 years and had gotten to know a great many successful politicians at the federal, provincial and local levels of government. One day he casually mentioned that he was good friends with the attorney general. Weston certainly wanted to be seen as someone who was extremely well-connected politically.

Weston enjoyed the cachet of being seen as a man of influence who had "the ear" of those in power. He considered his personal connections as integral to his station and status in life, whether in the public or the private sphere. For instance, he was not above using his self-perceived privileged status in his personal and professional relationships at work. Despite his limited knowledge and experience at MAG, he would frequently speak on all manner of issues and concerns at branch meetings. Although his oral delivery was impressive, his remarks often revealed, to those with any length of service in MAG, that he either did not understand the issues under discussion or that he had entirely missed the point.

In part, because Weston had, essentially, spent his entire career in the private sector before joining the public service, he frequently came across as the proverbial "bull in the china shop." Clearly, he was used to managing in an environment where those he worked with would quickly respond to his remarks and requests. When things did not go at the pace or in the way that he expected, he quickly became impatient and would respond in a curt or flippant manner. This was exacerbated by his gruff and unsophisticated demeanour. This may also have been due, in part, to his previous experience working in the private sector and/or his age and personality. Indeed, Weston's general conduct did not seem to endear him to many of his colleagues or to the staff in general. Stan Waters found that Terrence Weston seemed to be entirely oblivious to this fact. Indeed, he found, not surprisingly, that in Weston's own mind he actually believed that he was well liked and positively perceived by virtually everyone in MAG.

When Weston would speak with Waters he would always take an opportunity to point out how someone in the branch went out of his or her way to compliment him about something. He clearly wanted to leave Waters with the impression that Weston was not only well liked but, more importantly, that he was well respected by everyone who worked with him in the ministry. However, nothing could be further from Waters' own observations and impressions of how people responded and perceived Weston within the ministry. There were rumblings among the staff — in particular, regarding Weston's unrealistic expectations and domineering manner —nonetheless, Waters never received any formal complaints about Weston's conduct.

What was more troubling was the quality of Weston's overall work. His report writing was clearly deficient. He did not appear to be a "quick study" who could immediately grasp the fundamentals of his own job. His lack of research skills and his poor analytical abilities were also clearly evident. These deficiencies would require a great deal of effort on Weston's part to overcome within his mandatory probationary review period.

During the three-month review to assess Weston's progress in the branch, Waters pointed out these deficiencies and told him that he was not progressing as well as could be reasonably expected during this portion of his one-year probationary review period. When Weston heard this he immediately became defensive and suggested that Waters was dwelling on the negative and not considering sufficiently the positive contributions that he had been making to the branch and the ministry as a whole. He stated that he contributed to the branch by promoting a positive working environment among all his colleagues and staff. Waters asked him to elaborate on this and to give him some specific examples of how he was promoting a positive workplace. Weston stated that he was cultivating a positive workplace environment by generating "good will" within the branch. He mentioned the names of three or four people within the branch and the division that Waters recognized immediately as Weston's personal friends, whom he had known before he had come to MAG. Weston asked Waters whether anyone had made any complaints against him. Waters stated that he had not received any formal complaints, but that this was hardly the standard that ought to be used to determine whether anyone was contributing to a positive work environment. Waters emphasized that this was only the first three-month review and that there was plenty of time for him to adjust and demonstrate that he was making real progress and developing in the critical areas of knowledge of the MAG and his report writing.

At the conclusion of this meeting, Waters was not entirely sure whether Weston had accepted his assessment of his deficiencies or that he had accepted that it would take a tremendous effort on his part to overcome them in the nine months remaining on his probationary term contract.

Following the three-month review meeting, Waters noticed no appreciable change in Weston's behaviour in the office or in his substantive job performance. In fact, if anything, Waters appeared to be even more outspoken and troublesome. There was some change in his report writing; however, progress here was minimal at best. Waters also sensed that Weston began to look at him with some suspicion.

Shortly after the three-month probationary review meeting, Waters began to hear rumours that Weston was telling his colleagues that the attorney general had visited his home and that they had had dinner together. Waters also heard rumours that Weston was meeting with senior politicians at other levels of government as well.

At the six-month probationary review with Weston, Waters stated that he was still not making sufficient progress in his report writing. The deficiencies, he pointed out, had not changed. His report writing was still characterized by poor research and analysis. Weston became quite defensive and stated that Waters was being far too demanding of him in this regard. He stated that he had learned a great deal in the past six months at MAG and that there was a significant difference in his report writing from when he had first started. He claimed that his report writing had dramatically improved over this period. Waters stated that he agreed that some progress was evident but because his initial report writing had been so poor and deficient such "progress" could not even be considered.

Stan Waters pointed out that report writing was the essence of this job and that Weston had to demonstrate that he was capable of writing reports that were at the standards set by the Branch and MAG. Following this exchange Weston stated that he thought that he was being treated unfairly and that he might have to bring his concerns to the attention of higher authorities within MAG. He said that his contribution to the branch and the Ministry, in so many other ways, was being purposively overlooked or deliberately ignored.

Waters stated that he was welcomed to provide supporting evidence for his contributions to the branch and MAG. He said that he was not aware of any contributions that he had made to either the branch or the ministry that he might be referring to. He further noted that such contributions needed to be documented and that they could not simply be based on Weston's own assertions.

Waters also advised Weston that if he did not make significant progress in his substantive report writing that he would have to make a negative recommendation regarding either the extension of his contract for a further period of six months or for an appointment to a permanent position within the branch.

Weston stated that this was unacceptable and that he would take this matter to the highest authorities within MAG, if necessary. He felt that Waters was not only being unfair but that he was ignoring the reality of how things actually worked within government.

Questions

1. How should Stan Waters respond to Terrence Weston's claim of not only being unfair to him, personally, but ignoring the realpolitik of the public sector workplace?

2. What recourse does Terrence Weston have to address his concerns regarding his six-month probationary review at MAG?

3. What obligation, if any, does Stan Waters have to ensure that Terrence Weston meets the performance standards set by his ministry before the end of Terrence Weston's probationary period?

4. Has Stan Waters made a "career-limiting move" by advising Terrence Weston that he will not recommend that he receive either an extension of his probationary contract or an appointment to a permanent position without substantial progress in his report writing?

5. What are some of the most effective ways that public sector managers have to deal with employees who are, allegedly, well-connected politically?

Resource Materials

- Ontario Ministry of the Attorney General
  http://www.attorneygeneral.jus.gov.on.ca/english/about/

- Office of the Integrity Commissioner, Ontario
  http://lobbyist.oico.on.ca/dow/DOWweb.nsf/htmlDocs/home?Opendocument

- Public Sector Integrity Canada
  http://www.psic-ispc.gc.ca/index.php?lang+en

- Values and Ethics Code for the Public Service of Canada
  http://www.tbs-sct.gc.ca/pubs_pol/hrpubs/tb_851/vec-cve-eng.asp

- The Public Service Commission of Canada
  http://www.psc-cfp.gc.ca/index-eng.htm

Ambushed

Peter Archibald, director of the Horizontal Policy and Strategic Planning Division of the Policy, Planning and Priorities Directorate, Health Policy Branch, Health Canada, was planning for his monthly divisional meeting. He had carefully planned the draft agenda for the meeting. The main item for discussion at the meeting, without doubt, would be the preliminary consideration of the Departmental Report on Plans and Priorities. This was one of the division's major annual strategic planning exercises and it was something that required a great deal of Archibald's time and attention. The *Departmental Report on Plans and Priorities* was the key report that Treasury Board Canada (TB) used to assess whether Health Canada was spending its budget allocations on its stated priorities. Another important agenda item was the preparation of briefing materials for the next round of priority setting by the department. Archibald also thought it might be timely to do a roundtable discussion on the latest initiatives that might impinge on health policy from other departments across the federal government. It was important, he believed, to ensure that the division did not lose track of these initiatives and how they impacted on Health Canada's own plans and priorities.

Archibald was also considering whether any other matters needed to be raised at the monthly divisional meeting. There were always staff changes and other personnel matters that were brought up by one or more of the managers at the meeting. There seemed to be a number of staffing concerns as of late. One particular concern that impacted all branches in Health Canada was the competition for senior management positions. This competition seemed to preoccupy most of the junior managers in several of the branches, including the Health Policy Branch. The internal departmental competition was for four senior management positions, one of which was in the Horizontal Planning and Strategic Priorities Division.

Archibald had suffered without a senior manager for the Health Policy Development Unit within his division for over one year before Patricia Cartwright was finally selected to fill the position. This came as a bit of a surprise to a number of candidates in the competition. Cartwright was relatively new to Health Canada and she had served in a junior management position for only about one year before she won the competition. However, this also seemed to be the case for the other three senior management positions that were available in the competition. All four of these positions went to fairly junior managers. This upset many of those who lost out on the competitions for these positions, particularly, those managers who had faithfully served in their position for five or more years.

Archibald was aware of all the gossip and complaining that was going on among many of the candidates who had lost out on these senior management competitions. He attributed the rumours and gossip to the usual griping that goes on among the losing candidates. Nonetheless, he was somewhat surprised at the reactions of two of the losing candidates in his division, Mary Crosbie and Lorne MacKinley, two of his managers that he considered to be not only highly competent, but also quite sensible and usually unflappable. What came as even more of a surprise was that these managers, along with a number of other managers from other divisions, were considering filing a complaint with the Public Service Labour Relations Board (PSLRB) about the nature of the competition for these three senior management positions.

The senior management competition involved, essentially, a three-staged process. The first stage was a one-hour written test. The written test was based on an "in-basket exercise" that was designed to test the candidate's ability to prioritize their incoming files and correspondence, including, email. During the written test, the candidates also had to work through a scenario of having to deal with what is presented as either an emergency or something that required their immediate attention. The second stage was a full-day group exercise in problem solving and teamwork. The candidates were randomly broken up into teams and then each team was given a specific problem based assignment. The candidates were required to interact with their team members to come up with an optimal solution for their problem-based assignment. The facilitators of the group-based exercise not only acted as resources for the various groups, but also observed the intragroup and inter-group interactions and dynamics to assess the candidates on how well they interacted with others in a group context but also on their consensus building and leadership skills. The third and final stage of the competition, for the remaining short-listed candidates, was the personal interview. At each stage in the competition, candidates were screened out of the process.

Most of the candidates scored well on the "in-basket exercise." However, most of the remaining candidates were screened out after the group-based problem solving and teamwork exercise. For the third and final stage of the competition, only 10 candidates remained, from which only the four top-ranked candidates were offered one of the four senior management positions. In fact, out of the ten candidates who were interviewed for these available positions, seven were deemed qualified to fill the four vacant senior manager positions. The seven successful candidates were then ranked one through seven in terms of their overall performance in the competition. The remaining three were deemed alternates for the positions in the event that any of the top four candidates either turned down the offer of the senior manager position or left their position anytime within a two-year period.

The first four successful candidates on the qualified list were then offered one of the vacant senior manager positions. Not surprisingly, each of the successful candidates accepted the senior management positions. As noted, the remaining three persons on the qualified list would only be offered a senior management position if one of the higher ranking candidates refused to accept the position or they moved on to another position and the senior management position became vacant. As further noted, the list of qualified successful candidates remains valid for a two-year period after the conclusion of the competition. Neither Crosbie nor MacKinley made the qualified list of successful candidates for this competition.

The other major staffing issue centered on the expiry of the current collective agreement with the public sector unions, which was due to expire in three months. From various reports in the media and from the respective negotiating teams, there seemed to be little, if any, progress in the ongoing collective bargaining sessions. This had a direct impact on management–staff relations in a number of ways. Most notably, managers found work relations with their staff to be rather strained. This was exacerbated by the fact that Treasury Board had already approved a 9.5 percent increase in management salaries over three years. The government was offering the pubic sector unions an increase of only five percent over three years. This was perceived by many of the staff as insulting and not bargaining in good faith. Staff members could not understand how the government could provide management with a 9.5 percent increase over three years but only offer staff a five percent increase for this same period.

This was the environment in which Archibald was planning his monthly divisional meeting. A number of the other divisions within the branch had already held their monthly divisional meetings and he had not heard that anything too unusual had taken place at any of these. The other directors in the division did not alert Archibald about any branch or department-wide issues or concerns that he should prepare for at his own monthly divisional meeting.

Divisional meetings were scheduled for the entire day, from 9:00 a.m. to 4:00 p.m., with the appropriate health and lunch breaks. Most of the managers and staff used the breaks to go back to their offices to check their emails and to make telephone calls before coming back to the divisional meeting. Archibald always provided light snacks and refreshments before the start the divisional meetings to help launch the meeting day.

On this day, Archibald noticed that there were more staff at the meeting than usual. Although the monthly divisional meetings were not mandatory *per se*, all staff were encouraged to attend, particularly for those items on the agenda that had a direct bearing on their work. All managers, however, were expected to attend the meetings unless they were given a special dispensation by their director to be absent. Managers were excused from attending if there was some other more pressing matter, such as a pending report, that had to be completed as soon as possible. Peter Archibald noticed, in particular, that there were some staff members at the meeting that rarely, if ever, attended divisional meetings.

The meeting started well. Archibald had dealt with the first two items on the agenda when he then had a question from Crosbie regarding the recent competition for the senior manager positions in Health Canada. Archibald was somewhat surprised by this question, given that he was neither on the selection committee for this competition nor involved at any stage of the testing process. Nevertheless, he responded by giving the departmental line that the competition had been settled and that there was now a list of qualified successful candidates who would be called to fill those positions as the need arose. After Archibald finished answering this question there was another question on the subject from MacKinley, who wanted to know why Health Canada was using a flawed process for this competition. MacKinley went on to state that the criteria that had been set for the selection of senior managers specified such requirements as "experience," "relevant service within the department," "proven judgement and maturity" and he wondered why these qualities were given less weight or were totally ignored in the selection process.

Archibald stated that he was not aware that these specific qualities had been given less weight and stated that it was unfair to state that the selection committee ignored these qualities. Crosbie immediately jumped up and said that if that was the case, why is everyone on the qualified list under 40 years of age. Crosbie was one of the long-serving managers in Health Canada who was in her mid-fifties. MacKinley was also a long-serving manger in Health Canada and had just turned 50.

Crosbie then went on to state that, among the seven people on the qualified list of candidates, only two had served as managers for at least three years. She said that the other qualified candidates had served as managers for fewer than three years.

As Crosbie said all this, Archibald saw Cartwright's face turn red and she started to squirm in her chair. Cartwright was one of the top four qualified candidates who had won the competition and had been offered a senior management position in Archibald's division. Cartwright seemed to be visibly distraught.

MacKinley cut into Crosbie's remarks to ask why Health Canada would want to treat its long-serving and dedicated managers in such a dishonourable and reckless manner.

Crosbie then stated that the manner in which the selection process had been conducted smacked of age discrimination. She stated that a number of managers who had gone through these competitions before were feed up and not only considering a group action appeal but were seeking legal counsel to see whether a law suit against Health Canada would be appropriate. Archibald stated that all appeals and remedies would have to be exhausted within the government on this matter first before a civil law-suit could be taken to the courts.

At this point, there was a great deal of background discussion taking place among those present, and Crosbie and MacKinley had to raise their voices to be heard over the din of the meeting.

Crosbie retorted that the group of managers who had lost out in the competition would be exhausting all internal remedies and were in the process of filing a complaint with the PSLRB regarding the senior manager's competition.

Just as Crosbie finished stating this, Pearl Jones jumped out of her chair and stated that she was not surprised at how Health Canada and the senior executive within the public service had handled this competition. She said, "Just look at how they are handling the negotiations in the current round of bargaining with the public service unions."

Jones was a Clerk and local union steward in the division. She was widely recognized as a staunch union supporter and militant union activist. She went on to state that with the current attitude and approach to the negotiations for a new three-year collective agreement there would likely not be a settlement. Jones stated that the union would soon be holding a vote of the membership to decide whether to give the union executive committee the right to call for job action or a strike if a settlement was not reached before the current collective agreement expired. She reminded everyone that all union members had voted in favour of allowing the union executive committee to call a strike if the negotiations between the public service union and the government broke down or if they failed to reach a tentative settlement before the current collective agreement expired.

Archibald told Jones that she was out of order and that the monthly divisional meeting was not the proper forum for raising union business. He asked Jones to make her points at the next local union meeting. However, at that point, the proceedings were clearly disrupted and the meeting was in disarray. Everyone was talking at once and the noise level in the room was increasing. Archibald noticed the time on the wall clock was 9:45 a.m. and that they were still at least another 45 minutes from the first health break. This had never happened to him in a meeting before and he tried to think of what he should do next to calm everyone down and return to the items on the agenda.

Questions

1. If you were Peter Archibald, director of the Horizontal Policy and Strategic Planning Division, Health Canada, what would you do to try to restore order and decorum and to return to the agenda for the meeting? Explain why your actions would be the most effective way to proceed to achieve these ends.

2. Justify why you think Peter Archibald should have been able to anticipate this type of possible reaction at his monthly divisional meeting. Explain what Archibald could have done to avoid this type of confrontation and outburst at his meeting.

3. Are Mary Crosbie, Lorne MacKinley and Pearl Jones at fault for trying to hijack the monthly divisional meeting to further their own agenda? If so, would it be appropriate to impose any disciplinary measures on any of them?

4. Should Peter Archibald, as the chair of the monthly divisional meeting, bear any responsibility for the meeting deteriorating to the point that it did?

5. One of requisite skills for any manager is to be able to effectively chair a meeting, regardless of its size or composition. What insights does this case study provide for what public sector managers ought to do to ensure that they conduct an effective meeting that achieves all of their planned objectives?

Resource Materials

- Health Canada
  http://www.hc-sc.gc.ca/index-eng.php

- Human Resources and Skills Development Canada
  — Collective Bargaining
  http://www.hrsdc.gc.ca/eng/labour/labour_relations/index.shtml

- Public Service Labour Relations Board (PSLRB)
  http://www.pslrb-crtfp.gc.ca/intro_e.asp

- Canadian Union of Public Employees (CUPE)
  http://cupe.ca/

- Public Service Alliance of Canada (PSAC)
  http://www.psac.com/about/about-e.shtml

Copy Cat

Earl Warren, director in the Management Services Division in the Human Resources and Corporate Services Branch of the Canadian International Development Agency (CIDA), has been with CIDA for seven years. Previously, he had served as a director of the Management Services Division for four years. He was known throughout the Human Resources and Corporate Services Branch of CIDA as an exceedingly hard working, thoughtful and dedicated manager. The director general of the Management Services Division (MSD), Bill Crawford, relied on Warren for his advice on a broad range of administrative and management issues that impacted on the Division and, indeed, the entire Human Resources and Corporate Services Branch (HRCS). Warren came to CIDA from academe, where he had specialized in public policy and administration. He held a Ph.D. in public administration from the University of Toronto and had taught at several universities, including Queen's University and University of Ottawa, before he came to work for CIDA. Warren's academic background and experience made him especially well suited for the work he was doing for MSD in the Human Resources and Corporate Services Branch of CIDA.

Shortly after Warren arrived at CIDA, he was assigned to work on a number of high-profile projects at HRCS. Through his work on these high-profile projects he gained a reputation as an innovative thinker who was an effective team player. One of the advantages that Warren brought to these projects was his in-depth knowledge of organizational and management theories in public administration. He also brought a certain tenacity and drive to get the project concluded successfully and on time.

Connie Kennedy was also a director in the Management Services Division of HRCS in CIDA. She was one of Warren's colleagues. She had served in CIDA for about four years and had been appointed a director in the Management and Services Division the previous year. Kennedy struck Warren as being a highly ambitious person who was looking for the quick and easy way up the "corporate ladder" or organizational hierarchy. This was most evident, Warren thought, at the weekly divisional management committee meetings where it seemed that Kennedy never had a shortage of things to say.

Kennedy had a law degree from the University of British Columbia. Although she had been called to the bar in the province of British Columbia, she had never practised law outside the government. Her first job had been with the British Columbia public service in Vancouver. From there she moved to the Ontario Human Rights Commission in Toronto, before coming to CIDA and, eventually, to the Management Services Division. She was at least ten years younger than Warren.

Warren was always pressing aggressively for changes to improve the efficiency and/or the effectiveness of CIDA operations. He often promoted his ideas with Director General Bill Crawford and other director generals in the branch, such as Tyler Jarvis, director general of the Human Resources Division; Helen Fergus, director general of the Finance Division; and Percy Townshend, director general of the Administration and Security Division. Many of Warren's suggestions were not only sensible and practical, but they were cost effective and simple to implement.

Warren saw himself as an "ideas man" first and foremost as opposed to a promoter or someone who sold someone else's ideas to others. Sometimes his ideas were actually picked up, if not in whole then in part, by Crawford or the other director generals in the branch. More often than not, however, Warren found his ideas were being ignored by his superiors.

Warren was also a responsible manager who spoke less often than his colleagues at the weekly MSD Management Committee Meetings chaired by Director General Crawford. However, when he did speak his interventions were right on point and he had something significant to contribute to the discussion. Warren was a consensus builder, by nature, and often tried to persuade his management colleagues at these meetings to agree on a compromise. If, on the other hand, he had a strong view or opinion on an issue under discussion at these meetings, he would clearly state his position on the issue and do his best to persuade others to his point of view.

Kennedy, in contrast to Warren, seemed to lack internal consistency and focus. She was all over the map on issues from one week to the next. Indeed, it appeared at times that she was taking diametrically opposite points of views on the issues from week to week. Further, she had very few of her own ideas. She seemed to be recycling other people's ideas and trying to present them as her own.

About one year after Kennedy's arrival as a director of the MSD weekly Management Committee meeting, Warren began to notice that Kennedy was parroting his ideas on various issues. At first he thought it was flattering because he assumed she had heard him make these same points at previous weekly MSD Management Committee meetings or at other meetings. However, after awhile he realized that he had not presented any of these ideas in any public forum at CIDA.

In time, Warren also noticed that Kennedy was mimicking his actions as a manager. Again, initially, he considered this to be a compliment. After all, he told himself, "imitation was the highest form of flattery." But, in time, what he began to notice was that Kennedy was passing off Warren's ideas as her own. He found this to be rather unsettling.

Warren found this to be particularly so after he had realized that Kennedy seemed to be doing this on a regular basis. It seemed to him that she was scrutinizing his every move and doing everything he was doing. What Warren did not understand was where Kennedy was getting what he thought were his best ideas, since he did not share his innovative ideas with any of the other directors at MSD or in HRCS. The only possible source for his ideas, then, had to be from one or more of the directors general in HRCS. Warren assumed that someone was probably forwarding his emails with his suggestions for efficiency and effectiveness improvements to Kennedy.

Warren was confident that Kennedy was not getting his ideas from Crawford, director general of the Management Services Division. Crawford had an excellent relationship with and high regard for Warren, who he considered to be one of his most competent directors. Warren could not see how Crawford could gain from giving Kennedy his ideas. On the other hand, Crawford should have recognized that what Kennedy was suggesting in their weekly Management Committee meetings was coming straight out of his emails to the directors general in HRCS. Yet, Crawford never mentioned this to him either in the weekly Directors Management Committee meetings or in any of their one-on-one meetings. Warren did not think that it was appropriate, at the present time, to raise the issue with Crawford. Nor did he consider it the right time to challenge Kennedy with stealing his best ideas. He knew that if he did so, at best, it would sound that he was petty and, at worst, that he was absolutely paranoid of Kennedy. Consequently, Warren thought it would be better to wait for further developments before raising any concerns.

Warren doubted that Percy Townshend, director general of the Administration and Security Division, would be forwarding his emails to Kennedy. Warren knew that Townshend distrusted anyone outside his division and was very circumspect in all his email communications. Townshend was fond of saying that all electronic communications were retained and stored by the government of Canada and could be retrieved at any time. As the head of administration and security, Townshend would not want to be embroiled in anything involving emails.

Further, Warren did not think that Helen Fergus, director general of the Finance Division, would bother forwarding emails to anyone. Fergus stayed within her own realm of Finance and rarely, if ever, ventured beyond anything to do with the financial accounts. She was all business and played things by the book. Warren respected Fergus for her great integrity. Besides, he was aware that Helen Fergus did not know Kennedy very well, if at all.

Tyler Jarvis, director general of the Human Resources Division, was another matter altogether. Jarvis knew Kennedy before she came to CIDA. Apparently, they had worked together for a period of time when Kennedy was at the Ontario Human Rights Commission. Kennedy was also known to visit Jarvis in his office from time to time. Although Warren had no evidence or would ever likely come across any such evidence, he had a feeling that Kennedy was getting his best ideas directly from Jarvis.

Warren decided that he wanted to put a stop to Kennedy taking his best ideas and presenting them as her own. However, he still wanted to continue to present his ideas for improving HRCS and CIDA as a whole. He knew that he had a great deal to offer in this regard. It was not only something that he enjoyed doing, it was also something that he believed very strongly in — not only for CIDA, but for his own career within Canadian public service.

Questions

1. After reviewing a number of different possible options that Earl Warren has for resolving his dilemma, indicate which of these options he should adopt and why.

2. What should Earl Warren consider doing in the future to avoid having his best ideas stolen by others?

3. Justify why you think Director General Bill Crawford did not say anything about why Director Connie Kennedy's ideas were so similar to Earl Warren's.

4. Does this case study exemplify the old adage, "It is not what you know, but who you know that counts?" Discuss.

5. What lessons in public management and administration, if any, can be distilled from this case study?

Resource Materials

- CIDA
  http://www.acdi-cida.gc.ca/index-e.htm

- IPAC, *A Public Servant's Commitments*
  http://www.ipac.ca/PublicSectorEthics

- Kenneth Kernaghan, "The Ethics Era in Canadian Public Administration," Research Paper no. 19, Canadian Centre for Management Development, June 1996.
  http://www.ccmd-ccg.gc.ca/research/publications/complete_list_e.html#lectures

- Ethics NewslineR, A weekly digest of the worldwide ethics news (Published by the Institute of Global Ethics)
  http://www.globalethics.org/newsline

- Formal and Informal Communications Networks, Proz.com: The Translation Workplace.
  http://www.proz.com/kudoz/english_to_malay/psychology/1121175-formal_and_informal_communications_networks.html

Crossing the
Picket Line

The collective agreement between the Government of Canada and the public service unions had expired and the negotiators for both parties had failed to reach a tentative settlement. The local union presidents at Natural Resources Canada (NRCan) advised their members that the contract negotiations had failed. The local union presidents stated that since the public service unions were now in a legal strike position, the national union executive had called on its members to go out on strike. The local union presidents reminded their members that in a vote that was taken two months ago they had authorized strike action if a settlement was not reached by the end of the current round of contract negotiations. The national union president, the local union presidents stated, had called for picket lines to be set up at all entrances to Canadian government buildings. Only management and non-unionized employees and all those who have been designated as essential service staff would be allowed to cross the picket lines.

The assistant deputy minister (ADM) of the Corporate Management Sector of NRCan, Colin Hammerston, called a meeting to advise the directors general of his division of the protocol to be followed during the strike. The ADM said that all managers and non-unionized employees would be expected to report to work as usual and to perform their normal duties. He also said that all union employees designated to perform essential services would also be expected to report to work to perform their duties. The ADM observed that all union officials, particularly those who would be supervising the picket lines, were aware of this and were expected to cooperate fully.

Colin Hammerston also said that in a meeting with the deputy minister (DM) and other NRCan ADMs, it was made clear that all management and non-union staff and essential services staff would be expected to report to work and be on the job. In some instances, managers would be asked to perform functions or duties normally performed by unionized staff but this would only be to ensure that the most important and essential tasks at NRCan were still being performed during the strike. The ADM noted that although the strike was not expected to last a long time, the possibility that it could be a long, drawn out, strike was real, given that the two parties were currently so far apart on a number of key issues.

The ADM, Hammerston, further said that the DM wanted to ensure that management and non-unionized employees and those employees designated to perform essential services actually reported for work. Accordingly, he asked all ADMs to keep a daily log of all employees in their respective divisions who were required to report for work. Hammerston stressed that the DM stated that if anyone who was required to report to work failed to do so, without valid reason, then that person would have his or her pay docked.

A number of directors general then made the point that they had managers who strongly opposed, on principle, crossing a picket line. Vaugh Lester, director general, Financial Management Branch, stated that he had a manager who not only opposes, in principle, crossing picket lines but felt that it was morally wrong to do so. He noted that this manager was very involved with the public service union at NRCan before she assumed her management position. Hammerston replied that the DM was adamant that anyone who failed to appear for work, without a valid reason, would have his or her pay docked. Lester asked whether one's values and beliefs and moral conviction constituted a "valid reason" for not coming into work? Hammerston said that, as a manager and a non-unionized employee, Lester's manager would be obligated to come in to work. He stated that she has a responsibility and duty to come in to do her job. Hammerston asked Lester, "What about her moral obligation as a management employee to NRCan to come in to work? If she didn't want to cross picket lines then she should never have taken a management position."

Hammerston also stated that all management and non-unionized employees and those who had been designated as essential service employees would be provided with a letter signed by the DM to verify that they were authorized to cross the picket line. These letters were to be shown to the union officials on duty supervising the picket lines, and once shown, union officials would allow the person to cross the picket line.

Hammerston went on to say that the joint Management and Union Strike Planning Committee had had a number of meetings to ensure that the rights of both the union and management would be honoured. Hammerston stated that he did not anticipate any difficulties on the picket lines but, to ensure that everything ran smoothly and to address any problems that might arise, he stated that the ADMs had agreed to meet the first thing each morning. He also stated that a situation room had been set up to monitor all strike activities at NRCan and to serve as a central communication centre for receiving and disseminating information related to the strike. Hammerston also declared that the ADMs had agreed to assign their directors general to monitor each of the entrances in to the NRCan corporate head office building. The directors general would be assigned shifts on the picket line to ensure that all those who were authorized to cross the picket lines would be allowed to do so. Hammerston pointed out that if there were any problems on any of the picket lines then the directors general had to report this immediately to their respective ADMs.

Hammerston then asked each of his directors general to select a day and time slot when they would be on duty to monitor the picket line at their designated NRCan building entrance. Lester selected Tuesdays and Thursdays, 10:30 a.m. to 12:30 p.m.

When Lester went back to his office he called a meeting of his own managers. He outlined, in turn, the protocol to be followed for the strike. He also explained that all managers, non-unionized employees and any staff who were designated as providing an essential service were expected to report for duty at their offices and workstations throughout the duration of the strike. Lester further noted that all leave had been suspended for the period of the strike. He said that he would have to take attendance and file a report with the ADM on a daily basis. The DM, he explained, would dock the pay of any manager who did not report to work and did not have a valid reason for not doing so.

As Lester expected, Manager Carol Windsor stated, that everyone knew her position on crossing picket lines. Windsor stated that she could not cross a picket line on strong moral grounds. She said that, "It does not matter to me whether the union is right or wrong in its demands during these negotiation, I cannot cross a picket line because it would violate my most fundamental values and beliefs of the rights of workers in the collective bargaining process." Lester stated that if Windsor did not come in to work then he would have to report her as being absent and that her pay would be docked accordingly. Windsor said that this was not only petty and offensive but, worst still, it was disrespectful and forced people to violate their most fundamental values and beliefs.

Another manager asked whether it would be possible to work from home for the duration of the strike. Lester stated that management, non-unionized staff and those designated as essential service staff had a right to cross a picket line. There is no violation of the collective bargaining process for employees in these categories who cross the picket line. The Government of Canada also had a responsibility and duty to serve the people of Canada, irrespective of the work disruption caused by strikes. "NRCan cannot stop all its operations," Lester exclaimed, "there are people out there who are depending on us." The unions were aware of this, Lester observed, and that is why they recognized that essential service staff should be allowed to cross the picket lines.

On the first day of the strike, Lester did a walk about the office to note who had come in to work. To his surprise, he found that Windsor was in her office working. He asked her if she had any difficulties crossing the picket line. Windsor said, "Not at all. When I came to the office 7:00 a.m. this morning the picket line had not been formed. And, when I leave the office this evening at 6:30 p.m., the picket line will be gone for the day." Lester told her that he thought that this was very clever because it meant that she did not have to cross any picket lines or confront any of the employees who were out on strike. Lester asked Windsor whether this was merely a way of assuaging her conscience. After all, he noted, she had, in fact, come into the building and was working, which was, in effect, technically crossing the picket line. Windsor said that the DM did not leave her with any other options but to come in to work. She had to fulfill her responsibilities and duty as a manager in NRCan otherwise she would have been disciplined by having her pay cut. Windsor stated that this was unfair to all those whose values and beliefs deeply honoured, respected and supported the rights of workers. Windsor said the act of crossing a picket was antithetical to everything she held dear and to her deepest and most fundamental beliefs. She said that she clearly faced a moral dilemma. Windsor said that she knew that as a manager she also had the obligation and duty to report to work during the strike. She also recognized that as a manager that she had the right to cross the union's picket line. "The conflict between my responsibilities, duties and rights as a manager and my own deeply held personal principles, values and beliefs," she said, "have to be resolved or at least reconciled in some way."

Lester asked Windsor to explain how she managed to do this by coming in to work. Windsor said that she had spoken to one of the local union presidents, Casey Harrison, and told him that she would donate the pay that she earned for each day of the strike to the local union's strike fund. Windsor declared that she had spent a great deal of time thinking about how she could resolve her personal moral dilemma and the problem between her personal convictions and her responsibilities and duties to her employer and said that this was perhaps the best solution she could come up with. "Rather than have my pay cut and have this disciplinary measure on my personnel file, I decided to donate the pay that I would be earning during the strike to the local union strike fund." She further stated that by doing this she would not be compromising any of her principles, values and beliefs and, at the same time, she would be demonstrating her support for all public service workers who were out on strike. "This is one way that I can show my support for all our colleagues who are out on strike," she said. Lester was impressed with the solution that Windsor had come up with to resolve her personal moral dilemma.

Later that same day, Director General Lester took up his post at the NRCan entrance to monitor the activity on the picket line. When he arrived he noticed that there was a queue forming outside the entrance made up of NRCan managers and non-unionized employees. He recognized two of the managers that were speaking with the union officials who were supervising the picket line. The union officials seemed to be taking a great deal of time examining the DM's letter authorizing them to enter the building, as per the management union strike committee agreement. Lester thought that there was some sort of problem and went up to the union officials to find out what was going on. The two NRCan managers then advised Lester that the union officials were deliberately taking their time in letting people in the building. They said that the tactic they were using was questioning the authenticity of the letter that was issued by the DM to authorize their entrance. They further said that the union officials were letting in only one person about every 15 minutes. As a result, a queue was beginning to form outside the entrance to the building. There were about 10 people waiting to enter. They looked frustrated and angry that they were being made to wait needlessly outside in the cold.

Lester used his cell phone to contact Hammerston to let him know what was taking place on the picket line. When he got through to the ADM to advise him of this development, Hammerston responded by saying that the union was using this tactic at all the building entrances and, as a consequence, this was disrupting all NRCan operations in the building. The ADM said that he wanted all the directors general to meet him in the boardroom designated as the strike situation room in 10 minutes to address this problem. In the meantime, Hammerston said he wanted to go down and see what the situation was like at his particular entrance. Lester said that he would wait for him on the ground floor next to the elevators. He said that the union officials knew he was a director general because of the arm band that he wore. The arm bands were provided to the directors general for their shifts on the picket lines. He said that the union officials allowed him to cross the picket line without stopping him and without any difficulties.

As Lester was waiting for Hammerston on the ground floor next to the elevators he happened to run into Casey Harrison, one of the local union presidents. Lester asked Harrison why the union officials were delaying those who were authorized to enter the building. Harrison said that the union officials were just being thorough to ensure that everyone who had a DM's letter was entitled to one. He said that there was no obstruction of the movement of people in and out of the building only a slight delay. He acknowledged that it might inconvenience some people but it could not be helped. At about that moment, Hammerston came out of the elevator, and when he saw local union president Harrison he immediately went up to him and said, "Why are you obstructing managers from entering the building?" Harrison said that there was no obstruction, only a slight delay as the union officials checked everyone's credentials to ensure that they were indeed managers and entitled to enter the building. Hammerston then asked, "If that is true, then why are there growing queues at all the entrances into the building?" Local union president Harrison replied that there seemed to be problems with some of the letters that had been presented.

Hammerston became livid when he heard this. His face turned a bright red and he raised his voice so that the people standing outside the glass doors at the entrance of the building could hear him. "This is totally unacceptable! Stop playing games and making people stand in line for no reason! Why don't you start living up to your agreements!" Harrison stood for an instance looking at Hammerston in disbelief that he would treat him like a disobedient schoolboy. When he recovered, Harrison said, "You can't speak to me in that tone of voice! You may be an ADM around here but you still have to treat people with some dignity and respect. I find your comments and tone of voice unacceptable and I will file a complaint." Hammerston then quickly responded, "You are in the wrong and you know it! You better start letting my managers in this building or I will be the one who will be filing the complaint."

Lester stood there stunned. He had never seen Hammerston angry before, let alone worked up to such a degree that he was yelling at someone. In fact, he never thought that Hammerston was capable of such a thing because he always presented himself as such an easygoing and relaxed individual. This seemed to be entirely out of character for the ADM. Lester thought to himself that the strike had really gotten to Hammerston, and he wondered whether the ADM would be able to last until the end of the strike.

Questions

1. Justify why you think that Carol Windsor did or did not come to a practical solution to her moral dilemma on crossing the picket line.

2. Are Carol Windsor's well-known and strongly held beliefs against crossing picket lines likely to limit her career advancement in management? Explain and defend your answer to this question.

3. If ADM Colin Hammerston and local union president Casey Harrison filed complaints against each other, who do you think would likely win and why?

4. Describe what you think would be the likely outcome of ADM Colin Hammerston's outburst to local union president Casey Harrison on the strike situation at the NRCan building site.

5. Does Director General Vaugh Lester have a responsibility to report the ADM Colin Hammerston/local union president Casey Harrison incident to anyone in the ministry or elsewhere? Would it have been reasonable for Vaugh Lester to try and say or do something during this incident to try to "cool off" the two parties?

Resource Materials

- Natural Resources Canada (NRCan)
  http://www.nrcan-rncan.gc.ca/com/index-eng.php

- *The Canadian Encyclopedia* — Public-Service Unions
  http://www.thecanadianencyclopedia.com/index.cfm?PgNm=TCE&Params=A1ARTA0006555

- Public Service Labour Relations Board (PSLRB) — Collective Bargaining
  http://www.psc-cfp.gc.ca/index_e.htm

- Treasury Board of Canada Secretariat — Collective Bargaining
  Labour Relations and Compensation Operation Branch (LRCO)
  http://www.tbs-sct.gc.ca/lrco-rtor/collective/agreement-negociation-eng.asp

- Service Canada, Digest of Benefit Entitlement Principles, Chapter 8, Labour Disputes, 8.6.0 Participation.
  http://www.servicecanada.gc.ca/eng/ei/digest/chp8.shtml

Early Retirement

Ken Follette had been with National Defence Canada (NDC) for close to 10 years. He was a senior policy analyst with the Defence Research and Development Canada, where he had gained a reputation as a hard working and innovative policy analyst. Follette always took very good care of himself. He did not smoke or drink and he exercised on a regular basis. He was also careful with his diet and he never indulged in excess. He looked fit and younger than his age. Follette was rarely, if ever, away from work. Consequently, he accumulated at great deal of sick leave credit.

Follette reported to Sally Booth, director, at Defence Research and Development Canada (DRDC), located in the NDC's national headquarters in Ottawa. Booth was known to be an easy-going manager who had close personal relations with all her senior staff. She seemed to be particularly fond of Follette. It was well known in the office at DRDC that Follette and his wife would socialize with Booth and her husband. They seemed to be part of a close circle of friends.

Booth was much younger than Follette and would frequently seek his advice on many issues that she was confronted with, whether it had to do with staffing, administration or policy. Follette was happy to offer her his advice, given his varied background and many years of public and private sector experience. In fact, Follette was known for his strong ethical and moral values. He had studied in a theological seminary for three years before deciding that he would not enter the priesthood. Instead, Follette went on to earn a philosophy degree and then a master's in social work. He worked as a social worker for a number of years before he became the head of a number of non-profit social agencies. Eventually, Follette entered the public service and held a number of different positions before specializing in policy analysis.

Follette was close to his retirement. He did not want to retire and spend the rest of his life sitting at home and playing cards or golf. He saw himself continuing to work on a part-time basis as a consultant. This would not only supplement his pension income but also allow him to continue to work and stay involved actively in his policy community.

Another colleague and close friend of Follette was Roger Gauthier. Gauthier was another director in the DRDC and a colleague of Booth. Gauthier and Booth worked together on various management committees in DRDC, including the Regional Directors' Committee that was chaired by Gregory Gallagher, director general of DRDC. Gallagher was also a good friend of Follette. Like Booth, Gallagher was also known to seek Follette's advice from time-to-time on various issues impacting on DRDC and NDC.

It was well known among certain circles within DRDC that Gauthier was actively seeking an appointment on an administrative tribunal within the Canadian government or the government of Quebec. Indeed, this was particularly well known within Gauthier's unit within DRDC. It was also assumed, more generally within DRDC, that Gauthier was director general Gallagher's understudy and the person that he was grooming for his own position should he be promoted or move on. Gallagher would often assign Gauthier as the acting director general when he was away from the office, whether on vacation leave or on business-related travel.

Follette assumed the mantle of elder statesman not only because of his age and experience but also because of his diplomatic style. But perhaps even more important, Follette began to be seen as an elder statesman because of his wide network of personal contacts and influence. This was not lost on Gauthier who, when he had decided that he wanted to pursue an appointment on an administrative tribunal, immediately sought Gauthier's advice and assistance.

Gauthier told him that if he was serious about seeking such an appointment it would take him several years of concerted effort and lobbying. He stated that he would have to spend considerable time preparing his applications, testing and, then, interviews but, in addition, he also would have to spend time meeting the right people. Follette, of course, told his friend that he would assist him in any way that he could.

About one year before Follette was due to retire, people at DRDC noticed that he was away from the office for varying lengths of time. This was rather unusual for Follette, who had an impeccable attendance record. Naturally, people became concerned, and began to ask whether there was anything the matter with him. Booth, his director, reported that he was not feeling well and had to go to his doctor to get medical checkups and tests done. Follette then returned to the office and was there for only a few weeks before, once again, he was away on sick leave. Several weeks later, Booth told the staff in her unit that Follette was likely to be away on long-term stress leave. Needless to say, this came as a shock to most people when they heard this news. It seemed so unlike Follette. He never appeared to be stressed and he also seemed to be the picture of health.

Shortly after the news that Follette was now on extended stress leave and with no certainty of when or if he would return to work, Gallagher announced that Gauthier would be relieved of his unit responsibilities to be assigned to work in his office on special assignments and projects. No details were offered as to what special assignments and projects Gauthier would be assigned. Since there were no major initiatives or plans in the works at DRDC it was unclear exactly what Gauthier would likely be assigned to do in Gallagher's office. It was evident that a number of the directors at DRDC were caught off guard by the announcement.

In the ensuing weeks it became more and more evident that Gauthier did not seem to have any specific special assignments or project *per se*. He seemed to spend a great deal of his time in his office on the telephone or chatting with various directors, including, his good friend Booth. In time it was obvious that Gauthier was not saddled with any onerous duties or responsibilities. It also seemed that he was spending a great deal of his time in consultation with Booth. Booth's unit had taken on the responsibility for a high-profile project. Although she seemed to be handling it very well, it seemed that Gauthier was assisting her but only in what appeared to be a cursory and advisory capacity.

Other directors in the DRDC appeared to be burdened with their growing workloads, while Gauthier was unavailable and seemed preoccupied with other matters. It was not at all clear what work Gauthier seemed to be engaged in at the office for Director General Gallagher. Gauthier's time seemed to be his own. Although he was always at work during business hours, 8:30 a.m. to 4:30 p.m., he would never come in to work early or stay at work late. The few times that he was known to stay late were to attend social functions that had been planned for the office. It was not long before the directors, other than Booth, became resentful of the apparently "cushy assignment" that Gauthier had been given by Gallagher. There was speculation that Gallagher, Gauthier's close friend, had freed him of his director's responsibility so that he could spend more time trying to land his administrative appointment.

Ken Follette finally returned to the office seven months after he had gone on long-term stress leave. In fact, Follette did not return to the office until he had used all of his sick leave. When he did return to work he looked relaxed and refreshed and the same as ever. Some two months after Follette returned to the office, he retired from the public service. Naturally, with Follette so close to retirement and with so little time left, he hardly had sufficient time to finish off a few loose ends, sign off on his retirement package and clean out his office. Some thought it was rather fortuitous that Follette would experience his stress illness so close to his retirement. If he had not gone on his sick leave, he would have, of course, lost all his accumulated sick leave time on the day of his retirement.

At Follette's office retirement party, which had been organized by Booth, Gallagher gave a brief speech about how valuable and hard working an employee Follette had been to the office and how much he would be missed by all those at DRDC when he retired. Gauthier also spoke on the occasion, saying how much he personally valued Follette's advice and how productive he was over his years with DRDC. When Follette spoke, he said, that he was going to take a holiday with his wife but that he did not intend to retire fully; he said that he enjoyed working and wanted to take on new challenges and work on a part-time basis.

One year after Follette's retirement, staff at DRDC noticed a familiar face in the office. Follette was seen walking around the office. It was later learned that he had gotten a small contract to work on a research and development project for DRDC. The contract required Follette to come to the office three days a week, and he was provided with his own office and staff support. It seemed that he would report directly to Gallagher.

Shortly after Follette's return to the office, it was announced that Gauthier was appointed to a five-year term as a Member of the Veterans Review and Appeal Board of Canada (VRAB). He was also granted a leave of absence from the DRDC for the duration of his term on the VRAB.

Questions

1. Explain why you think that this case study is or is not aptly titled.

2. What, if anything, is wrong in the scenario(s) outlined by this case study? Are private interests superceding the public interest in this case study?

3. Justify who, if anyone, is most at fault in this case study. Would it be Director General Gregory Gallagher, Director Sally Booth, Director Roger Gauthier, Senior Policy Analyst Ken Follette or any other person(s) or group(s)?

4. What type of organizational behaviour does this case study exemplify?

5. Would you say that this scenario is more prevalent in the public sector than in the private sector? Justify your answer.

Resource Materials

- National Defence and the Canadian Forces
  http://www.forces.gc.ca/site/home-accueil-eng.asp

- National Defence — Defence Ethics Program — Defence Integrity Framework
  http://www.ethique.forces.gc.ca/index-eng.asp

- National Defence and Canadian Forces Ombudsman
  http://www.ombudsman.forces.gc.ca/au-ns/index-eng.asp

- Public Sector Integrity Canada
  http://www.psic-ispc.gc.ca/index.php?lang=en

- Public Servants Disclosure Protection Act
  http://laws.justice.gc.ca/en/showtdm/cs/P-31.9

Negotiating Annual Budget Targets

Patrick Hastings was reviewing the monthly statistical reports to determine whether his unit would make its budget commitment for the year. The statistics for the current month indicated that he and his staff were not likely to make this month's budget target unless they had an outstanding last week to finish the month. However, the year-to-date statistics were strong with three months to go before the end of the current fiscal year. If they continued their current production level, it was likely that they would make their overall budget target for the year. Hastings knew this meant that his unit would have to continue to work hard to ensure that this would happen. He knew that he would have to keep his team motivated for the remainder of the year and hoped that none of his key personnel took sick leave, for any extended period of time, in the next three months.

Hastings was very proud of his unit's record for meeting or exceeding its annual budget target. Since he had been appointed the director of the unit, more than four years ago, the unit had met or exceeded its annual budget target for each of these fiscal years. He considered this to be an important measure of his unit's excellent performance under his leadership and management.

Naturally, he wanted to maintain his unit's excellent performance record and his own reputation as a good manager.

However, Hastings was concerned about the forthcoming meeting with his division's director general, Walter Stanton, and the new assistant deputy minister (ADM) of his branch, Katherine Smith, on his unit's budget targets for the next fiscal year. The new ADM had a no-nonsense reputation and was also known for her aggressive and confrontational style. Smith was also reputed to be a very tough and a clever negotiator who gave up very little and expected to get a great deal in return. Stanton, on the other hand, who he knew very well, was more open and flexible in negotiations. After all, he had to work directly with all the directors in his division on a daily basis and he was also intimately familiar with all of the trials and tribulations of running a unit. Stanton had been a unit director for many years himself, before he was promoted to his current position as the director general of the division. In contrast, Smith was still "learning the ropes" of the operations of her branch. Before coming to the ministry she had been the director general of another ministry and she appeared to be on a very steep "learning curve" for both her new ADM position and for her assignment as head of the branch in her new ministry.

Hastings asked his administrative assistant, Gloria Spencer, to do a draft of his unit's budgetary targets for the next fiscal year based on the budget targets that were set for the current fiscal year. Stanton had already provided him with the resource assumptions that he should use for his unit for the total person years (PY) staff positions and the materiels budget for such things as supplies and photocopying, etc. He also held several meetings with his unit's managers to ensure that he had a good sense of where they all stood in terms of their individual resources levels, including staffing and the challenges that they would expect to face in the next fiscal year.

In his last round of meetings with his managers, Hastings was able to get a good sense of what his unit was likely able to produce in the next fiscal year. Spencer sat in on all of these meetings and incorporated the individual managers' estimates into the overall production target estimates for the next fiscal year. The next day Hastings sat down with Spencer to review her final overall production target estimates. These were, in fact, slightly higher than the production target estimates for the current fiscal year. Patrick Hastings was somewhat surprised, given that the staffing and materiel budget assumptions that he had received from Walter Stanton were lower than what he had to work with for the current fiscal year. He asked Spencer whether she was confident that they could make these production targets for the next fiscal year. Spencer stated that all things being equal, and barring any unforeseen staffing problems or surprise budget cutbacks during the course of the fiscal year then, she was quite confident that their unit could achieve the estimated production targets. Hastings said that he was not at all comfortable with the estimated production targets.

Hastings stated that if he presented these estimated production budget targets to Stanton and Smith they would not be satisfied and would want to set them even higher. He said that knowing Stanton, he would want to add an additional 20 percent on any budget target that he presented. He also mentioned that everything he knew and heard about Smith had led him to believe that she might want to have the unit's production targets bumped up by at least 25 to 30 percent. Hastings stated that he would have to assume that whatever budget target he presented to the director general and the ADM would be increased by at least 20 percent. This would leave the unit in a very difficult position and in danger of not meeting its production targets for the coming fiscal year. It also meant that the staff in the unit would have to work a quarter to a third harder than they were working currently just to try to get close to these unreasonably high production targets.

Hasting stated that he would rather set the estimated production targets lower than he knew the unit was capable of achieving in order to be confident that it could achieve these figures. If they exceeded the budget targets, then the unit would be seen as a group of overachievers and as exceeding their commitments and expectations. He said that he would rather be seen as that than as underachievers who could not make their fiscal year production targets. Accordingly, he directed Spencer to reduce the estimated production targets that she had presented by 20 percent; he would use these projected production targets in his meeting with Stanton and Smith.

The meeting to set his unit's production targets for the next fiscal year was held in Smith's office. Stanton started by congratulating Hastings for his unit's performance in the current fiscal year. He said that his unit was only one of three in the division that would likely make its production targets for the current fiscal year. He said that the other four units in the division would not likely make their production targets. One unit, in particular, he said was not performing very well and would come well below the production targets they were committed to achieving. However, he stated that the division as a whole would meet its overall production target for the fiscal year, thanks to the performance of the three units that would not only make but, in all likelihood, exceed their production targets for the current fiscal year. Smith also complimented Hastings on his unit's contribution to the division and its good work in meeting and, hopefully, exceeding its production targets.

Smith then stated that she was disappointed with the estimated production targets for his unit for the coming fiscal year. She said that she thought that these figures were far too low, particularly given the unit's strong performance in the current fiscal year. Stanton also said that he thought the figures could be higher than those that Hastings had submitted.

Hastings thanked Smith and Stanton for their positive comments and their congratulations for his unit's strong performance over the current fiscal year. However, he said that the estimates he had presented for his unit's production targets for the next fiscal year were based on realistic estimates of what he thought his unit could deliver, given the resource assumptions that Stanton had provided him. He also pointed out that he expected a higher turnover in his unit's staff in the next fiscal year due to retirements and maternity leave. He said that two of the unit's most senior members were scheduled to retire in the middle of the next fiscal year and that this would have a dramatic impact on the production levels of his unit. He also noted that he had already received notice from another staff member that she would be on maternity leave in June and would not return to work until the following June, at the earliest.

Hastings also stated that he had been very fortunate during the current fiscal year because his unit averaged only two days per month of lost staff time due to illness. The average over the past five years, he noted, had been three-and-a-half days per month of lost staff time due to illness. He stated that the current fiscal year was likely an anomaly and that next fiscal year the average lost staff time due to illness would likely be at or above the 3.5 days per month average of the past five years. Moreover, he stated that with the ministry's new initiative and offer to provide junior staff with ongoing in-house training he expected more staff to request additional training in key areas such as personnel management, budgeting fundamentals, computer skills upgrading, and so on. Furthermore, he stated that there had been persistent rumours that the ministry was going to introduce a new central computer accounting systems program that would, if introduced next year, require intensive training on the part of key staff and a period of adjustment that would cascade throughout the ministry and have an inevitable dampening affect on overall productivity. Given all of the forgoing, Hastings stated, his unit would be fortunate, indeed, if it was able to achieve the estimate production targets that he had submitted.

Stanton stated that the rumours about the new central computer accounting system program for the ministry were just that nothing more than rumours and that this should not be included as a factor in any estimate of production targets for the next fiscal year. Hastings made a special note of the fact that Smith did not wish to comment on this point. Stanton also stated that the new ministry initiative to provide ongoing in-house training had built-in controls to limit the number of junior staff that could take these courses at any one time from each division within the ministry. Further, he reminded Hastings, that these courses could be taken only with the approval of the director generals on the recommendation of the staff member's director. Hastings stated that he was aware of the approval process but stated that he could not very well refuse to allow his hard-working junior staff members to take these opportunities for professional development, if they put in their requests, especially, when other units and divisions are doing so. He note that these in-house week-long training programs were one of the few perks that he could offer his unit's promising junior staff members.

Smith intervened and stated that she thought that his unit could produce at least 25 percent more than the estimated production targets that Hastings had submitted. Hastings replied that with all due respect this was asking far too much from his own unit. He noted that his unit was one of the few units in the division that had consistently met or exceeded its production targets. He stated that his staff should not have to be rewarded with more work than they were already doing when other units were not pulling their fair share of the division's workload. He stated that increasing his unit's estimated production targets by 25 percent would seriously damage his unit's morale to the point that it could have a damaging effect on production for the balance of this current fiscal year, let alone the coming fiscal year. He also stated that this would be putting him in a near impossible position of having to try and sell these new production targets to a unit that already felt that it was being pushed to the limit. On the contrary, Hasting declared, would it not be better to address the under-performance of the other four units in the division than to continue to press those units that are consistently meeting and/or exceeding their production targets?

Smith stated that she would be looking at this in due course. Nonetheless, she said that all the units had submitted estimated production targets below what she thought they were capable of achieving. Hastings noted that he had not seen the budget estimates submitted by the other units and could only speak for his own unit's submissions. He stated emphatically that his unit would be hard pressed next fiscal year even to make his projected production targets and that increasing these by 25 percent would be merely setting his unit up for failure.

Stanton said that perhaps a fair compromise for his unit would be to increase the estimated production targets by 20 percent rather than 25 percent. Hastings stated that this, too, was far too high to expect from his unit and something he would have a very difficult time selling to the managers and staff. He added that with the anticipated high staff turnover rate next fiscal year and the planned hiring of new employees, which would require considerable time training, this would have a further negative effect on his unit's productivity.

Smith stated that the deputy minister (DM) had told her the other day that he anticipated the possibility of a small budget cutback across the government in the next few months. She pointed out the DM thought that the ministry could make up this budget cutback by imposing a hiring freeze on indeterminate positions for the first six months of the next fiscal year. Stanton stated that this was the first that he had heard of this possibility. Hastings asked whether this possible hiring freeze would also be imposed on determinant positions. Smith replied that it would not. The DM, she remarked, made a definite point of saying that the ministry would not have to resort to limited contract hires to meet any budget cutbacks.

Stanton then asked Hastings whether he could sell a 15 percent increase to his estimated production targets for the next fiscal year. Patrick Hastings stated that he would be more comfortable selling a 10 percent increase to his estimated production targets. However, if the budget cutbacks were implemented it would be unlikely that he would be able to achieve even his original estimated production targets.

Smith then directed Stanton to set Hastings' production targets at 15 percent above those that he had submitted. In light of this dramatic increase in his unit's production targets for the next fiscal year, Hastings asked whether he could have an equivalent increase in his unit's staff and materiels budget for next fiscal year. Smith said absolutely not.

Questions

1. Was there a clear winner and a clear loser in these negotiations for setting annual production targets for Patrick Hastings' unit? Explain how and why you determined who, if anyone, won or lost in this scenario.

2. Critically assess Director Patrick Hastings' strategy for negotiating his unit's production targets with Director General Walter Stanton and ADM Katherine Smith.

3. What were the most important factors that impacted on the outcome of this negotiations scenario?

4. What, if anything, could Patrick Hastings have done differently to ensure a better outcome for his unit in these negotiations?

5. What lessons can be drawn from this negotiations scenario about the operation of the budgetary process in public organizations?

Resource Materials

- Allan M. Maslove, "The Budgetary Process," *The Canadian Encyclopedia.*
  http://www.thecanadianencyclopedia.com/index.cfm?PgNm=TCE&Params=A1SEC817408

- Abhinay Muthoo, "A Non-Technical Introduction to Bargaining Theory?" *World Economics,* Vol. 1, No. 2 (April–June, 2000), 49–66.
  http://privatewww.essex.ac.uk/~muthoo/simpbarg.pdf

- Mike Moffatt, "What are Game Theory and Bargaining Theory," About.Com
  http://economics.about.com/cs/studentresources/f/game_theory.htm

- Sergio Poggione, "Negotiation Skills," Presentation to the American Society of Access Professionals, Orlando, Florida, March, 2008.
  http://www.capa.ca/ASAP-2008-Negotiation.ppt#1

- Stephen Cohen, *Negotiating Skills for Managers.* Toronto: McGraw-Hill Professional, 2002. ISBN:0071387579
  http://books.google.ca/books?id=1GGAnrNyqQEC&dq=negotiation+skills&source=gbs_summary_s&cad=0

Restructuring the Regional Office

There were persistent rumours circulating in the Pacific Regional Office of Fisheries and Oceans Canada (FOC) that a major restructuring of the regional office was imminent. The most pressing concern among the staff members was where they would likely end up following the restructuring. It had been evident for months that a downsizing was likely to take place. Several years earlier, the demands on the Pacific regional office were such that it had been decided that a separate office in Victoria, British Columbia, should be opened. However, with current budgetary cutbacks and the change in priorities, this office would have to be folded back into the main Pacific regional office in Vancouver, British Columbia.

At present, there were eight major work teams operating on functional lines within the Pacific regional office. The satellite office in Victoria was considered to be the ninth team, but because it was situated in a separate office, some distance away, it operated with greater autonomy than any of the other teams. This was partly due to the type of work that this team was expected to do and was also due to its relative size in comparison to other teams. The Victoria team grew to be larger than any of the work teams in the Pacific regional office partly because the regional director general was able to visit the office only about once or twice each month. In effect, it operated as a separate mini-Pacific regional office of FOC.

The other eight work teams had the regional director general, Joyce Weatherall, immediately on hand and she and her staff were constantly available and frequently dropped by to speak with the respective team managers on all manner of issues and concerns. The Pacific regional office had also, initially, carved out a separate budget for the satellite office in Victoria. No other work teams in the Pacific regional office had a separate budget. However, the satellite office in Victoria had a budget that was limited to only three years, and its budget allocation was coming to an end in a matter of a few short months.

The situation in the Victoria satellite office was also substantially different because it was primarily staffed with determinant and temporary employees whose terms were slated to end when the three-year funding for the office was due to expire. Needless to say, the morale in the Victoria office was significantly worse than the morale in the main office in Vancouver. Most of the employees in the satellite office knew that they would be losing their jobs.

The work team manager in the Victoria office, Tom Carlton, was concerned, particularly, with executing effectively his office closing strategy. Indeed, there were rumours that he was also working on his own personal "exit strategy" to another position in FOC.

A three-year stint as work Team Manager in a separate satellite office situated in Victoria was very appealing to Carlton, when Weatherall had first broached this subject with him some four years earlier. Carlton saw this as an opportunity to gain valuable management experience leading what was, in essence, a separate, albeit, smaller version of a regional office. He assumed that this would make it easier for him to move up the FOC hierarchy at the end of the three-year assignment. But, the position had proved more demanding and challenging than he had anticipated and it seemed to have worn thin over the last three years.

Weatherall had carefully considered a number of possible scenarios for restructuring the Pacific regional office. The one that she found the most attractive and the least disruptive was the scenario that saw the nine work teams reduced to six.

From the outset, everyone knew that the work team in the satellite office in Victoria was only temporary. There were no issues with the unions because many of the staff in the satellite office were, in fact, contract and/ or temporary employees who were unrepresented by the unions. It was unfortunate that the Pacific regional office and FOC were going to lose a number of employees from Victoria who had proven to be very capable and hard-working staff. Many of these employees were certainly much better than many of the employees in the Vancouver office, but there was nothing that Joyce Weatherall could do about that because the Vancouver office employees were indeterminate and unionized. Management could not pick and choose who went and who stayed. The few indeterminate staff who were in Victoria would have to be relocated and resume their former positions and be incorporated within the new restructured Vancouver operations.

In order to reduce nine work teams to six, the indeterminate staff on the work team in Victoria would have to be found a home on one of the other teams in Vancouver. However, staff members should not, ideally, be incorporated into one of the work teams that would eventually also be folded into another work team. Surely, no permanent staff member should be expected to make more than one move during the Vancouver restructuring.

Weatherall thought that she was fortunate that one of the work team managers in the Vancouver office was slated to retire before the end of the year. In the preliminary planning for the inevitable restructuring some months before, she had spoken to work team manager, Kendall Grant, about the possibility of merging his work Team with another one. Given Grant's pending retirement, he was naturally very open to the suggestion. Indeed, he welcomed it because this would allow him to reduce his own workload gradually so that he could devote more of his time to planning his departure from the public service and determining how he should spend his retirement. It would also give him an opportunity to consider other post-retirement employment possibilities.

Grant's advice was that the most natural fit for his work team was a merger with Wayne Reynolds' work team. He also pointed out that he worked well with Reynolds and that he would probably be open to the suggestion of gradually taking on the responsibility for his work team. The only thing he was concerned about, Grant said, was that Reynolds would probably not welcome his own increased workload. Weatherall stated that the workload increase for Reynolds would be temporary at best, since there would be an inevitable reduction in the size of the new merged work Team down to its normal size. She told Grant that she would have to speak to Reynolds about this possibility.

When Weatherall spoke with Reynolds, he said that he was not surprised at the suggestion of merging his work team with Grant's. He stated that he agreed with Grant's opinion that there was a natural fit between their two work teams. However, he said that meant that he would have to manage a new work team that would be twice as large, essentially, as his current work team which would hardly be fair. Weatherall stated that the new merged work team would not actually be twice as large because not all the staff on Grant's work Team would be merged with his work Team.

Weatherall noted that there would be a number of retirements and other transfers out of Grant's work team. The staff turnover rate, she said, on Grant's work team has been higher traditionally than the other work teams in the Pacific regional office. She added that she was also aware that there would be a number of pending transfers from his work team. Overall, Weatherall said, she expected that new merged work team would be about 50 percent larger than Reynolds' current work team.

Reynolds stated that the real challenge would not only be in managing a larger work team but in handling the merger of the two, which would not only be time consuming but would also take a great deal of careful planning and execution.

Weatherall stated that she agreed that this was perhaps the most difficult part of the challenge in the merger of the two work teams and was precisely why she thought that Reynolds could benefit by having an additional staff person added to his office. She stated that he would need someone to assist him for at least six months to handle all of the administrative details that would inevitably arise in the merger. Weatherall said that she was prepared to second one of her administrative assistants, Patsy Griffiths, to work with him for the next six months on this critical part of the task. Reynolds replied that he appreciated the additional staff support. Nonetheless, he said that he was not certain whether a six-month secondment of an administrative assistant would be sufficient support to manage the merger. Weatherall reminded him that Grant would not formally retire from the public service until the end of the year and that he would be able to assist him with executing key aspects of the merger. She stated that this would have to be worked out very carefully between Grant and himself, so that there would be a clear division of labour in their tasks; otherwise, it could potentially be a formula for disaster. Weatherall said that she wanted to make it clear that Reynolds would have the overall responsibility for managing the merger of the two work teams.

There was one work team in the Pacific regional office that was the least productive among the nine work teams. Weatherall knew that this work team would have to be merged with another. However, there did not seem to be a natural fit with this team with any of the others. Deborah Horace who was the youngest and most inexperienced manager in the Pacific regional office managed the least productive work team. Weatherall was acutely aware that Horace would be very disappointed if her work team was merged and she lost her first management opportunity.

When Horace had been appointed a work team manager, about a year earlier, she was given the assignment to try and turn around the least productive work Team in the Pacific regional office. Weatherall decided to give her this assignment, in part, because there were few other viable options available at the time, but also because she wanted to see whether Horace was up to the challenge. Although Horace made some marginal improvements in her work team's overall operations, there was only a negligible improvement in the team's overall productivity.

Allan Campbell managed the most productive work team in the Pacific regional office. Indeed, Campbell was known as a tough, no-nonsense, manager who was also respected, if not well liked by his staff. Weatherall knew that Campbell would likely be disappointed if he was not called upon to take on the challenge of merging his work team with one of the others in the Pacific regional office.

When Weatherall met with Campbell, she asked him if he would be willing to take on a huge but important challenge. She said that she needed a talented and proven work team manager to take on the critical task of not only merging two work teams, but also of increasing the overall productivity of the newly-merged team. She explained that she wanted Campbell's team to merge with Horace's.

Weatherall said that everyone in the Pacific regional office was well aware that Horace had the least productive work team in the office and that something needed to be done about this situation. The critical challenge, she noted, would be to raise the staff's productivity on Horace's team while merging them in with his own to create an entirely new work team that would be more productive than the two existing work teams.

Campbell said that this was a major challenge indeed! He noted that there were a number of real concerns with many of the staff on Horace's team and that it could take some time to straighten these out before there could be any signs of productivity improvements. He also noted that there was a potential risk that rather than bringing Horace's staff to a higher level of productivity, they could end up bringing down the productivity of his own work team instead, to the detriment of the Pacific regional office's productivity as a whole. Moreover, this challenge would require the necessary resources and support to organize and to implement properly.

Campbell asked Weatherall what support staff and other resources she would be able to provide him if he took on these challenges in the suggested work team mergers. Weatherall stated that Campbell's personal administrative support staff would be immediately doubled. She further informed him that Horace had a secretary and an administrative assistant who would be assigned to him for as long as he thought he could use the additional staff support. Campbell thought that this probably would be sufficient staff support but he said that he did not want Horace's administrative assistant because he considered her to be part of the problem on her current work team. Campbell suggested that she be reassigned to another work team manager. In fact, he stated that he wanted, specifically, Grant's administrative assistant. He said that Grant was due to retire and that everyone knew that his administrative assistant was one of the reasons why Grant's team was so efficient. Weatherall said that this could be arranged. Campbell asked why Weatherall neglected to mention anything about how the proposed merger would affect Horace.

Weatherall stated that she planned to assign Horace the task of leading and managing the entire Pacific regional office restructuring. However, she would do so under her personal direct supervision. She said that she saw this as a real development opportunity for Horace, who needed an opportunity to work directly with all of the successful work team managers in order to observe them and to learn how they managed their work Teams.

Campbell also asked Weatherall whether any decision had been made about staff members who would be returning to the Vancouver regional office from the Victoria satellite office. Weatherall said that Carlton would return to Vancouver for only a short period to ensure that everyone from Victoria was reintegrated in to the Pacific regional office. Carlton would only be back in Vancouver for about one month before he is seconded to FOC headquarters in Ottawa to work on a special assignment. Weatherall said that Carlton put in a request for a transfer to Ottawa some months ago. She noted that he would like to do some policy development and planning work for at least one year after the intensive operational management and administrative work that he had been doing for the past three years.

Campbell remarked that all the managers in the Pacific regional office might be making the same request after the restructuring was completed. Weatherall laughed and asked him whether his new work team could use any of the returning indeterminate staff from the satellite office in Victoria. Campbell said he would have to go over the list of staff to see whether there was anyone that he wanted. He asked Weatherall what Carlton would do for the month that he would be back in Vancouver, before going on his special assignment in FOC headquarters in Ottawa. Weatherall told Campbell that Carlton would be assigned to her office because she would be short staffed. She said that she would be assigning one of her most capable administrative assistants, Patsy Griffiths, to work with Reynolds for the next six months. She also wanted Carlton to assist her with planning all the "nitty gritty" details that are necessary to ensure that the Pacific regional office restructuring is a success.

Questions

1. Critically assess Joyce Weatherall's "change management" strategy for restructuring the nine work teams into six work teams in the Pacific regional office of FOC.

2. What would you consider to be the greatest obstacles that Wayne Reynolds and Allan Campbell would likely face when they attempt to merge Kendall Grant's and Deborah Horace's work teams with their own?

3. Justify who you think has the most challenging assignment in the Pacific Regional Office restructuring among the following three managers: Wayne Reynolds, Allan Campbell or Deborah Horace.

4. Explain why you think that Joyce Weatherall has or has not made a serious error in assigning Deborah Horace, her least experienced manager, with the overall responsibility for restructuring the Pacific regional office.

5. Is it fair to conclude that work team manager Tom Carlton was rewarded for his work in successfully managing the startup and the winding down of the Pacific regional office's satellite office in Victoria?

Resource Materials

- Fisheries and Oceans Canada
  http://www.dfo-mpo.gc.ca/index-eng.htm

- Guidelines for Organizational Design, Free Management Library,
  http://www.managementhelp.org/org_thry/design.htm

- "What is Organizational Design?"
  http://www.inovus.com/organiza.htm

- The Center for Organizational Design
  http://www.centerod.com/

- Team Building/Employee Empowerment/Employee Involvement
  http://humanresources.about.com/od/involvementteams/
  Team_Building_Employee_Empowerment_Employee_Involvement.htm

- Canada Public Service Agency
  Public Service Modernization Act (PSMA) Change Management Tools
  http://www.psagency-agencefp.gc.ca/arc/smp-gps/cm-gc/menu_e.asp

Running for Cover

Benjamin Gallant, director of the Taxpayer and Business Assistance Section of the Saskatchewan Regional Office of the Canada Revenue Agency (CRA), was responsible for a team of 10 professionals, largely accountants, who worked in his section. He reported to Peter Shell, regional director, who, in turn, reported to Laurent Trembley, deputy commissioner for Program Management in CRA's headquarters in Ottawa.

Gallant had a good working relationship with Shell, his immediate supervisor, and Trembley, his supervisor's immediate supervisor. Both were regarded as excellent managers in the CRA. Indeed, Shell frequently called on Gallant to serve as the acting regional director when he was required to travel outside the Saskatchewan regional office on business, usually to Ottawa for senior management meetings or for training purposes.

For the past six months the CRA's regional office seemed to be getting a great deal of attention and scrutiny in the media. The CRA commissioner was making an effort to respond to the media by issuing news releases and letters to the editor to try to correct some of the misperceptions that seemed to be widely disseminated by the media. The media seemed to be interested especially in the fact that the CRA appeared to be handling taxpayers differently from one regional office to the next. It was alleged, for instance, that the Ontario regional office applied a strict interpretation of various provisions of the *Income Tax Act*, while the Quebec regional office applied these same provisions in a more liberal and generous manner. The allegations were that the same rules and regulations of the *Income Tax Act* were being applied and interpreted differently in the different CRA regional offices across the country.

The media was also quite interested in the fact that there seemed to be different productivity levels in the CRA regional offices across the country. For instance, it was alleged that the British Columbia regional office was the most productive regional office in the country, in terms of processing tax returns, while the Atlantic regional office in Halifax was among the least productive regional offices in Canada. All of this was having, as one might imagine, a devastating impact on the morale of the CRA staff across the country. Some staff members took great umbrage at what they described as a "media smear job" against the CRA, and they demanded that the Commissioner and the board of management immediately address the accusations levelled against the CRA in the media.

Gallant noticed that the media in Regina had also raised a number of concerns regarding the CRA's Saskatchewan regional office. The newspapers broke a story that there were allegations that certain CRA employees in the Saskatchewan regional office were not dealing fairly with all taxpayers. One newspaper story even alleged that CRA employees in the Saskatchewan regional office were accepting inducements to ignore income-tax violations on the part of certain taxpayers. This story broke on a Friday morning on what appeared to be a slow news day. Gallant considered this to be typical of the type of news coverage that the CRA had been getting over the past few months.

Later that same day, Peter Shell called Benjamin Gallant to tell him that he had to attend an important meeting for CRA regional directors in Montreal next week. He stated that Deputy Commissioner Trembley called him and insisted that he and all the other CRA regional directors had to attend this meeting. Shell then asked Gallant whether he would be willing to serve as the acting regional director during his absence from the office. Shell stated that he would have to be away for the entire week. Gallant replied that he would be happy to serve as the acting regional director during the week he was away.

Gallant considered these Acting Regional Director assignments to be important opportunities to demonstrate his senior management capabilities. He also saw the acting regional director assignments as professional development opportunities or a type of "on-the-job training" for senior executive positions within the federal government. He enjoyed these assignments because it also gave him a chance to interact with more people and to address different issues than he usually had to address as the director of a section of the regional office.

On the Monday afternoon of the following week, Gallant received a call from a senior communications officer in Ottawa, who said that he had received information from his sources that the media would be carrying a story on the Saskatchewan regional office the next day. He said that the story would likely be along the lines of what was covered locally about how certain staff members in the regional office were handling particular tax violations. He advised Gallant to be prepared for the media calls to come into his office the next day.

When Gallant got off the telephone, he thought that he should immediately inform Shell of this development. However, when he tried to contact Shell at his hotel in Montreal he found that he was not there so he left him a brief message. He also contacted the local public relations officer in the Saskatchewan regional office, who told him that he had gotten the same information from Ottawa and that he was trying to find out what the content of this story was likely to be from his own local sources in the media. Gallant then notified the other directors in the regional office about this and advised them to be prepared for possible media inquiries the next day.

The next day two major daily newspapers carried front-page stories that alleged that two or more staff in the Saskatchewan regional office were under investigation by the Royal Canadian Mounted Police (RCMP). The newspapers alleged that these officials were under criminal investigation for receiving payments from a number of firms that owed sizeable amounts in back taxes.

When this story broke there was a great deal of consternation among the staff in the Saskatchewan regional office. There was also a great deal of speculation as to who in the regional office was the subject of the RCMP's investigations. This had, of course, a devastating effect on the morale in the Saskatchewan regional office. Staff absenteeism increased dramatically as employees called in sick or failed to report to work. There was also an increase in the number of last-minute leave applications for staff members who, suddenly, wanted to take vacation leave.

Rumours were rampant throughout the Saskatchewan regional office. One such rumour was that someone or perhaps a few people within the Regional Office were leaking information to the media. There were rumours that also suggested that whoever was leaking information to the media was also making allegations of misconduct against fellow co-workers. Since no one in the Saskatchewan regional office had been approached, apparently, by anyone from the RCMP, there were also rumours that the RCMP was conducting an undercover operation within the office and that everyone was under investigation.

Benjamin Gallant immediately tried to contact Shell and found that he was not at his hotel. He had not responded to his previous telephone message. Gallant, as the acting regional director, also tried to contact Tremblay, and again was unable to do so. When he contacted Tremblay's office in Ottawa his staff stated that he was at the regional directors' meetings in Montreal and they, too, could not seem to contact him.

Gallant then started to get barraged with telephone calls from CRA headquarters in Ottawa. At the same time, a stream of people began coming into his office to speak to him about the newspaper articles and to get further information about what was allegedly taking place in the regional office. His secretary, Alice Hamin, was inundated with telephone calls asking to be connected immediately with the regional director and requesting an appointment as soon as possible.

Hamin had worked with Gallant for three years. Hamin was an experienced secretary who had worked with other senior executives in her career. She was able to screen and prioritize incoming telephone calls and manage the flow of staff who came by to see him. One of her strengths was to be able to deal with all types of people. She was firm, but also extremely tactful, particularly with especially difficult personalities. Hamin was quite accomplished at dealing with people who would try to storm down the hallway demanding to see Gallant. Irrespective of the person's rank or position, she could invariably defuse or deflect the situation without the person losing face or being embarrassed. However, the flow of incoming calls and people was so great on this occasion that even Hamin had to put a sign on Benjamin Gallant's office door that stated, "Busy, Please Do Not Disturb."

One of the calls that Hamin immediately put through to Gallant late on Tuesday afternoon was from the CRA commissioner, who told Gallant that he was very concerned about the local newspaper articles and that he too was receiving a constant stream of telephone calls from the national media outlets who were following the story. At this point, he stated, he could not confirm or deny anything. He had contacted the commissioner for the RCMP to find out whether there was an ongoing investigation in the Saskatchewan regional office or any other CRA regional office or offices. He also asked Gallant whether he was able to contact Shell or Tremblay. Gallant said that he had not been able to do so. The commissioner said he should not worry because he had a call scheduled with both of them in the next half-hour and that he would be calling him back immediately after he spoke with them first about the latest developments in the situation. The commissioner also said that if Gallant managed to obtain any information on this story or if there were any further developments from his end that he should call him immediately. The commissioner gave Gallant the number for his private line and told him to call him no matter how late it was, day or night. Gallant reminded the CRA commissioner that Ottawa was two hours ahead of Regina.

About one hour later, Gallant got a call from Shell, who said that the commissioner and general counsel of the CRA had briefed him on the media situation. Gallant asked Shell how everyone in the regional office was coping under the strain of the media onslaught and the news of the possible RCMP investigation. Gallant stated that situation was not very good. The staff morale had hit rock bottom and office productivity had dropped significantly. Shell expressed that he was worried about the possibility of staff leaks to the media. He said that a general email should be sent to everyone in the office, instructing them that the only person in the regional office who is designated to speak to the media is the public relations officer. Shell stated that the media was known to try to contact staff at random simply to get information from whomever they could. He stated that sending this general email to everyone in the department was vitally important.

Shell informed Gallant that he would not likely be able to return to the regional office until Thursday at the earliest. He said that the meetings in Montreal were going well and that the deputy commissioner was still insisting that he remain at the meetings, if at all possible. Shell also stated that the deputy commissioner was also going to call Gallant after their telephone call.

It was about 7:00 p.m., Regina time, when Deputy Commissioner Tremblay called Gallant. Tremblay's first question was whether there was any further news or developments at the Saskatchewan regional office. Gallant replied that there were no further developments and Tremblay also said that he was waiting for the commissioner to get back to him about any information that he was able to get from the RCMP. Gallant stated that the situation in the regional office was not good. Productivity would likely be affected by this situation for some time to come. The deputy commissioner stated that he expected as much but that the regional office would have to do its best under the circumstances. He said that it was important to try and ensure that there are no unauthorized communications to the media regarding this story and that a general email should be sent to all staff as soon as possible. He added that the CRA was reviewing its policy regarding media relations to ensure that all the staff at the CRA were familiar with the rules and regulations regarding contact with the media.

Deputy Commissioner Tremblay then told Gallant that he should contact him as soon as there were any further developments in this news story.

It was 8:00 p.m. when Gallant finally finished his call with the deputy commissioner. He was beginning to wonder whether he should have agreed to serve as acting regional director for Shell on this occasion. He also began to wonder why the meetings in Montreal were so important that Peter Shell had to remain there for the entire week while Gallant had to deal with this major crisis.

Questions

1. Assess what risk or risks, if any, Benjamin Gallant likely faces as the acting regional director during this crisis at the Saskatchewan regional office.

2. What should Benjamin Gallant do, in his capacity as the acting regional director, to weather this crisis at the Saskatchewan regional office? Your recommendation should be mindful of the situation with the media and the public, regional office staff, and senior management at headquarters in Ottawa.

3. In retrospect, justify why you think Benjamin Gallant should or should not have accepted this acting regional director assignment.

4. What are the likely long-term implications of this crisis on the Saskatchewan regional office and the CRA? Explain what, if anything, can be done to address these possible long-term effects on the Saskatchewan regional office.

5. What lessons "crisis management" within the public service does this case study exemplify?

Resource Materials

- Canada Revenue Agency (CRA)
  http://www.cra-arc.gc.ca/menu-e.html

- Royal Canadian Mounted Police (RCMP)
  http://www.rcmp-grc.gc.ca/

- Public and Media Relations, Free Management Library
  /http://www.managementhelp.org/pblc_rel/pblc_rel.htm

- Insurance Bureau of Canada, "Controlling Costs with Risk Management"
  http://www.ibc.ca/en/Business_Insurance/Risk_Management/

- Crisis Management, Free Management Library
  http://www.managementhelp.org/crisis/crisis.htm

Superior Subordinate

Nancy Nicholson, Director, Planning and Operations Secretariat in the Department of Government Services, was reviewing her plans for a major world conference of the International Government Planners Association (IGPA), which was going to be held in Paris, France, in one week's time. The deputy minister, Suzanne Poulette, had asked her to take on the challenge of undertaking a major planning initiative on behalf of the IGPA. She had been engaged in this project for several years. It involved a number of government officials in other countries, such as, the United States, Australia, the United Kingdom, Sweden, The Netherlands, France, and Denmark. Since the IGPA was a voluntary international professional association, Nicholson was doing the work on this project largely on her own time. She was not given any time off from her normal duties and responsibilities in the Planning and Operations Secretariat or from other management responsibilities in the Department of Government Services.

Nicholson reported to Lawrence Kent, Director General of the Strategic Management Branch of the Department of Government Services. She also reported to Gerald Pollard, the Assistant Deputy Minister of the Management and Policy Division, through Director General Kent.

Nicholson's management colleagues in the Management and Policy Division envied her because she had the opportunity to be involved actively with the

IGPA and to work on an interesting international project. They also envied her because she also had an opportunity to do some international travel. Because Nicholson was doing work that was assigned to her by Deputy Minister Poulette and was directly relevant to the work of not only her division but also the department, her travel and related expenses were covered by the Department of Government Services.

Nicholson had been given this assignment by the deputy minister some four years before either Kent or Pollard were appointed to their current positions. However, Pollard considered the IGPA project something that fell directly under his responsibility. When he first assumed his assistant deputy minister (ADM) position, Nicholson spent a great deal of her own time briefing Pollard and his staff on the IGPA and the project that she was involved with for the IGPA. However, as a new ADM, Pollard was so busy dealing with the challenges of his new position that he did not have the time to devote to the IGPA and was very pleased that Nicholson was on this project. He also realized that Nicholson was heavily involved in the IGPA and had built a broad network of international contacts in the professional association and that this network of personal contacts was absolutely vital to the overall success of the project. Nonetheless, he was determined to eventually assume the responsibility for this project and the IGPA file within the Department of Government Services.

Director General Kent also wanted to get involved with the IGPA and eventually play a greater role in this international professional association. However, he knew that Nicholson had the mandate of the deputy minister with respect to her involvement in the IGPA and that, at least for the time being, ADM Pollard was content to have Nicholson engaged in the IGPA. Moreover, Kent knew that Nicholson was a model manager who was doing an excellent job as the director of the Planning and Operations Secretariat. In fact, it was generally acknowledged in the division that one of the reasons that Nicholson had been asked to take on this assignment by Deputy Minister Poulette was because she was such an outstanding manager who had performed exceptionally well in her position.

In fact, it was generally known that Nicholson was an acknowledged expert in the planning field. She had taught at the University of Toronto and at York University before taking up her current position in government. She had completed her Ph.D. in Operations Management at the renowned Harvard Business School, and she had a number of publications on the subject to her credit. Deputy Minister Poulette, of course, did not overlook these impressive credentials when she decided that Nicholson would be ideally suited for this particular assignment.

ADM Pollard was well aware of Nicholson's educational background and her outstanding reputation and performance in his division, but he felt that his own educational background and work experience compared favourably with those of Nicholson. Pollard was a lawyer and member of the Quebec Bar. Before entering government service he had his own successful law practice. After he entered government service, he went on to earn a master's degree in International Affairs at the Sorbonne University in Paris, France. He also had extensive experience with international legal professional associations. He was about 10 years older than Nicholson and was confident that in the long run his many more years of practical and government experience gave him a decided advantage over Nicholson.

ADM Pollard was determined that he should also attend the IGPA world conference in Paris, France, since Nicholson worked in his division and not only reported to him but also because her project fell directly in line with his own responsibilities as the ADM of the Management and Policy Division. Pollard raised this with DM Suzanne Poulette in one of his weekly bilateral meetings. He made the case that since Nicholson's involvement with the IGPA project came under his Division's budget line and he was ultimately responsible for the budget, he should also be directly involved with the IGPA and Nicholson's international project. DM Poulette accepted his rationale and approved his participation in the forthcoming IGPA world conference. In fact, Poulette welcomed Pollard's involvement in the IGPA because she wanted the Department of Government Services to play a greater role internationally, including professional associations such as the IGPA.

Nicholson also welcomed Pollard's participation in the IGPA and her project. She was also very pleased that the Department of Government Services wanted to play a greater role on the international stage. She thought that this would not only benefit the department but she also thought that the department had a great deal that it could offer and contribute internationally as well. This was especially true, she thought, for those members of the IGPA and from other international associations who were from the less developed countries of the world.

Although Pollard wanted to assume responsibility for the IGPA file and project, he was preoccupied with other more pressing work for his division and the department. He found that the hectic pace of his responsibilities as the ADM of the Management and Policy Division left him little time, if any, for much else. Accordingly, he found himself relying more and more on Nicholson for the work on the IGPA file and project. Nicholson found that Pollard was disengaged entirely from the IGPA file and her participation in the project. At times, in fact, he seemed totally disinterested. For instance, whenever she wanted to speak to him about the IGPA project he was either unavailable or did not return her calls. The same applied to her emails to him about the IGPA project. Pollard rarely, if ever, spoke to her about the IGPA or the project she was working on in preparation for the forthcoming world conference. Nicholson found herself speaking to Pollard's executive assistant about the IGPA project more often than not. Nonetheless, whenever Pollard wanted to meet with Poulette, he insisted on a briefing note from Nicholson so he could update the DM on the IGPA project. Indeed, any time that Pollard needed any information on the IGPA or wanted to speak on this subject at departmental meetings, he insisted that Nicholson provide him with either a briefing note or speaking notes on the subject.

Nicholson spent many hours of her own time working on the IGPA file and project in preparation for the world conference in Paris. Several weeks before the world conference, she prepared a briefing and preparation book that she thought would be useful for coordinating her participation at the meeting. When it was completed, she felt that she was completely ready for the IGPA world conference.

When she arrived at the airport to take her flight to Paris she happened to meet Pollard, who also happened to be on her same flight. During the course of their conversation in the departure lounge, Pollard happened to notice Nicholson's briefing and preparation book. Nicholson was happy to show it to Pollard who, when he saw it, asked whether he could have a copy of it for his own use. Nicholson said that she would be happy to arrange to get a copy of her briefing and preparation book for him to review on their flight to Paris. Pollard said that he was annoyed at his staff for not preparing something similar for him. He said that his staff only put together his travel itinerary and the IGPA world conference program and IGPA general meeting agenda but nothing more. Nicholson's briefing and preparation book contained everything that one would need for the IGPA world conference broken down into an easy-to-follow daily schedule of meetings and panel sessions that she was planning to attend and background materials and notes for each IGPA meeting she was invited to attend.

This was Pollard's first IGPA world conference and he only knew a few people who were present, and most of these people only by name. On the other hand, Nicholson knew most of the IGPA world conference participants from her work on the project. As it happened, she took the time to introduce Pollard to all of the key people at the conference. Pollard was quite surprised to see how many people that Nicholson knew. He was even more surprised to see how well regarded she was by these government officials from all parts of the world. They all greeted her very warmly and complimented her for all the work that she was doing, not only on the project but also for the IGPA.

Since Nicholson was taking a lead role on the project and reporting the findings and results of the work on the project at the IGPA world conference, her name was listed in the IGPA program. A copy of her report, on behalf of the international working group, was also contained in the IGPA world conference programme. When Nicholson presented her report to the IGPA world conference in one of the main plenary sessions and was complimented publicly by the president of the IGPA and some of the other executive officers of the IGPA, Pollard was beginning to get concerned.

Pollard did not like to see someone who was several levels below him in the public service hierarchy getting all of the attention and recognition at an international conference. He thought that Nicholson's role should be that of any other subordinate. Their job, he thought, was to make him look good and not to go out of their way to bask in the limelight. Pollard felt upstaged by a subordinate in his own division.

Nicholson certainly did not expect to receive all of the accolades or attention from her international colleagues at the IGPA world conference. She was encouraged by all of the positive feedback that she was receiving but she was more concerned about having her report approved and accepted by the IGPA membership at the general meeting. She was, in fact, so busy with the details of the IGPA world conference that she did not at first notice all of kudos that she was receiving from senior members of the IGPA. Nor did she notice the troubled look on Pollard's face every time someone complimented her on her work on the project. It eventually, however, did come to her attention as well as the attention of other IGPA members at the world conference.

On the third day of the world conference, during a health break, a senior official from Finland, who she had known for many years, came up to her and said that she was doing an outstanding job for the IGPA and they were all very fortunate to have her participating in the association. But then her Finnish colleague cryptically added, "You have done a really good job, but perhaps *too* good of a job." Nicholson was surprised by this comment. She wondered what it meant.

Later that day during a plenary session, she was sitting next to Pollard in the audience when the president of the IGPA again complimented Nicholson on her outstanding work on the project. She noticed that ADM Pollard stirred in his chair at the remarks and looked visibly upset.

Questions

1. Explain whether Nancy Nicholson needs to concern herself with Gerald Pollard's reaction at her doing so well at the IGPA world conference.

2. Is Gerald Pollard's reaction to Nancy Nicholson petty and small, or is he justified, in any way, to expect that Nancy Nicholson would have done more to raise his profile at the IGPA world conference?

3. This case study examines the dynamics of superior/subordinate relationships and the issues between those in positional authority versus those who wield influence due to their skills and abilities and/or the situational context. Analyze the relative power of Nancy Nicholson and Gerald Pollard from a role analysis of their positional authority and influence in the IGPA and the Department of Government Services.

4. Does this case study exemplify the truism that subordinates in an organization who publicly outperform their superiors do so at their own peril?

5. Does this case study also exemplify the importance of subordinates in an organization always having to be cognizant of managing upward; that is, managing their superiors to maintain positive working relationships?

Resource Materials

- Michele C. Wierzgac, "The Power of Informal Networks: The impact of forming a cozy klatch is vast," *Meetings West*, (March 2005).
  http://www.meetingsfocus.com/displayarticle.asp?id=4661

- "Sociologists define informal networks as the web of relationships that people use to exchange resources and services (Cook 1982; Scott 1991; Wellman 1983). Informal networks are distinct from formal networks in that they are not officially recognized or mandated by organizations and in that the content of their exchanges can be work-related, personal, or social (Ibarra 1993)." Gail M. McGuire, "Gender, Race, and Informal Networks: A Study of Network Inclusion, Exclusion, and Resources," Department of Sociology, Indiana University — South Bend, Indiana, January 2000.
  http://www.iusb.edu/~sbres/randd/frgsample.PDF

- Francis J. Yammarino and Allan J. Dubinsky, "Superior-Subordinate Relationships: A Multiple Levels of Analysis Approach," *Human Relations*. 1992; 45:6, 575–600.
  http://hum.sagepub.com/cgi/content/abstract/45/6/575

- Poonan Sharma, "Social Capital," *Phila: A dialogue of caring citizenship*
  http://www.philia.ca/cms_en/page1136.cfm

- Social Capital, *The Encyclopedia of Informal Education*
  http://www.infed.org/biblio/social_capital.htm

- The Art and Science of Leadership
  http://www.nwlink.com/~Donclark/leader/leader.html

The Distasteful Salary Negotiations

Helen Baker had received a letter from the vice-president academic at Eastern State University that the president of the university had approved her appointment at the rank of assistant professor in the department of sociology. This was extremely good news. Baker had completed her doctoral degree in sociology at Stanford University in California four years ago and had taught at several universities in Canada before applying for an academic position at Eastern State University. The vice-president academic's letter stated that the dean of the faculty of social science would be contacting her to discuss the terms and conditions of her appointment.

Baker waited anxiously for the dean of the faculty of social science to call her about her appointment and to discuss her starting salary. She had finished her teaching assignment at Southwestern University two months ago and was now living on her savings. Although she knew that the appointment was not due to start until June 1, in about two months time, she wanted to get things settled as quickly as possible. She was keeping herself busy doing research and writing. The University of Texas Press was interested in publishing her doctoral dissertation, but did not want to publish it in its current form. The editors suggested that it be revised for publication to make it more suitable for a broader academic and general public market. She was also working on a book review and a journal article.

Baker considered herself very fortunate because although she had only recently completed her Ph.D. she already had managed to have a number of academic publications to her credit. She also had delivered three conference papers at a number of academic conferences over the past four years. In addition, she had gained valuable teaching experience since she had completed her doctoral dissertation. Unfortunately, she was only able to land contractually limited term (CLT) appointments for two years each at other universities before she won the competition for the tenure-stream academic position at Eastern State University. Baker thought that she had a good interview with the departmental hiring committee but she suspected that it was her academic publications that had really made the difference in why she was selected for the position over the other candidates who had applied.

Getting her research work published was by no means an effortless task. As a new scholar just starting out without a permanent position and no ready access to research funding, she had found it difficult to do extensive research. Since she had to devote a great deal of her time to teaching there was little time left for research and for writing.

As a contract employee at two different universities, Baker had been pleased to be getting valuable teaching experience in her field of study and expertise. But, one of the hazards of CLT appointments was that employees often found themselves teaching new courses as they moved from one university contract to the next. In the last four years, Baker had to teach six courses that she had never taught before; this required a great deal of time and effort in course design and development as well as lecture and assignment preparation. She had also found that CLT appointments meant that you would have to teach larger classes. This meant that CLT appointees often had a much heavier workload grading student assignments, tests and examinations, including, of course, the time spent meeting and consulting with students.

One of the things that Baker was looking forward to was the stability of teaching the same courses from one academic term to the next rather than having to teach entirely different courses each term. Naturally, she was also looking forward to having a salary she could rely on for the foreseeable future.

When Baker did not hear from the dean of the faculty of social science at Eastern State University, Lois Beatty, she decided to call her office. To her surprise, she was put through immediately to Beatty, who greeted her warmly and welcomed her to the faculty of social science and to Eastern State University. Beatty said that she was meaning to call her but had been extremely busy at this time. She also said that she would have her administrative assistant call Baker to set up a time when they could discuss the terms and conditions of her appointment. Jenny Perkins, Beatty's administrative assistant, called Baker the next day to set up a meeting for the coming week.

Baker came to the dean of the faculty of social sciences' office at the appointed time. However, she was left waiting for about 20 minutes before Beatty greeted her warmly at the door of her spacious office. Beatty was quite friendly and personable and offered Baker a drink. Baker asked for some water and, then, was escorted to Beatty's private meeting room, which was attached to her main office.

They sat across from each other at the boardroom table and, after some preliminary small talk, Beatty stated that it was very good to have Baker joining the department of sociology. She mentioned that the faculty of social science was hiring at least 10 new faculty members this year. She also pointed out that the faculty was experiencing significant financial constraints in a number of areas, particularly in its research funding. Beatty emphasized that she had to be very careful that she stayed within her various faculty budget lines or she would end up hearing from the central university administration.

Beatty went on to point out that Eastern State University offered an excellent benefits package for all its employees. She added that a full teaching load in the department of sociology was six half courses a year. This did not include, she noted, graduate student supervision of theses or dissertations. Beatty then said that she was happy to offer a teaching load reduction of two half courses or one full course for her first year of teaching. She indicated that this reduced teaching load was intended to allow new faculty members an opportunity to get their research underway. Beatty stated that the new faculty members were expected to seek their own research funding to maintain their research program, and she also said that the university would, of course, provide a computer and office.

Beatty then said that the starting salary for the position would be $60,000 per year. Helen Baker was taken aback at the starting salary offer. At first she did not know what to say. But then she stated that she had earned $65,000 per year teaching at Southwestern University on a CLT appointment.

Beatty went on to say that new faculty would also receive research start-up funds in the amount of $3,500 to cover their first year research expenses. This was offered to help new faculty members to not only initiate their research as soon as possible but to assist them with raising their own research funds.

Beatty then asked Baker how much she was currently earning. Helen Baker had to admit that her CLT appointment had expired at Southwestern University and that she was not currently employed.

Beatty saw that Baker was disappointed and perplexed with her salary offer. Beatty suggested that Baker might wish to consider contacting the university's faculty association and also talk to Anne Banks, the Chairperson of the department of sociology. Beatty also suggested that she and Baker hold another meeting next week to continue their negotiations on the terms and conditions of her appointment and the starting salary.

Baker was unhappy at how things had transpired in her meeting with the dean. She had expected that the starting salary offer would be considerably higher than $60,000 per year. She contacted the faculty association at Eastern State University and spoke with Lisa Shilling, one of the senior staff members in the faculty association. Baker told Shilling that she was just appointed to the department of sociology and was negotiating her starting salary and the terms and conditions of her employment at the university. Baker stated that she was negotiating with the dean of the faculty of social science, Lois Beatty. Shilling chuckled and said that Beatty was a tough negotiator. She said that she wished her the best of luck in her negotiations. Then, Shilling bluntly asked her, "So, how much do you want for a starting salary?" Baker said that she had been struggling with this and was not entirely sure what to ask for in a starting salary. She said that she had been expecting to get at least $70,000, but said that the reason she was not certain what to ask for was that she assumed that there would be an upper limit for starting salaries for assistant professors at Eastern State University. Shilling stated that there was no upper limit for a starting salary. She noted that it varies from individual to individual and what they bring to the university and with their level of research and teaching experience. Shilling suggested that Helen Baker read the material on the faculty association's website on negotiating a starting salary. She said that the material would help in Baker's negotiations.

Baker took Shillings' advice and went to the faculty association's website and read all the materials available for new appointees. She found that the average salary for assistant professors at Eastern State University was $65,000. This was considerably higher than the salaries at many other universities, but slightly lower than a number of other universities, including, Southwestern University. Nonetheless, Baker felt that with her previous university teaching experience and her publication record, at this stage in her career, she should be earning at least the average salary for an assistant professor at Eastern State University, $65,000. In fact, Baker felt that she should be earning much more than the average salary for an assistant professor, given her years of teaching experience and her publication record. She felt that her starting salary should be at least $70,000.

Baker also visited the chairperson of the department of sociology and spoke to her about starting salaries in the department. Anne Banks said that it had varied considerably over the past five years. She observed that the starting salaries for new hires, without a completed Ph.D., were substantially less than those with many years of teaching and research experience and an extensive publication record. She also noted that the department had hired a number of very experienced criminologists in the past couple of years who had worked in government for many years. She stated that these very accomplished practitioners and academic sociologists had commanded fairly high salaries and because their skills were needed in developing a specialized certificate and degree program in criminology within the department of sociology. However, she noted, these special appointments were the notable exceptions and atypical for the department and in the faculty of social science.

Banks also remarked that Beatty can be a difficult negotiator and that her faculty also had been hit with a number of cutbacks over the past couple of years and that it had really had to struggle to keep its budget in line with the university's targets. She further noted that Beatty had very little flexibility on the salary front. Banks also informed Baker that the faculty association had just negotiated a new contract with the university and there would be a three percent salary increase as of April 1. She suggested that Baker might wish to try to include this increase in any starting salary that she manages to settle with the dean.

At their second meeting, Dean Beatty told Baker that she had reconsidered the starting salary offer and said that she was prepared to offer $62,000. Baker said that she had reviewed the statistics available for the average salaries for assistant professors at Eastern State University and found that the average annual salary was $65,000. She said that she felt that given she had a completed Ph.D., with four years of teaching experience and a publication record, she should be earning considerably more than the average annual salary for assistant professors. She stated that she, in fact, thought that her starting salary should probably be $70,000. Beatty replied by stating that the average salary for assistant professors includes all assistant professors at Eastern State, whether they were in their first year of service or their sixth year of service. She said that the average starting salary for first-year assistant professors was considerably lower than $65,000. Baker said that the difference between what Beatty was offering and what she was requesting was only $3,000.

Baker then asked whether it would be possible to raise the research start-up grant funding from $3,500 to $5,000. She noted that she has an extensive research agenda planned for the next several years and that $3,500 was well below what she needed to cover her research costs. Beatty said that she had a limited research budget and $3,500 is what all new hires would be offered. She said that she was prepared to see whether that amount could be increased, but it would depend on how many new positions were filled in a number of faculty departments over the following weeks.

Baker then asked if her teaching load of six half courses a year could be reduced to four half courses a year for at least the first three years. She said that this would allow her to be able to concentrate more of her time on research and writing and publication, in preparation for her consideration for tenure and promotion. Beatty said that she would not budge on this issue because of the tremendous costs involved in reducing the teaching loads for faculty. She said that she could offer a reduced teaching load only in her first year of teaching.

Baker asked whether it would be possible then to have some stability in the courses that she would be teaching over the next three years. Beatty stated that this was a matter that would have to be addressed at the departmental level and with her departmental chairperson, Anne Banks. Baker said that she did not want to be faced with teaching nothing but new courses over the next three years. She stressed that it took a great deal of effort and energy to mount new courses each term and that it would be a huge benefit if she could teach the same courses for the next few years. Beatty stated that from her experience in serving on the faculty's Tenure and Promotion Committee that it was rare for tenure-stream professors to have taught more than six different courses over their careers. However, this was something that she would have to discuss with Banks.

Beatty stated that she wanted to settle this negotiation by the end of the week, if possible. She said that she likely would be away for at least the first part of following week and, perhaps, longer. She went on to say that if she did happen to be away, she would have one of her associate deans contact Baker to present her with the final offer. However, she said that she would send Baker an email outlining what was finally approved in terms of starting salary and start-up research funding and other terms and conditions of employment.

By the end of the following week, Baker had not received an email from Beatty. She began to get concerned and wondered whether there were any difficulties. As her anxiety level rose with each passing day, Baker decided to contact Beatty to see why she had not sent her an email. When Baker called, Perkins answered the telephone and told her that Beatty was on a business trip. Perkins said that she would advise Baker as to when her contract had been approved by the vice-president academic.

Another week went by and Baker had still not had any communication with Beatty or her administrative assistant, Perkins. Baker then decided it was necessary to contact Perkins to find out whether the vice-president academic had approved her contract. When Baker reached Perkins on the telephone, she was told that the vice-president academic had, indeed, approved her contract and that someone in her office would be sending it to her shortly. Baker was, of course, quite relieved to hear that the vice-president academic had approved her contract offer.

The following day, Baker received a surprise call from Beatty's associate dean, Heather Tindal. Tindal asked, "You must be quite anxious to conclude your contract?" Baker said that quite frankly, yes, she was anxious to conclude matters. Tindal then said that while the vice-president academic had approved everything, there was nevertheless a slight problem. She said that the start-up grant funding for research could only be $3,200. Tindal also said that they would mail the offer to her today and that it had to be returned to the dean's office within 15 days.

When Baker received the offer, it was for a salary of $62,000 per year. However, it did not include the forthcoming negotiated increase of 3 percent that faculty members were to receive with the new contract that came into force several weeks later. As Tindal had stated, the start-up grant funding was only $3,200. Baker read and reread the offer at least four times before she decided to speak to the faculty association senior staff member, Lisa Shilling.

After Baker outlined the offer from the university, Shilling stated that Baker would have to decide whether she was prepared to accept the offer or try to negotiate further for a higher salary and research start-up grant.

Questions

1. Explain why you think Helen Baker should or should not accept the offer tendered by Eastern State University?

2. Analyze the negotiating approach and style of Helen Baker and Dean Lois Beatty and justify why you think one or the other has a more effective approach or style and is, hence, a better negotiator.

3. Justify why you think the faculty association representative, Lisa Shilling, gave Helen Baker proper advice and assistance throughout these negotiations.

4. On the facts of this case study, is it reasonable to say that Eastern State University made a fair offer of employment to Helen Baker? If so, why, and if not, why not?

5. What, if anything, could Helen Baker have done differently to affect a higher starting salary and start-up research grant offer from Eastern State University?

6. Are there any lessons or principles of public not-for-profit sector negotiations that can be drawn from this case study?

Resource Materials

- Heidi Burgess, "Negotiations Strategies," January 2004, BeyondIntractability.org
  http://www.beyondintractability.org/essay/negotiation_strategies/

- Brad Spangler, "Best Alternative to a Negotiated Agreement (BATNA)," The Conflict Resolution Information Source, June 2003.
  http://crinfo.beyondintractability.org/essay/batna/?nid=2370

- Susan Ireland, "Salary Negotiation's Guide"
  http://www.susanireland.com/salaryguide/index.html

- Salary Negotiations
  http://www.crummer.rollins.edu/career_management/skills/salary.PDF

- Bargaining Theory of Wages, *Encyclopaedia Britannica*
  http://www.britannica.com/EBchecked/topic/53211/bargaining-theory-of-wages#tab=active~checked%2Citems~checked&title=bargaining%20theory%20of%20wages%20—%20Britannica%20Online%20Encyclopedia

The Fluid
Management
Committee

Henry Jackson was only recently appointed as the regional director of the Toronto office of the Ministry of Correctional Services. Before he entered government service he had served for many years in private legal practice with various law firms in downtown Toronto. In addition to his law practice, Jackson spent a great deal of time volunteering with various organizations that promoted the rights and advocated on behalf of those who had been allegedly wrongfully convicted as well as those who were appealing their denial of parole. For a period of time, in fact, he had served as the president of a nationally-known organization promoting the rights of the wrongfully convicted. When Jackson first entered government service, his appointment did not go unnoticed. He was seen as a high-profile lawyer who was well connected within the criminal law field as well as with key interest groups within the policy field. But, this quickly dissipated and over the years he seemed to work in relative obscurity within the Ministry of Correctional Services (MCS) and he did not seem to distinguish himself through outstanding performance within the ministry. Consequently, it was somewhat surprising when he won the competition among a very strong field of candidates to become the regional director of the Toronto office of the MCS. One of the most surprising features of his selection, in comparison to many of the other candidates for the position, was his lack of any "hands on" management experience in government.

Prior to Jackson's appointment as the regional director, there had always been a weekly managers' meeting that was chaired by the regional director. Jackson, of course, continued the weekly managers' meeting when he assumed his new position because these meetings were vital to ensuring the effective coordination among the respective units in the Toronto office. The weekly management meetings also allowed the managers to plan and implement key activities and initiatives throughout the year and also served as a sounding board for dealing with sensitive personnel issues and concerns.

Jackson had never attended one of these weekly management meetings before his appointment. As the new regional director, however, he now found himself in the position of having not only to participate in the meeting, but chair it as well. Jackson thought he would start things off on the right foot by holding the meetings over the lunch hour and into the afternoon. He directed his administrative assistant to order sandwiches and beverages for all the managers and indicated that the lunch should be served at the outset of the meeting.

Jackson wanted to make everyone as comfortable as possible, particularly given that some of the managers had competed against him for his new position. He expected that there could be some ill will and resentment among some of those managers who had lost out on the competition. Furthermore, he was well aware of his lack of overall management experience and his unfamiliarity with many of the concerns and issues that the managers were struggling with in order to meet their monthly and annual operational budgetary targets.

Jackson decided that the first few meetings would be rather informal affairs to allow for some time for him to familiarize himself with the issues and the various personalities that he had to work with in his new position. At the first weekly management meeting, the managers were pleased to see that the new regional director was providing lunch, something that his predecessor had never done during his tenure. The meeting was also quite informal, and there was a free-flowing discussion covering a broad range of topics. No one bothered with recording the minutes of the meeting and everyone went away quite pleased with the outcome. The ice had been broken and all the managers appeared to be getting along quite well. Fortunately, there were no crises that had to be addressed and the overall office productivity appeared to be satisfactory. The next weekly meeting was much the same. It was quite informal and any manager was free to raise whatever topic of concern they might wish to have discussed and, hopefully, resolved. Again, lunch was provided and no minutes were recorded.

What was remarkable was that this continued to go on week after week, month after month. When one of the managers went on an extended month-long leave, he designated one of his staff to fill in for him during his absence. Charles Hampton, the acting manager, was very pleased to attend his first weekly managers' meeting. He had always wondered what important issues were being discussed at these private and confidential meetings, and he found his first weekly managers' meeting to be very interesting. A number of issues were discussed and debated by the managers at the meeting. He found the regional director to be a quite generous, flexible chair who allowed issues to be discussed at full length with little concern for time and the relative importance of the topics under discussion. It seemed that the meeting spent as much time on what he considered to be a minor matter as it did on the clearly more important and substantive matters that the Toronto office had to deal with and address.

When Hampton attended his second weekly managers' meeting, he was again struck by the informality of the meeting. After the first half hour, he realized that the managers were discussing the same issues that they had discussed in the previous week. It also appeared that they were not coming to any resolution on any of the issues that were being discussed and that nothing was being decided. Furthermore, without an agenda the meeting appeared to lack any orderly discussion of pertinent issues or concerns.

Furthermore, it did not seem as though Jackson was acting as the meeting chair but, rather, seemed to be participating in the discussion and adding his comments just like the other managers. He seemed oblivious to the need to chair the meeting and to ensure that a decision be reached on each of the items under discussion. Moreover, he was either ignoring the fact that these same issues and concerns had been discussed the previous week or he was suffering from a loss of memory. However, at one juncture at the meeting Hampton realized that Jackson was reciting the same points that one of the managers had made the previous week on the same item that was again being endlessly discussed in that day's meeting.

Following the meeting, one of the other managers must have noticed the look of consternation on Hampton's face and said that he should not be too concerned about these weekly management meetings because it had been happening every week since Jackson had been appointed the regional director.

Questions

1. Why, in your opinion, has Henry Jackson not adopted the usual trappings of a meeting, such as an agenda, minutes, resolutions, action items, and so on?

2. What, if any, are the advantages of this type of meeting style?

3. What does this type of weekly management meeting format reveal about Henry Jackson's management approach and leadership style?

4. Explain why you think that this type of weekly management meeting format is effective or not.

5. What are the long-term implications for using this type of meeting format for the overall effective and efficient administration of any organization?

6. Explain why you think Henry Jackson's managers have not requested changes to the way the weekly management meetings are conducted.

Resource Materials

- Managing Meetings, Free Management Library
  http://www.managementhelp.org/grp_skll/meetings/meetings.htm

- Carter McNamara, "A Basic Guide to Conducting Effective Meetings," Free Management Library,
  http://www.managementhelp.org/misc/mtgmgmnt.htm

- University of Illinois, Extension, Local Government Topics, "Effective Meeting Management"
  http://www.extension.uiuc.edu/factsheets/LGIEN%202002-0016.pdf

- Andrew E. Schwartz, "Group Decision-Making," *The CPA Journal,* August 1994.
  http://www.extension.uiuc.edu/factsheets/LGIEN%202002-0016.pdf

- Methods of Decision-Making, The Foundation Coalition,
  http://www.decs.sa.gov.au/ods/files/links/Methods_for_Decision_Makin.doc
  www.foundationcoalition.org

The Forgotten Incident

Ever since Christine Thorpe arrived in her new position she seemed annoyed, disappointed and resentful. She had left her previous job as a high school teacher to join the government. It was rumoured that she had inherited a great deal of money just after she took the job. This rumour was perpetuated by the fact that Thorpe never tired of telling people at the office that she "did not need this job, unlike other people in the workplace." It also seemed to be reinforced by her bellicose attitude and her apparent resentment of other colleagues who she seemed to perceive as either incompetent or lazy. This was quite apparent to everyone after Thorpe stood up at a meeting of the entire office and challenged the director general on a number of issues with respect to how she had been treated personally regarding her benefits. The director general seemed to be very uncomfortable with her questions in this forum. It was latter learned that the director general had met with Thorpe several days before the meeting and that he had explained to her that he could not address her concerns because they were dictated by departmental policy and that he did not have the discretion to make any exceptions for any employee.

Shortly after this meeting, Thorpe had an exchange with her manager's administrative assistant, Patricia Banks, which quickly escalated when Thorpe thought that Banks was being deliberately uncooperative and obstreperous. Thorpe immediately lost her temper and raised her voice over Banks' and used profanity that was heard by everyone in the immediate area. Thorpe then retired to her office and closed her door. Shortly thereafter, Clara Fraser, a staff supervisor, knocked on her door to see whether she could try to resolve any misunderstandings that may have arisen during this incident. Thorpe then had a heated exchange with Fraser that was not directed at her but at Banks' manager. Again, Thorpe raised her voice and repeatedly used profanity to describe her manager. She stated the manager was insensitive, irresponsible and trying to work everyone to exhaustion. Even though Thorpe's office door was closed, her loud voice could be heard in the adjoining offices and by the staff who were situated in workstations outside her door.

While Fraser was meeting in Thorpe's office, Harry Jacobs, the director of the unit and Banks' manager, came by to speak to his administrative assistant. Jacobs immediately noticed that Patricia Banks was visibly upset and obviously had been unnerved by something. Banks explained what had happened in the exchange with Thorpe. She advised Jacobs to stay away from Thorpe, who seemed to be out of control. Banks explained that Thorpe had been yelling at her and using foul and abusive language, much of it directed against him, in particular. She also stated that Fraser was meeting with Thorpe at this very moment and that it was perhaps best if he left not only the office area but the building. Jacobs declared that he had no intention of leaving the office and would deal with the matter after he spoke with Fraser.

Shortly thereafter, Fraser dropped by Jacobs's office. She seemed physically shaken by the experience of meeting with Thorpe. Fraser said that she had had a conversation with Thorpe about the exchange that took place with Banks and she could not believe the profanity and foul language that came out of Thorpe's mouth. She said that she had worked previously in the provincial penal system with young offenders and that she had heard a lot of foul language and profanity but that she had never heard such abusive vitriol even while she had worked with young offenders. Moreover, she said that the profanity was directed personally against Jacobs.

Fraser then stated that she wanted to speak to Jacobs off the record and in the strictest confidence. She repeated that Thorpe had threatened to do whatever she could in her power to ensure that Jacobs's career would be ruined. She said that, "If I were you, I would watch out for her. She is out to get rid of you." Fraser said that in all her social-work experience she had never experienced anyone, male or female, who had used such foul and abusive language and had openly made threats like this before. Jacobs thanked her for her comments and for intervening in the situation and stated that he would have to address the matter with Thorpe.

Jacobs then went to Thorpe's office but found that she was not there. He called her on the telephone and left her a voice message, indicating that he wanted to speak with her as soon as possible. He also sent her an email, requesting that she meet with him as soon as possible to discuss what had transpired in the office that morning. About an hour later, Jacobs received a reply email from Thorpe stating that she would be available for a meeting at 1:00 p.m. that afternoon.

Thorpe came to Jacobs's office at 1:00 p.m. for the meeting. Jacobs began by asking Thorpe what had transpired that morning and why the staff in the office and, in particular, Banks appeared to be so visibly upset. Thorpe replied that an exchange had taken place between her and Banks regarding the assignment of her files but that she could not recall a heated exchange nor the use of any foul language. She also confirmed that she had met with Fraser but, once again, she did not have any recollection of any yelling or the use of profanity or any inappropriate language.

Jacobs then told Thorpe that these types of exchanges in the office were unacceptable and that he could make arrangements to have her transferred to another unit to work with another manager if she did not like working in his unit. He said that he would give her several days to consider this possibility and to discuss the possibility of a transfer with any other manager. Thorpe was then excused from his office.

Jacobs then contacted the director general and briefed him on the entire incident and the outcome of his meeting with Thorpe. He stated that Thorpe claimed no recollection of a heated exchange with either Banks or Fraser nor did she remember using profanity or inappropriate language in the office. He also stated that he had not received any formal complaints from any of the staff in the office. Jacobs told the director general that he would notify him immediately if anything further developed regarding this incident.

Questions

1. Was this incident handled appropriately by Christine Thorpe's manager, Harry Jacobs? Justify your answer.

2. If not, what should he have done differently to handle and address this incident?

3. Are any disciplinary measures necessary and appropriate to address this particular incident?

4. What role, if any, do you think that the director general has in addressing this incident?

5. Given the circumstances, should Christine Thorpe transfer to another unit?

6. What will have to be done, as a result of this incident, to help resolve the tensions and the negative impact on morale within the unit?

Resource Materials

- Susan M. Heathfield, "Workplace Conflict Resolution: People Management Tips," Managing Your Human Resources, About.com
  http://humanresources.about.com/od/managementtips/a/conflict_solue.htm

- Kim Squires, Bridget Brownlow, Tara Erskine, "Resolution of Workplace Conflict: A Legislated Approach as Compared to a Proactive and Preventative Approach," Saint Mary's University
  http://www.caubo.ca/annual_conf/presentations/2007%20Eng
  Resolution_of_Workplace_Conflict_by_Bridgette_Brownlow_and_Kim_Squires_and_tara_erskine.ppt#1

- mti, Mediation Training Institute International, Managing Difficult People, Bibliography
  http://www.mediationworks.com/mti/certconf/bib-difficultpeople.htm

- Treasury Board of Canada Secretariat, Guidelines for Discipline
  http://www.tbs-sct.gc.ca/pubs_pol/hrpubs/TBM_11B/discipline01_e.asp

- City of Toronto, Human Resources Procedures/Guidelines, Complaint Procedures
  http://wx.toronto.ca/intra/hr/policies.nsf/9fff29b7237299b385256729004b844b/
  b56b633e5572ee618525746e006a2656?OpenDocument

The "Grifter"

The branch director general, Stephen Woods, transferred Nelly Jenkins to Graham Collins' unit shortly after she had finished her formal orientation and training in the agency. Collins, Jenkins' manager, found her to be a friendly and pleasant person when he was introduced to her. He had this same impression of her after he had a chance to speak with her at length at a meeting that was held in his office. Collins informed Jenkins that, like all new employees, she would be allowed to ease into her position in the unit over the next few weeks and months. He pointed out that she would be assigned some light duties and that she would be given a full orientation and briefing on how the unit operated within the branch and agency. He also informed her that she would be assigned a mentor, Gerry Norris, one of the most experienced staff members in his unit. He noted that Gerry Norris had extensive experience in training new employees. Before he joined the public service, Norris had worked for more than a decade as an elementary school teacher. His formal training and experience as an educator made him ideally suited for the task of mentoring new employees.

Before Jenkins was hired at the agency, she worked in a related field with a well known and respected non-governmental organization (NGO). She had served with the NGO for more than 12 years and had accrued a substantial degree of seniority there. Jenkins also seemed to have had a good reputation as a responsible employee with the NGO. When she came to work for the government, she came with the seemingly high regard and recommendation of her former supervisor at the NGO.

Collins was in the habit of stopping by the new employees' offices in his unit to see how they were adjusting to their new positions. From time to time, he would stop by Jenkins' office to see how well she was adapting to her new surroundings and responsibilities in the unit. During his brief visits to Jenkins' office, he learned that her husband worked in a senior management capacity in the private sector and that she had two young children. He also learned that she had a close friendship with another new employee at the agency, who had been assigned to another unit in the branch. Interestingly enough, her friend in the other unit also had been employed previously at the NGO where Jenkins had worked before she entered the public service.

Collins was also monitoring Jenkins' progress in a number of areas, including her case assignments, and he found that she seemed to be pro-gressing slowly in a number of areas. Although it was evident she was not having a great start, he did not consider this to be too unusual. It often took new employees time to adjust to their new work routines and to get fully up to speed on case assignments.

Collins also got regular reports from Jenkins' mentor, Norris, on how well she seemed to be progressing in her work generally. Norris noted that she was progressing much slower than expected, given her background and experience in the field and given that she had worked for so many years with a relevant and well respected NGO. He pointed out that she seemed to have difficulty writing case reports. Both Collins and Norris agreed that this was something that they would try and work on with Jenkins in order to help her accelerate her development in this key area.

Report writing was an essential part of the work in Collins' unit and something that everyone was expected to be able to do well, and, indeed, to become more proficient at over time. This was commonly understood by everyone in the unit and the branch. In fact, Collins had made a point of stressing this in his very first meeting with Jenkins.

Several weeks after Jenkins' arrival, Collins happened to meet her in the hallway and they had a brief conversation. Jenkins mentioned that she was actually on a leave of absence from the NGO where she had worked and that she could return to her former position there at any time. Collins had suspected that this was probably the case but he was, nevertheless, somewhat surprised to hear her state this so explicitly to him. His impres-sion was that she was trying to send him a clear message that she did not care much for her current job in the government.

Collins also found Jenkins' attitude to be atypical of most new employ-ees. For instance, on one occasion she had invited a private citizen, a per-son who was not employed with the government, to a restricted area within the office. When Collins spoke to her about this breach in the rules, she pleaded ignorance and stated that she was unaware that what she was doing was against regulations. Collins mentioned this to Stephen Woods, the branch director general, and they both thought that they should give her the benefit of the doubt because she was new. It was agreed that Collins would speak to her about the incident to ensure that she was fully aware of the regulations and to make it clear that she could not bring anyone from the general public in to the restricted office areas.

Several months later, Collins and Norris had a meeting to discuss Jenkins' progress in adjusting to her new position. Norris reported that in the past three months since Jenkins' had arrived in the unit, she had only managed to complete two very short written case assignments. He pointed out that she had yet to complete any full reports. When Collins asked him why this was the situation, Norris stated that he was not entirely certain. He said that he noticed that she spent a great deal of time on the telephone when she was in her office. Most of the calls seemed to be of a personal nature rather than on agency business. He also noted what seemed to be a lack of focus on the task at hand. Norris said that Jenkins was not managing her time effectively and, consequently, this was impacting her productivity. He also observed that she was not grasping some essential concepts necessary to perform well in her position. In other areas, however, he noted she seemed to perform very well and above what one would expect for a new employee. It appeared that her progress was mixed at best. Nonetheless, it was encouraging to see that there appeared to be some progress in some areas. They both agreed that Jenkins was probably preoccupied with personal matters involving her young family and, as a consequence, it was taking her longer than usual to adjust to her new surrounds and work responsibilities. Collins noted that she was absent from work on a number of occasions because she had to look after her children when they were ill. He also noted that she had been away on sick leave for at least one week in the past three months. He stated that she, in fact, had used all of her personal leave days and that she had used more than the allotted sick leave that she had accumulated to that point as a new employee.

About a week after Collins had met with Norris, Jenkins requested a meeting with Collins. At this meeting, Jenkins said that she and her husband wanted to take four weeks annual leave that summer, which she said that she was entitled to, starting in two months time. She pointed out that this was something that the family had been looking forward to for several years. She noted that her brother had invited her family to visit him in California, where he was hosting a family reunion. Everyone in her immediate and extended family was looking forward to attending the "Jenkins family reunion," which had not been held for many years. Jenkins gave Collins her leave request form and asked him to approve it.

Collins knew that Jenkins' request for annual leave happened to come at a crucial time in her development as a new employee. There were serious concerns with her report writing, her difficulty grasping key concepts, and her low productivity. Nevertheless, Collins approved her vacation leave request. Collins was aware that, technically, Jenkins was not actually entitled to four weeks vacation until she had been employed with the agency for a full year. Nonetheless, it was customary to grant new employees their vacation leave before their entitlement period. On the other hand, Collins thought that a vacation at this time might be beneficial because it would provide Jenkins with an opportunity to address any personal issues that she might be facing that were impacting on her overall poor performance.

In the period before Jenkins took her vacation leave, there did not seem to be any progress in her adjustment or development. Norris stated, again, that there appeared to be a lack of focus on her work and that her lack of time management were still major concerns. He reported that she seemed to be constantly on the telephone engaged on personal matters, rather than agency business.

Upon Jenkins' return from her vacation, she came to Collins and stated that she had to say that she was thinking of filing a complaint against Wilber Comings, the professional development officer who had been responsible for her orientation and training when she had first joined the agency. She asked Collins whether he had seen Comings' report on his overall assessment of her abilities and performance and his comments about the areas that she needed to make further progress in, following her initial formal orientation and training with the agency.

Collins stated that he had received a copy of Comings' report when she was on annual leave. Jenkins complained that Comings was not treating her fairly. Indeed, she stated that a number of people who had taken their initial agency orientation and training with him were considering filing a complaint against him. She mentioned her close friend in the other unit of the branch was also thinking of filing a complaint against Comings. Collins said that this was the first time that he ever heard anyone wanting to file a complaint against Comings, a long-time employee of the agency who was considered to be a very good professional development officer and who had an easy-going personality. Jenkins stated that his report was biased and unfair and that it put her in a very poor light. She said that she would let Collins know whether she would be filing a formal complaint against Comings.

Collins contacted Stephen Woods, the branch director general, to advise him of this possibility and to find out whether he was aware of any complaints that may have been filed against Comings. Woods was surprised by these accusations of bias and unfair treatment against Comings. He said that he was unaware of any other complaints against Comings, and said that this was the first time that he was aware of even the possibility of filing a complaint against him for any reason. He went on to say that knowing Comings as he did, he thought that such accusations would prove to be completely groundless.

Collins also met with Norris to determine whether he had heard any grumblings about Comings among any of the new employees. Norris stated that he had heard that a few of the new employees had some concerns about a number of issues that had been raised, apparently, during the agency's orientation and training program for new employees. Norris further stated that he thought that his mentoring assignment with Jenkins appeared to be going well. Norris, however, also stated that he was still concerned about the progress Jenkins was making in a number of key areas, principally, in her report writing.

Shortly after his meeting with Jenkins and meetings with Woods and Norris, Collins received a copy of one of Jenkins' first reports for his unit. The report was short and concise. Collins was pleasantly surprised by the report, and although he had a number of minor concerns with part of the report's analysis, he thought that it displayed significant progress on Jenkins' part. When Collins met with Norris to review Jenkins' progress to date, he mentioned her report and he was surprised to hear Norris state that the report was in large part the work of someone else, even though the only name that appeared on the report was Jenkins. He stated that this report was not indicative of her report writing abilities. As far as he was concerned, he noted, Jenkins was not making much progress, if any, in her report writing.

Several days later, Jenkins' submitted a five-page letter attacking Comings' report on her performance during the agency's orientation and training program and her progress in the unit over the past several months. Jenkins stated that she had had to defend herself against the biased and unfair assessment that she had received from Comings. She also stated that she did not want to have anything more to do with him. As Collins read Jenkins' letter, he realized that it seemed to be written with the assistance of legal counsel. It was evident that Jenkins had either retained legal counsel in the preparation of this letter or had the advice of a lawyer friend in drafting it. Collins had read and reviewed a number of reports that Jenkins had written to date and he knew, instinctively, that this letter was not written by Jenkins without the assistance of someone with a legal background.

In a meeting that was held with Comings, Norris and Collins, it was noted that the five-page letter seemed to be the work of a lawyer. The letter was written in a very formal and legalistic manner. Norris was confident that Jenkins had not written this letter, while Comings was very concerned by it because it challenged his assessment of her performance to date, which he claimed was entirely straightforward and fair. Although Jenkins' letter did not make any direct accusations of bias or unfairness against Comings, it challenged a number of negative statements that were found in the body of the report and its conclusions. The letter, however, clearly implied that his assessment was biased and unfair, without expressly stating so.

Nelly Jenkins had been at the agency now for about six months, but she had been on vacation leave for a full month during this period. She had also exhausted all of her sick leave credits and personal leave credits. Compared to the cohort of other new employees who had been hired at the same time as Jenkins, she was far behind in a number of key indicators, the most important being her written reports. For instance, the average number of reports that were produced by the cohort of new employees in the agency over this period was four. Jenkins had managed to write one report only during this entire period, and, in fact, doubts were raised about whether she had actually written this report and whether it had been written largely with someone else's assistance.

It also seemed that Jenkins had managed to ingratiate herself with a number of colleagues in her unit. She met regularly with a number of female colleagues over lunch, and it appeared that she may have managed to secure their support with respect to her ongoing battle with Comings. A number of her male colleagues were also supporting her in various ways by assisting her with her work. Collins also noticed that Norris was beginning to change his view of Jenkins' performance and the reasons she was well below the expected level for new employees in the unit.

Norris stated that Jenkins was under a great deal of stress from her experience of having worked with Comings. He then went on to say that he found Comings' report to be far too critical. At the same time, Norris felt that it was perhaps time to end his mentoring assignment with Jenkins. He stated that he had worked with her far longer than he had worked with other new employees and that he had tried to address a number of areas of her performance, but he had been unable to make much progress with any of them and that it was perhaps time for someone else to take on this responsibility. He suggested that since Jenkins got along well with Jill Grant, in the legal affairs section, that perhaps Grant could work with her to address these areas of concern.

Collins contacted Woods to discuss Jenkins' development and progress in his unit. He pointed out that Jenkins had filed a five-page letter challenging Comings' report and that Norris had requested that he be relieved of his mentoring responsibilities with Jenkins. Collins stated that he was very concerned about Jenkins and her impact on his unit. He also pointed out that Jenkins made a point of advising him that she was on a leave of absence from her previous position with the NGO. He mentioned that Jenkins did not seem to be focused on her work, she lacked basic time-management skills and spent an inordinate amount of time on the telephone, dealing with what appeared to be personal matters rather than agency business. Her major weaknesses, he noted, were her report writing and her overall lack of productivity.

Woods then turned to Collins and asked him how they could best address Nelly Jenkins' situation. Collins thought very carefully before giving his answer.

Questions

1. Explain what advice Graham Collins should give to Director General Stephen Woods on the situation of new employee Nelly Jenkins?

2. Are there any obvious and/or reasonable explanations for Nelly Jenkins' apparently poor performance in Graham Collins' unit?

3. What response should Wilber Comings make to Nelly Jenkins' five-page detailed reply to his report on her overall performance during her initial orientation and training session?

4. Explain why you think that Grahan Collins did or did not manage new employee Nelly Jenkins effectively.

5. "Grifter" is slang for a person who engages in swindling or cheating. Is this case study appropriately titled? Justify your answer.

6. What public administration and management lessons, if any, can be drawn from this case study on new employee orientation and training?

Resource Materials

- HRM Guide, "Origins and Interpretations"
  http://www.hrmguide.net/hrm/chap1/ch1-links3.htm

- Treasury Board of Canada Secretariat, Performance Objectives/Review
  http://www.tbs-sct.gc.ca/tbsrp-prsct/foiard-rpafvi/fm-gf/sht-res/por-oer/menu-eng.asp

- Performance Review Tips/Tips for Conducting a Better Performance Review, BCjobs.ca
  http://www.bcjobs.ca/re/hr-resources/human-resource-advice/recruitment-and-retention/perfor-mance-review-tips—tips-for-conducting-a-better-performance-review

- Carter McNamara, "Basics of Conducting Employee Performance Appraisals," Free Management Library
  http://www.managementhelp.org/emp_perf/perf_rvw/basics.htm

- Mentoring, Free Management Library
  http://www.managementhelp.org/guiding/mentrng/mentrng.htm

The Interview

The members of the interview team consisted of Robert Stillman, manager for the Ontario region of the National Parole Board of Canada (NPB), Eileen Billingsgate, Ontario regional director of the NPB, and Wayne Garrison, a representative from the community at large. Stillman was the only appointed member of the NPB. He had served on the NPB for eight years and as the manager of the Ontario region for the last four years. Billingsgate was a permanent civil servant who had worked for the federal government for her entire career and she had been hired immediately after she had graduated from Queen's University with her honours B.A. in sociology. She had started her career with the civil service in Corrections Services Canada (CSC) as a junior clerk. After 10 years with CSC, she had been hired to work with NPB as an administrative officer. Five years after she had come to the NPB, she was appointed the Ontario regional director of the NPB. She had served in this capacity for the last three years. Garrison was a retired parole officer who had been appointed as a representative of the community to serve on the NPB hiring committee several years ago. His entire working life had been spent in the criminal justice system, and he was knowledgeable about all aspects of the work of the NPB.

The interview team was in Toronto conducting interviews for the entire week. The team members planned to interview at least six candidates each day, three in the morning and three in the afternoon. They hoped to complete a minimum of 30 interviews during their one-week stay in Toronto. They knew that they had a hectic schedule that left them little time to do anything other than conduct their in-depth interviews with the prospective candidates. From past experience, they knew that they had to schedule one or two extra interviews per day if they hoped to complete their target of 30 completed interviews for the week. There were invariably one or two candidates each day who either cancelled at the last minute or who were "no shows." Occasionally, though, all the candidates appeared as scheduled and this meant that the team members had to stay past 5:00 p.m. to finish all the interviews that were on the schedule for the day.

The interviews lasted about one hour, which gave the interview team an opportunity to see the prospective candidates and listen to how they responded to each of their questions. The interview team had about 15 minutes between each interview to do a quick assessment of the candidate's responses to their questions and to prepare for the next interview.

As a well-seasoned interview team, the team members were used to conducting week-long marathon interview sessions. Generally, they were able to assess the quality of the candidates fairly easily and quickly. They rarely, if ever, disagreed on the assessment of the candidates they interviewed. They used a set, structured questionnaire for all their interviews. Each of them took their turn asking the same set of questions to each of the candidates interviewed and they recorded the candidate's responses directly on their copies of the questionnaire.

After the first two or three interviews at the beginning of each week of interviewing, the process became routine. Each member of the interview team went through his or her questions in a methodical manner. There was a certain pace and rhythm for each interview, and it took only one or two questions for the interview team to find this pace and rhythm and to rapidly go through the entire questionnaire.

On Wednesday morning at about 10:30 a.m., the team members saw their second candidate of the day, Jeremy Sanderson. Sanderson was a lawyer with 20-years experience working in the criminal justice system. The bulk of his law practice was defending clients who had been charged with all types of crimes but largely misdemeanours and petty offences. Occasionally, he would get cases involving more serious offences, such as robbery, battery and, on the rare occasion, murder. He had also appeared before the NPB on numerous occasions representing his clients at their parole hearings, so he was familiar with NPB hearings and how they operated in practice.

All those seeking an appointment to serve on the NPB were required to first submit an application indicating why they qualify for the position and whether they wished to be appointed as a full- or a part-time member of the NPB. Applicants also had to include a copy of their curriculum vitae. If they met the minimum qualifications for serving on the NPB, they were invited to do a written test that lasted one hour. The written test was designed to see how well the applicant could analyze a case involving an application for parole and to write a decision. All those applicants who passed the written test were then invited for an interview.

Sanderson recalled that when he took the written test there were about 30 applicants in the room for his test session. He found out that for the last round of administered written tests there were four test sessions held per day in Toronto. He was also informed that these test sessions were held over two consecutive days. Sanderson realized that there must have been at least 240 applicants who wrote the written test in Toronto, alone, over those two days. He knew that the written test sessions were also held in other cities across the province, such as Ottawa and Kingston. He also knew, of course, that appointments to the NPB were very competitive and that the screening process for applicants was long and complicated.

When Sanderson entered the interview room, Garrison, Billingsgate and Stillman shook hands with him and introduced themselves. Their first impression of Sanderson was that he was a middle-aged man who looked somewhat older than they had expected. He was dressed neatly in a jacket and tie and had a pleasant voice. He also had the appearance of a successful lawyer and professional.

Stillman chaired the interview and invited Sanderson to sit down across from them. Stillman began by welcoming Sanderson to the interview and telling him that each of them would be asking him questions from a standard questionnaire that would be put to all the candidates for a position on the NPB. He told Sanderson that if he did not hear or understand a question that was being asked that he should immediately ask the person to repeat it. He also said that all of the candidates would be required to go through a RCMP security clearance and criminal background check. Stillman informed him that the NPB would also be contacting his references as well and mentioned that Sanderson should be getting a letter within about two weeks indicating whether he was selected to go on a list of qualified candidates for the NPB that would be presented to the solicitor general of Canada. The Government of Canada would then select its preferred candidates from the list of qualified candidates to fill any vacancies on the NPB from Ontario. He stated that this list of qualified candidates would be valid for two years.

Stillman then asked Sanderson what he considered to be the most important qualifications for the position of member of the NPB and why he thought he met these qualifications. Sanderson replied that he thought that one of the most important qualifications for the position of member of the NPB was the ability to make decisions. He said that to be a successful member of the NPB you must be a good decision-maker. He noted that as a successful criminal lawyer he was required to make important decisions and exercise effective judgement each business day, which would also be a necessary quality for any NPB member. Jeremy Sanderson noted that it was important to be able to assess evidence. He stated that at NPB hearings, members must carefully listen to the testimony that inmates presented in order to be able to assess the credibility of the evidence adduced in order to make a sound decision. As a trial lawyer with 20 years experience, he stated that he not only had good listening skills but that he could effectively question witnesses. Jeremy Sanderson continued by saying that the final quality necessary for being a good member of the NPB was to be an effective communicator. Verbal and written communication skills were absolutely vital for this position. He reiterated that his qualifications as a successful criminal lawyer made him an excellent communicator.

Stillman then asked Sanderson to indicate what he thought of conditional release and to explain its relevance to the NPB. Sanderson said that conditional release was essential to ensure that inmates had an opportunity to work toward the goal of rehabilitation and, once they were ready, to effectively integrate back in the community. He said that conditional release was, in fact, part and parcel of the NPB and the very essence of its work.

Eileen Billingsgate then asked Jeremy Sanderson what he would do if he was a member of the NPB and he needed to get some advice about the *Corrections and the Conditional Release Act.* She said, "Let us assume that you have friends who are police officers or parole officers. Would you call your friends to get this information and to seek their advice?" Sanderson replied that he would not contact any friends to get any information about the act or anything else that involved the NPB. Rather, he said that he would seek the advice of legal counsel on the NPB.

Garrison then asked Sanderson to explain the relevance of the NPB as an independent administrative tribunal. Sanderson stated that it was essential to the NPB. He said that no member of the NPB should be making decisions out of either "fear or favour," but, rather, exclusively on the merits of each case that they were asked to decide.

Stillman asked Sanderson whether he was willing and able to relocate to Kingston, where all the major detention facilities were located in Ontario. Sanderson responded that he did not have any problem with relocating to Kingston from Toronto.

Billingsgate asked him whether he had ever observed a NPB hearing. Sanderson said that he had actually participated in numerous NPB hearings. He said that the most recent one had been in the Warkworth Institution to represent an inmate at his parole hearing. He pointed out that he was very familiar with parole hearing procedures.

Garrison then asked Sanderson what he would do if he were a member of the NPB sitting on a high profile case and the media was paying a great deal of attention to the parole hearing. Would Sanderson consider, Garrison asked, public opinion as relevant to his decision in this case? Sanderson declared that he would have to consider the media and its coverage of this high-profile case. However, he also would have to consider the source of the reporting and whether that source was presenting a particular bias and promoting his or her own agenda. As for public opinion, he stated, this was also very important because knowing what the community standards were was critically important in the decision-making process. He noted that if the NPB ignored "community standards" it did so at its own peril. If the public were opposed to the decisions of the NPB, it would lose eventually the support of the Canadian public and undermine its own standing with the public. This did not mean, however, that the NPB could ignore the law or precedent, but it had to be sensitive to the public and what it considered to be within the acceptable bounds of the community that it served.

Billingsgate asked Sanderson whether he considered it necessary and important to be sensitive to the cultural backgrounds of inmates who appear before the NPB. Sanderson stated that he thought that this was critical for making sound judgments in parole applications. If a board member ignored the cultural background of an inmate then he or she would not be able to grasp or fully understand the inmate's situation or testimony. Sanderson declared that over the past 20 years he had had clients from all sorts of cultural and racial backgrounds. In order to represent those clients, he said, he had to be able to comprehend and appreciate their different cultural backgrounds. Sanderson pointed out that he had refined his "cultural sensitivity" skills over the years by taking professional development courses offered by the Law Society of Upper Canada in this area.

Garrison asked Sanderson how he would feel if he had sat on a case involving a sex offender who was seeking parole and he had decided to grant the person parole and the person had gone on to commit another sexual assault while out on parole. Sanderson said that he would, of course, feel terrible about it. But, he continued, he would only have decided to grant the person parole if he had been entirely satisfied that the evidence before him indicated that the inmate was rehabilitated and that strict conditions were imposed on his parole. Sanderson said that this way he would not have any difficulty in defending the decision he had made to release this inmate. He said that he would also point to the strict conditions imposed on the inmate's release in an effort to try to protect the community. In other words, Sanderson stated the decision to release this person on parole was not only legally sound and fair but was defensible in the media and before the Canadian public. That was not to say, he noted, that all decisions would prove, in the end, to be the right ones.

Stillman stated that this brought the interview to a close and he asked whether Sanderson had any questions that he would like to ask.

Questions

1. Justify your assessment of the performance of the interview team conducting this interview. Which of the three interviewers, in your opinion, did the best job?

2. Justify your assessment of how well Jeremy Sanderson performed at this interview.

3. Explain why you think Jeremy Sanderson will or will not receive a letter indicating that his name will appear on the list of qualified candidates for possible appointment to the NPB.

4. Comment on this interview procedure for assessing whether applicants are qualified for appointment to the NPB. Indicate the advantages

and disadvantages of this interview procedure and whether you think it can properly assess whether an applicant will make a good member of the NPB.

5. Structured interview questionnaires are among the most common interviewing techniques for assessing candidates for positions within the public service. What are the pros and cons of using a structured interview questionnaire for assessing a candidate's suitability for a position? What, if any, alternatives might be better suited for interviewing prospective candidates for public service positions?

Resource Material

- National Parole Board (NPB)
  http://www.npb-cnlc.gc.ca/about/abt-eng.shtml

- Canadajobs.com, Job Interviews
  http://www.canadajobs.com/articles/category.cfm?Category=Job%20Interviews

- General Guidelines for Conducting Interviews, Free Management Library
  http://www.managementhelp.org/evaluatn/intrview.htm

- Administrative Tribunals, *The Canadian Encyclopedia*
  http://www.thecanadianencyclopedia.com/index.cfm?PgNm=TCE&Params=A1ARTA0000044

- The Canadian Council for Administrative Tribunals (CCAT)
  http://www.ccat-ctac.org/en/

The Messy Office

Jennifer Lewington went to see her manager, Gerald Stevenson, to report that she had inspected Bart Matting's office and had found it to be a workplace hazard. She said that when she had inspected his office she had found his desk completely covered in paper, folders and files. The top of the desk was not visible, she said, with all of the paper, memos, files, newspapers, books, pens, pencils and other things piled on top of the desk. She said that it looked like someone dumped a large pile of paper a foot deep on top of Matting's desk and that the paper seemed to be in total disarray.

Lewington further stated that, perhaps, worse still was the number of files and folders that were on the floor in Matting's office. The bookshelves in the office were also piled high with papers and folders. Given the present state of the Matting's office, she said, it is no longer safe for staff to go into his office to either drop off or to retrieve files or other material. She told Stevenson that she would have to declare Matting's office a "workplace hazard" if he did not clean up his office. In particular, she noted that the floor space in his office would have to be cleared so that people could walk in and out of his office to drop off and retrieve files, mail, memos and the like.

Lewington stated that Matting would have to be cited for having an unkept office that, potentially, was hazardous to all employees, including Matting himself. As a consequence, she noted, staff would be warned to stay out of his office until it is properly cleaned and all of the files and papers were cleaned off of the floor.

Lewington also told Stevenson that there had been a number of staff who had been injured at the office over the past year due to unkept workstations, file rooms and offices. She cited the example of Tanya Belko, administrative assistant, who had been lifting a box of files off a shelf in the file room when she fell backward and struck her head on the shelf immediately behind her. She said that Belko was now off work and was on long-term disability as a consequence of her head injury. Lewington indicated that it was uncertain when she would be able to return to work, if at all.

Lewington also cited the example of Robert West, file clerk, who had been carrying a number of files when he slipped on some papers that had never been picked up from the hallway floor. When West fell, he twisted his left ankle and missed two months off work as a consequence.

Lewington stated that both of these accidents could have been prevented. As the Workplace Health and Safety officer, she said that it was her responsibility to ensure that her section of the workplace was safe for all employees. She said that Matting's office was probably one of the worst offices that she had seen in her eight years of service with the government. She also said that she could not understand how anyone could work in an office that was in such disarray. There hardly appeared to be any room for anyone to sit down in a chair and work at the computer in that office, she said.

Lewington stated that she would be filing her report to the Joint Management and Staff Workplace Health and Safety Committee on the deplorable condition of Bart Matting's office. She noted that if Matting did not clean up his office in the next several days that appropriate disciplinary measures ought to be applied.

A copy of the citation that she had filled out for Matting was then handed to Stevenson. He said that he would speak with Matting about this as soon as possible and definitely before the end of the day.

Stevenson and Lewington then went to inspect Matting's office together. Attached to the door of Matting's office was a notice advising staff that the office was off limits because of its current state and condition. The notice also advised the occupant that the office was a workplace hazard and should be cleaned up immediately.

Stevenson and Lewington knocked on the door and there was no answer. When they opened the door they looked at what could only be described as an unmitigated disaster. There were books and files piled in each corner of the office, and the desk was barely visible. The top of the desk was completely covered in paper and overflowing with newspapers, memos, files and folders. There was not one inch of space available for anyone to work from on the top of the desk. The floor was also covered with files and stacks of paper except for a small footpath that had been left for someone to walk from the doorway to the chair, which was situated behind the desk and immediately in front of a computer.

Stevenson said that he had to agree that this office was a complete shambles and that it constituted a workplace hazard. He stated that this was clearly unacceptable and that he would speak with Matting to ensure that his office was properly cleaned up immediately. Lewington thanked him and went on her way.

Stevenson taped a message on Matting's office door requesting that he stop by his office to discuss the Workplace Health and Safety Officer's declaration that his office constituted a workplace hazard. About an hour later, Stevenson went by Matting's office and found him busy cleaning the papers stacked on his desk. He had already made some progress in doing so. Gerald Stevenson stated that he was glad to see that he was cleaning his office. He said that he wanted to speak to him in his office at his earliest convenience. Matting replied that he would come to his office in the next half hour. He went on to say that he was nearly finished cleaning off the top of his desk.

When Matting came to see Stevenson, he said that he should have never let his office get in such a state but that he had been under a great deal of pressure as of late. Matting stated that his two adopted children had been experiencing some difficulties at school and that his wife was ill and, as a result, he had had to spend a great deal of time dealing with these family crises. He said that with a number of project deadlines at work and the family pressures at home, he had let things slide in terms of the state of his office.

Stevenson told Matting that he had never been known for having the cleanest office in the building but he had never seen it in such a bad state. He told Matting that Lewington was very concerned that someone who came into his office might slip and fall and seriously injure himself or herself. He said that Lewington was also concerned about Matting, himself, possibly suffering a personal injury given the awful condition of his office.

Stevenson also noted that Matting had not been meeting his project reporting deadlines, which was probably due, in part, to the current state of his office. Stevenson asked Matting how it was possible for him or anyone else, for that matter, to find a particular file that might be in his office. He stated that he thought that Matting was probably wasting a great deal of his time merely trying to locate a particular file or paper, but Matting insisted that this wasn't so. While he acknowledged that he was having difficulties meeting his project reporting deadlines this was due, he insisted, to his personal family situation and to the complexity of the tasks that he had been assigned at work, rather than the sorry state of his office.

Stevenson stated that his immediate concern was to ensure that Matting's office was cleaned up before Lewington, or anyone else from the Joint Management and Staff Workplace Health and Safety Committee, dropped by to see his office. Stevenson reiterated that his office not only had to be cleaned up, but it had to remain that way. He told Matting that once the Workplace Health and Safety officer cited someone for a messy work space, then that person would be monitored for a long period of time. He said that repeated citations and violations of the Workplace Health and Safety Committee regulations could result in disciplinary measures. Stevenson also stated that failure to comply immediately with the current citation could also result in disciplinary measures.

Matting responded that he would like to be relieved of his current workload and deadlines in order to ensure that he can meet the requirements of the citation of the Workplace Health and Safety officer. He said that he would also need this relief in order to deal with his ongoing family problems.

Questions

1. Explain why you would or would not grant Bart Matting's request to be relieved of his current workload and reporting deadlines if you were his Manager, Gerald Stevenson.

2. Is Gerald Stevenson, Bart Matting's manager, at fault in any way for the state of Bart Matting's office?

3. Bart Matting's messy office may be symptomatic of a number of underlying difficulties that he is currently facing. What can Gerald Stevenson do to assist Bart Matting in addressing these underlying concerns and difficulties?

4. What would be the appropriate disciplinary measures that should be imposed if Bart Matting fails to comply with the Workplace Health and Safety officer's citation that his office constitutes a "workplace hazard" that needs to be cleaned up as soon as possible?

5. Is a tidy and clean office reflective of a well-organized and efficient person who is on top of his or her work?

Resource Materials

- Rhymer Rigby, "An Organized Mess?" B2B International, "In defence of the messy workstation," *The Financial Times*, May 28, 2008.
  http://www.b2binternational.com/b2b-blog/2008/09/09/an-organised-mess/

- _____., "In defence of the messy workstation," The Financial Times, May 28, 2008.
  http://www.ftchinese.com/story.php?lang=en&storyid=001020295&page=2

- Workplace Hazards, Ontario Ministry of Labour
  http://www.labour.gov.on.ca/english/hs/faq/faq_4.html

- Top Workplace Hazards, Ontario Workplace Safety and Insurance Board
  http://www.wsib.on.ca/wsib/wsibsite.nsf/Public/TopWorkplaceHazards

- Workplace Safety Committee, Workplace Safety Tool Kit,
  http://nonprofitrisk.org/tools/workplace-safety/nonprofit/c1/committee.htm

- Department of Occupational Health and Safety, Occupational Health and Safety Management System, York University, January 1999, revised September 2002.
  http://www.yorku.ca/dohs/documents/obtsmangsys.pdf

- David A. Good, *Accountability in Government,* Notes for a Presentation to the Annual Conference of the Financial Management Institute, Vancouver, British Columbia, May 29–31, 2005
  http://publicadmin.uvic.ca/research/pdfs/dag_fmi_may05.pdf

The Meticulous Chairperson

Jessica Thomas was thrilled to be appointed chairperson of the Regional Professional Development Committee (RPDC). She had served as a member of the RPDC for nearly four years before she was asked to take on this responsibility. It was evident that she had done a good job as a member of the RPDC. She was considered to be a conscientious member of the committee who not only attended meetings on a regular basis but also made a substantial contribution to the development of various training programs for all staff in the regional office. She was also considered to be a good trainer in her own right. RPDC members were expected to serve as trainers and workshop facilitators whenever required and she had faithfully done this at least two or three times a year over the past four years.

Before joining the government, Thomas had worked as a college instructor who specialized in public administration and management. She had also published in the field. So when she joined the government it was only natural that she would want to contribute to the professional development and training programs in her regional office. Indeed, management assumed that she would be willing to serve on the RPDC.

When Thomas assumed the chair of the RPDC she faced at least two major challenges. The first was that her regional office was undergoing a major restructuring. In fact, it was doubling in size because it would soon be merging with a sister regional office situated nearby. Combining the two offices was clearly a major undertaking. It meant that the separate regional offices would have to be brought together physically and relocated in a new building. It also meant that the two offices would have to merge their operations, meaning there no longer would be the requirement for two regional directors, two registrars, two senior counsels, two libraries, two mailrooms, and so on.

This was clearly not welcomed news for those who would be losing their jobs and required to transfer to new government departments or agencies. The office merger created a great deal of uncertainty in the minds of the staff because it was unclear who would end up where in the restructured single regional office. Those who were happy with the status quo and the current arrangements were fearful that they would be assigned to another unit and a new supervisor and co-workers they did not know. Likewise, those who were not satisfied with their current arrangements feared they could possibly end up in a work situation that was worst than their current one. There were also separate unions representing the employees in the two regional offices who were very concerned about the possibility of job loss and, of course, the loss of their members.

Needless to say, the current state of morale in the two respective offices was not high. At the same time, the pace of activity at each regional office seemed to be escalating. The merger required, of course, a great deal of planning and preparation as well as effort, but the staff members were also expected to continue to perform their usual work to maintain productivity. Although there was some time allowance for the inevitable workplace adjustment built into everyone's work schedule, for most people this involved packing their office belongings for the physical move to the new location. However, this did not allow for any of the inevitable disruptive effects of the pending restructuring.

One of the first organizational mergers in this restructuring was to combine the two separate regional professional development committees in the two regional offices. This, in effect, meant that the RPDC would double in size from six members to twelve. However, it also meant that the RPDC would have to combine its professional development and training programs for the staff in the two offices that were to be organizationally and physically united in their new location.

Complicating matters further was the fact that the two regional offices were not identical in many key respects. Although the two performed essentially the same functions and tasks, they had developed, over time, specializations and expertise in particular fields and areas. Consequently, in some respects, the two regional offices were very different. They also relied on each other's relative expertise to take the lead in their developed fields of specialization and areas of expertise.

In fact, the two offices were known, both by the staff and their clients, for different things. These differences were appreciated by some people who thought that there were qualitative distinctions in the operation of the two regional offices. Statistically, it appeared that one of the offices was certainly much more productive than the other. Qualitative measures were more problematic and less reliable than quantitative measures, but even with some of the qualitative measures the more productive regional office seemed to score higher than the other office. This long-standing rivalry and competition between the offices engendered resentment among the respective staff that did not seem to bode well for a quick, smooth and easy amalgamation.

Thomas's second major challenge was to revamp the professional development and training program itself, in order to make it more relevant and meaningful for both the professional and administrative staff. The RPDC was criticized frequently for presenting professional development and training sessions that were too theoretical and impractical. It was also criticized for being irrelevant for the needs of the staff in the professional cadre. A common criticism seemed to be that when expert guest speakers were brought in for the monthly professional development (PD) meetings they were poorly briefed in advance of the sessions and had no sense of what it was actually like working in these regional offices. As a result, the guest speakers' remarks and comments would often sound either naive or overly simplistic. Over time, this resulted in high absenteeism among the professional staff at the PD meetings. Typically, most staff would attend a PD meeting for only part of the morning session and then not return for the balance of the program. Some staff members routinely did not bother attending PD sessions because they claimed that they would rather get caught up on the work in their office than sit in a PD session that they found to be dull, irrelevant and, occasionally, confusing or, worse still, misleading. Thomas considered this second major challenge to be far more difficult than the first.

Thomas also knew that she would have to get to know at least half of the members of the newly combined RPDC who were in her sister regional office. She was well aware of the differences and the unique working cultures that existed between the offices. She worried about a number of things, including whether the two RPDCs would be able to merge into a single cohesive functional group. She was also concerned about the informality that had characterized the manner in which the RPDC had operated when she was a member. The RPDC seemed to operate with little more than a hastily drawn-up agenda that was circulated at the last minute before the committee meeting was scheduled to commence. Thomas thought that it would be necessary to add further structure to committee meetings.

Bearing this in mind, Thomas decided that she would spend a fair amount of time considering what items should be included. She also thought that it would be better to attach a name to each item of the agenda so all the committee members would know who would be responsible for commencing the discussion on each item on the agenda. She also wanted to make sure that for the first meeting that everyone on the committee felt welcomed and had an opportunity to meet each other. To facilitate this, she managed to persuade the regional director to provide refreshments as well as some treats, muffins and cookies, to help break the ice and to give everyone an opportunity to socialize.

The first meeting of the RPDC went extremely well, she thought. There was a good attendance and everyone appreciated the refreshments and snacks. Thomas also thought that there was a lively and interesting discussion on a number of items on the meeting agenda. The RPDC also agreed to move forward on a number of items. She was favourably impressed with a number of new members of the RPDC that she had never met before.

Thomas thought that it would be important to capture as much detail of the meeting as possible and to include these in the minutes. She thought that this was necessary in order to ensure that everyone on the RPDC was aware of what had been discussed and why those present at the meeting had reached the decisions that they did. She made a point of highlighting the items that had been resolved for each item of the agenda and to include an "action" item for each resolution. For instance, if the RPDC had resolved to plan and to organize a particular training program then the "action" item would specify what action was necessary to put the training program into place and who on the RPDC was responsible for carrying this out. Since the RPDC chairperson was not given any secretarial support, the task of preparing the minutes of the meeting fell to its chairperson. Thomas took fairly detailed notes during the RPDC meetings and then she had to transpose these into the minutes of the meeting. She found that this took a great deal of her time because the minutes usually ended up being about four to five single-spaced pages in length.

Thomas thought that these detailed minutes were absolutely essential to ensure that everyone followed up on his or her commitments in the RPDC meeting. She also thought that the detailed minutes were essential to ensure that no one became disorderly because this would become part of the record of the meeting. She also felt that the detailed minutes provided the necessary formal structure and professionalism to the proceedings at the meetings.

Thomas also found that the agenda for her RPDC meetings was evolving, over time, to include a certain standard format. For example, she incorporated the "action" items from the detailed minutes directly on the agenda for the next meeting to ensure that those who were responsible for a particular action item would have an opportunity to report back to the committee on their progress in completing the action items that were approved by the RPDC. She thought that this was necessary to ensure that RPDC members not only met their timelines for carrying out the professional development and training programs that they had committed to delivering, but that they were also held accountable to the RPDC for their performance. She also wanted to make sure that any items that had not been resolved in the previous month's meeting were not forgotten or lost from meeting to meeting until they were actually finally resolved. The detailed minutes of the meetings, she thought, facilitated this process because everyone on the RPDC could follow the discussion on these items from one meeting to the next so that the same concerns, issues, points and arguments would not have to be made and repeated month in and month out. It also helped, she thought, in building a consensus on an agenda item in the RPDC because everyone would know who said what and, therefore, knew where everyone stood on an issue. It was often clearly evident from her detailed minutes of the RDPC meetings who had presented the most persuasive arguments on an issue. She thought that this also helped to save the RPDC's valuable time and made the meetings more efficient.

Thomas's detailed and formal approach to the agenda and the minutes took a great deal of effort and time on her part. It was undoubtedly characteristic and reflective of her administrative and management style as the chairperson of the RPDC.

Thomas was not a forceful or assertive chairperson who imposed her ideas or will on the RPDC. She was a responsive and reactive person by nature and someone who shunned the spotlight. She consciously preferred and adopted a consensual leadership approach. Although she had her own ideas for professional development and training initiatives and how they should be delivered, her preference was to introduce these into the flow of the discussions in an indirect and subtle manner. She saw her role as chairperson of the RPDC as "the neutral arbiter" who allowed a consensus to emerge and for others to take the lead on key initiatives and projects.

After a number of months, members of the committee were making comments about how detailed the minutes of the RPDC meetings were and they were asking Thomas how she was able to recall all the details of the discussion that took place at the meetings. She also received comments on how detailed the agenda for the RPDC meetings were as well. However, she also began to get comments that the meetings were too open-ended and were lasting far too long. Thomas was mindful of these concerns but she was relieved that there was no criticism about the lack of cohesiveness in the newly-merged RPDC.

The criticisms she was hearing seemed to be levelled at her personally, rather than at how the new committee was working. There also seemed to be some real success at the PD meetings that were now being held jointly for the two regional offices. The PD meetings now included all of the staff of the two respective regional offices that would soon be merged and working together in the same building. This seemed to generate a new life and excitement in the new RPDC's PD meetings and its professional development and training programs.

Nonetheless, Thomas found that her duties as the chairperson of the RPDC were now consuming more and more of her time. In addition, she was concerned that her hard work and devotion, as the RPDC chairperson, to ongoing professional development and training in the regional office was not being fully appreciated by senior management and that it was beginning to affect her other job responsibilities.

Questions

1. How can Jessica Thomas resolve her dilemma? She is spending increasingly more time on her role as RPDC chairperson, apparently an important yet under-appreciated and thankless task, that may now be affecting her other job responsibilities.

2. Justify why you think or do not think that Jessica Thomas is spending too much of her time preparing detailed minutes and agendas for RPDC meetings.

3. Is Jessica Thomas's consensus leadership style best suited to address the two major challenges confronting the new merged RPDC for these two Regional Offices?

4. How would you go about assessing Jessica Thomas's performance as the RPDC chairperson?

5. From the information presented in this case study, what would you say are Jessica Thomas's strengths and weaknesses as the RPDC chairperson? What skills, if any, would you recommend that Thomas improve substantially in order to dramatically enhance her performance as chairperson?

Resource Materials

- Meeting Minutes Template, wtamatap
  http://www.wtamatap.com/sdlc/meetingminutes.html

- Ben Leichtling, "Consensus Leadership is a fad beginning to fade," *East Bay Business Times,* Friday, August 13, 2004
  http://www.bizjournals.com/eastbay/stories/2004/08/16/smallb6.html

- Organizational Culture, Free Management Library
  http://www.managementhelp.org/org_thry/culture/culture.htm

- Manage Your Work, Don't Let It Manage You: Tips for Managing Your Time and Getting Ahead, Annette Nellen at San Jose State University
  http://www.cob.sjsu.edu/facstaff/nellen_a/time_management.htm

- Stuart C. Gilson, "How to Make Restructuring Work for Your Company," Harvard Business School, Working Knowledge, October 1, 2001
  http://hbswk.hbs.edu/item/2476.html

The Offensive Comment

Jordan Michaels was a program analyst in the finance and administration division of the Corporate Services Branch of the Treasury Board of Canada Secretariat (TBS). He had been in this position for the past four years and reported to Phillip Gaston, the director general of the Finance and Administration Division.

Michaels was nearing his retirement after serving with the Canadian government for nearly ten years. Prior to joining the public service, he worked in the insurance field. He considered himself to be very well educated, and had completed his undergraduate and graduate degrees in the United States before coming to work in Canada. He completed his Ph.D. in economics at Cornell University and his ambition was to work in a senior executive capacity in the private sector.

Michaels was a proud man who did not like anyone to think that he could be easily intimated or pushed around. In fact, if he thought that anyone was trying to take advantage of him or was trying to put him in a negative light he would respond instantly. He had a quick, sharp wit and often displayed an equally quick temper. But he also had a personable and humorous side. He liked to engage in light banter and friendly conversation with colleagues and administrative staff. Over time, however, people became wary of Jordan Michaels because they knew that his light, humorous side could change instantly to truculent disdain. At times, he could be overbearing and openly resentful. This seemed to get Michaels into difficulties from time to time. Not everyone liked to work with him for this very reason. Indeed, some colleagues would studiously avoid doing so. The staff often neglected approaching him to deal with minor administrative matters out of fear that they might get involved in a gruff and distasteful exchange.

Michaels' general grumpiness seemed to be exacerbated by his deteriorating health. Gaston noticed that Michaels appeared to be taking more sick leave than normal. He also noticed that Michaels seemed to be avoiding people at work. When he walked by his office of late, he noticed that his door was always closed.

One day he received a telephone call from Michaels's son, who said that his father had to be rushed to the hospital because he had experienced chest pains. He said that his father would have to remain in the hospital for at least several days while the doctors ran a series of tests. Michaels remained in the hospital for about a week and a half before he was allowed to go home.

It was not until about two weeks later that Gaston got another call from Michaels' son, stating that his father would not be able to return to work for at least another two weeks. He also said that his father was continuing to receive treatment and that it was likely that he would have to have heart surgery. He said that he would keep Gaston apprised of his father's situation and get back to him.

By this point in time, Gaston realized that Michaels had depleted all of his sick leave. This meant that unless he was granted an exceptional sick leave extension provision from the secretary of the Treasury Board, he would no longer be getting his regular salary. The secretary of the Treasury Board had the authority to provide a one-time-only special dispensation to employees to continue to receive their salaries while they were on long-term sick leave. This provision was used in those situations where an employee experienced a serious illness and would suffer an undue hardship from loss of salary due to their medical condition.

Gaston contacted Michaels' son to advise him that his father had exhausted his sick leave and would have to apply to the secretary of the Treasury Board to try to obtain an exceptional sick leave extension provision if he wished to continue to receive his regular salary. He explained that this was a one-time-only special dispensation that, if granted, could not be used by him ever again. Michaels' son said that his father would apply for this provision because he could not afford to continue without receiving his usual salary.

Michaels submitted his application to obtain an exceptional sick leave extension provision to the secretary of the Treasury Board. Gaston recommended that the secretary of the Treasury Board grant Michaels this benefit, which could only be used once for a maximum of 180 days. On

Gaston's recommendation, the secretary of the Treasury Board decided to grant Jordan Michaels the special dispensation.

Subsequently, Gaston learned that Michaels had open-heart surgery. Following Michaels' successful operation, he remained in the hospital for about one month before he was sent home to recover and continued to receive ongoing treatment and therapy. It was another four months after the surgery that Gaston got a telephone call from Michaels, who stated that he would be ready to return to work in two weeks time. He said that his doctors had told him that he could return to normal duties at work. Gaston said that he was very pleased to hear that Michaels was doing so well and that he wanted to return to work.

After the telephone call, Gaston advised the human resources staff that Michaels had contacted him and that he was doing well. Gaston said that Michael's doctors had advised him that he could return to work to resume his normal duties in two weeks time. The human resources staff were pleased to hear that Michaels was doing so well and that he wanted to return to work. They said that Michaels would have to call human resources to complete some required paper work when he returned to the office. They also pointed out that they would need a medical note from his physician stating that he was medically fit to return to work.

Several days later, Gaston contacted Michaels to inform him that the human resources staff wanted him to complete some paper work on his return to the office and that he would also require a medical note from his physician. Michaels did not understand why a medical note was necessary. He said that he was perfectly fine and that he thought it was absurd that human resources would require him to provide a medical note from his physician. Gaston suggested that he contact the human resources staff directly so that they could explain what they required upon his return to work.

Michaels called a few days later to tell Gaston that he spoke with the human resources staff and that he was still at a loss as to why a medical note was required. Gaston could tell from Michaels' tone of voice that he considered this request to be both frivolous and offensive. He stated that he was capable of working and that it was his own decision to return to work and that a medical note from his doctor was totally unwarranted under the circumstances.

Gaston then consulted with the human resources staff, who stated that this was their standard practice in these types of medical circumstances. They noted that Michaels was far from being a young man and he had just had major heart surgery. The human resources staff further stated that it was their obligation to ensure that he had medical authorization from his physician to return to work. They said that they did not want the TBS to be held liable should anything happen to Michaels, because of his medical history, when he returned to work. They stated that a mere verbal statement, on his part, that he was well was just not sufficient. They insisted on having the letter from a medical physician who could attest to his medical fitness to return to his normal work duties. The human resources staff also indicated that they had explained all this to Michaels and his son.

When Michaels returned to work he still had not provided the human resources staff with his medical report as requested. They contacted Gaston to remind him that this was still required and to advise Michaels that his doctor's note would have to be submitted to them as soon as possible. Gaston then approached Michaels to tell him that the human resources staff were insisting that a medical note was still required. When he did so, Michaels got visibly upset and said that all of this was unwarranted. He also said that his condition was a private matter between himself and his physician and that he had no intention of providing a medical note. Gaston said that this matter was out of his hands. It was not his requirement but the requirement of the TBS. Michaels said that he wanted to speak to the human resources staff, once again, about all these needless bureaucratic requirements. Gaston stated that he was more than welcome to do so.

Later in the day, Michaels came to Gaston's office demanding to see him. He stated that he just finished a meeting with the human resources staff and that they were still insisting on a note from his physician. He said that this was nonsense and that he expected Gaston to support him on this because he had no intention of providing a medical report. Gaston told him that he could not do this for the reasons they had already discussed. Then Michaels stated, "Now, aren't you the jack ass!" Gaston was quite shocked at what he thought he had just heard Michaels say. Michaels continued to say that this was all a needless waste of his time and an additional stress on him. Gaston could see that Michaels was visibly upset when he walked out of his office.

Gaston was still recovering from Michaels' off-the-cuff remark and trying to decide what he should do next.

Questions

1. What should Phillip Gaston do regarding Jordan Michaels' offensive remark?

2. Who would you say is at fault in this situation and why? Is Jordan Michaels right on insisting that a medical note or letter from his physician is unnecessary?

3. What are the consequences, if any, should Phillip Gaston choose to ignore Jordan Michaels' offensive remark?

4. Does Jordan Michaels have any obligation in these circumstances? What should Jordan Michaels do to resolve the situation?

5. What lessons, if any, in public management and administration can be distilled from this case study?

Resource Materials

- Treasury Board of Canada Secretariat (TBS)
  http://www.tbs-sct.gc.ca/tbs-sct/index-eng.asp

- University of Western Australia, HR Policies and Procedures
  http://www.hr.uwa.edu.au/policy/toc/performance_management_of_staff/
  conduct_workplace?childfx=on

- Mike Russell, "Code of Professional Conduct: Dealing With Inappropriate Conduct in the Workplace," January 26, 2008, jobing.com
  http://sandiego.jobing.com/blog_post.asp?post=8390

- Citizenship and Immigration Canada, Code of Conduct
  http://www.collectionscanada.gc.ca/webarchives/20060304010854/http://www.cic.gc.ca/english/
  research/workplace/code.html

- Canadian Association of University Teachers (CAUT), "Standing up to bullies at work"
  http://www.academicwork.ca/en_career_articles_details.asp?cID=14

The Sharp
Manager

If anything, George Mitchell was a survivor. He had served as manager of the operations branch of the Supply and Services Division of the Ministry of Transportation for close to 10 years. He was considered to be a bright and clever manager who was seemingly able to work well with everyone. But, on the other hand, he was no one's fool. Those who were not pulling their weight in the operations branch immediately heard from Mitchell. Whenever any major project or change within the division was being contemplated or discussed senior management would suggest that the proposal first be "run by" Mitchell to see what he thought about it. In meetings, senior managers were frequently heard asking, "Well, what does George think about this proposal?"

Mitchell was famous for his "walkabouts." It seemed like everyone in the division and, in fact, the entire ministry, seemed to know him. When he walked around the various offices in the division, staff would greet him and he would always have a joke or an interesting and humorous story to tell. All sorts of people would also come by his office just to talk to him or to seek his advice on all matter of things. There was no doubt that he seemed to be very well informed about what was happening throughout the ministry. Well before any general announcements were made, Mitchell would be known to tell a select few in his branch about the latest information that would likely be announced soon. If he thought impending change was a good idea and that it would work well, he would be sure to let you know, and, if he thought, it was a bad idea and would be a disaster he would also tell you. Mitchell was certainly not shy to voice his opinions on certain matters. He appeared to have an uncanny sense of which way the wind was likely to blow and who in the Ministry was likely to support which initiative or change. He always took or ended up on the side of the majority, the winning side.

When Walter Salter was first hired by the Ministry of Transport, he was not assigned to work in the operations branch, yet one of the first managers he met was Mitchell. Salter came to the Ministry of Transport by way of the University of Saskatchewan, where he had taught various civil engineering courses. Salter had enjoyed a successful research and engineering career at the university, but he wanted to have public sector work experience, applying his engineering expertise to "real life," practical engineering transportation problems. Mitchell was aware of Salter's academic and research background and thought that he would make a good addition to his branch.

Shortly after Salter had settled in to his new office, Mitchell was seen dropping by Salter's office to speak to him. It was not long before Mitchell was also seen taking coffee breaks with Salter and, shortly thereafter, it appeared that the pair had become good colleagues and friends. Mitchell made a point of not only introducing Salter to staff around the office but to other senior managers within the division as well as the ministry. Salter's manager did not consider this unusual in any way and seemed to welcome Mitchell's frequent visits to his area of the office.

After a time, Salter noticed that Mitchell was seeking his advice on various technical points in his area of expertise. Initially, Salter considered this to be flattering, given that he was relatively new to the ministry. However, he soon found that Mitchell was also sharing private information regarding a number of people and incidents, in not only his own Branch, but in other branches in the ministry. This was presented in such a humorous and light manner that it seemed to be nothing more than idle office gossip to Salter. However, over time, Salter found that Mitchell was beginning to seek his advice not only on technical engineering issues but also on the personnel and management issues that he had to deal with in his branch as well.

About one year after Salter had arrived in the Ministry of Transport, he found himself transferred to the operations branch. He welcomed the move not only because of the seemingly positive relationship that he had with Mitchell, who would serve as his new manager, but also the opportunity to work on a number of interesting and challenging engineering projects that were being run by the operations branch of the ministry. Not long after Salter was transferred to the operations branch he found himself in a daily routine of meeting with Mitchell for a coffee break shortly after his arrival in the office at 8:00 a.m.. This would be followed by lunch with Mitchell at about 1:00 p.m., often times with other members of his branch.

Because Mitchell was a person who arrived in the office at 7:00 a.m. each day, he usually left the office at 3:00 p.m.. Mitchell rarely worked beyond his required seven-and-a-half-hours per workday. He would routinely drop by Salter's office to share with him the latest issues that he was confronted with at senior management meetings that day or the personnel issues that he and other managers had to address within the branch or throughout the ministry. Often Mitchell would invite him for a coffee break as he made his way to the subway for his daily commute home.

Over time Salter also found that Mitchell was assigning him more and more work to do. On top of all this, Mitchell was also requesting his detailed comments on a number of items that Salter knew were being sent to Mitchell for his comment by the deputy minister's office. Salter suspected that any suggestions or comments that he was making were being sent to the deputy minister's office as Mitchell's own ideas and commentary, without any attribution to him.

At other times, Salter felt like he was briefing Mitchell for his next senior management meeting as he presented his own creative ideas for dealing with various technical, administrative and management issues and concerns that impacted not only on the branch but the entire ministry.

Salter liked Mitchell, not only because he was an interesting personality, but because he now considered him also to be a friend. Nonetheless, he could not help but feel that Mitchell was taking advantage of his position as his manager but also their friendship. The manager/friendship dichotomy was getting blurred. Furthermore, even though Salter found he could handle the additional workload and that he enjoyed discussing the management and personnel issues that Mitchell shared with him, he was beginning to feel that his manager was perhaps taking unfair advantage of him.

Questions

1. Describe how you would classify George Mitchell's management style, and explain why you think that he is or is not taking advantage of Walter Salter.

2. Is it possible to separate friendship from a manager/subordinate relationship in the workplace?

3. What is the best course of action for Walter Salter in this situation?

4. Should George Mitchell be acknowledging Walter Salter's contribution to his performance as a manager?

5. What course of action would you recommend to avoid employees getting drawn into these types of manager/subordinate/friend relationships?

Resource Materials

- Transport Canada
  http://www.tc.gc.ca/en/menu.htm

- Australian Institute of Management, Queensland and Northern Territory, "Professional Code of Conduct for Managers"
  http://www.aimqld.com.au/membership/conduct.htm

- The Career Place, Career Development Resources for UC Berkeley Staff, "Code of Conduct for Supervisors and Managers"
  http://thecareerplace.berkeley.edu/supscode.htm

- CBC/Radio Canada, Corporate Policies, Code of Conduct
  http://www.cbc.radio-canada.ca/docs/policies/hr/conduct.shtml

- Abbi F. Parets, "Who's the boss? Tips for managing friends," TechRepublic Inc., 2001, builderau.com
  http://www.builderau.com.au/strategy/businessmanagement/soa/Who-s-the-boss-Tips-for-managing-friends/0,339028271,320268699,00.htm

- Tom Rath, "Can Employees be Friends with the Boss? Gallup Management Journal (Excerpted from *Vital Friends,* Gallup Press, August 2006)
  http://gmj.gallup.com/content/23893/Can-Employees-Be-Friends-With-the-Boss.aspx

The Thoughtful Gift

Jason Allison, the director general of the program and services branch of the Environment Canada, was reviewing the progress of three of his new managers who had been with his Branch for the last several months. Gregory Lyons was the manager in charge of the Conserving Biodiversity Program. Harry MacMillan was the manager in charge of the reducing the impact of pollution program and Jill Porter was the manager responsible for supporting the sustainable development program. Among these three new managers, it was now evident to Allison that Lyons was clearly the best-performing manager and that Porter was the worst-performing manager of the group. MacMillan's management performance fell somewhere in between the other two managers. Allison was satisfied with the performance of two of his three new managers and knew that he did not have to worry about Lyons's and MacMillan's management skills and abilities.

Allison also noted that Porter was falling further and further behind in her work. More critically, he noticed that the staff in her section were missing important details in their work and that there were a number of outstanding complaints from program clients and beneficiaries, principally that they were not getting their program funds on time and that the monitoring reports on their projects were inaccurate. Allison also noted that Porter's weekly management reports were far from thorough and that, occasionally, entire sections of the reports were either missed or incomplete.

Allison had met with Porter on a number of occasions, which he had carefully documented, to try to determine why she and her section were performing below expectations. He decided that an in-depth meeting would be necessary to go over her most recent weekly management report, that he had found to be unsatisfactory, and to try to determine what could be done to address the serious performance issues that seemed to be plaguing her and her section.

Porter, expecting the worse with her meeting with the director general, came prepared. Allison had given her advance warning that the meeting was going to address the performance issues within her section and the concerns he had with her weekly management reports. Porter was ready for a spirited and aggressive defense of herself and her section. She began by stating that she was responsible for managing one of the largest program budgets in the branch. She pointed out that there were currently 10 major projects underway in addition to 12 others that her section had to monitor on an ongoing basis. She said that on an annual basis the Supporting Sustainable Development Section was responsible for processing and reviewing over 100 applications for ongoing and new project funding. This alone consumed a great deal of her administrative support staff's time. Furthermore, she noted that her Section had twice as many staff as MacMillan's Reducing the Impact of Pollution section and nearly 20 percent more staff than Lyon's Conserving Biodiversity section. Consequently, she noted that her workload was proportionately higher than either MacMillan's or Lyon's workloads.

Porter went on to say that her section had been commended for its program innovations in sustainable development over the past year. She pointed to a number of positive letters and remarks that she had received from a number of her program clients. She acknowledged that there had been a number of complaints as well but these had to be balanced with the positive comments and compliments that her section had received.

Porter further noted that prior to her arrival as manager of the section, there had been a sizable turnover in staff. She reminded Allison that her section had lost two very experienced and productive project supervisors who had been promoted to other positions within the ministry. She further noted that there had been a number of retirements among the administrative staff, which had created delays in the processing of new applications for funding.

Porter also acknowledged that as a new manager, who had been on the job for only several months, she was still trying to get comfortable in her new position. She said that it seemed that she was forced to be dealing with major and minor crises on a daily basis in her section. As a consequence, she had very little time to do much of anything else.

Allison noted that even though Porter's section had one of the largest budgets in the branch she and MacMillan and Lyons were all responsible for a comparable number of projects within their respective sections. In fact, he noted that Lyons managed 25 projects and MacMillan managed 26 projects compared to Porter's 23 projects. However, he did acknowledge that she was responsible for managing 10 major projects compared to

MacMillan's seven and Lyons' eight. Nonetheless, in terms of the number of projects and their relative size, he stated, the three managers seemed to have the same workloads. With respect to staff, Allison agreed that she had responsibility for twice as many staff as MacMillan's section and 20 percent more staff members than Lyons' section. But, he noted, there was a reason for this and that was to deal with the many more new applications that the Supporting the Sustainable Development Section received on an annual basis in comparison to the two other Sections. He acknowledged that over the past decade, the Sustainable Development section had, in fact, had to manage many more projects and clients than other sections in the branch. But, he said, that this had changed over the past three years as evident by the comparable number of projects presently being managed by the three new managers. With many of the reporting and monitoring procedures and systems now being done online, there was no longer a need to have as many administrative staff as in the past. He said that other managers were complaining that they did not have the same level of staff support as her Supporting the Sustainable Development section. He said that this was an ongoing concern that the assistant deputy minister for their division would likely address in due course.

As a matter of fact, Allison pointed out, that Porter had more personal staff support than any other manager in the branch. He noted that in addition to Porter's Secretary, she had two administrative assistants and an administrative clerk supporting her office. He said that MacMillan and Lyons only had one secretary and one administrative assistant.

Allison said that the Supporting Sustainable Development section had won kudos for its innovative programming over the past year, but these innovations had been put in place before she had assumed her position as the section manager. He also acknowledged a relatively high turnover in her section over the past several months but stated that all managers were faced with these types of staff changes over time and have to learn to cope with the loss of key personnel. He said that succession planning for key positions was absolutely essential.

Allison then turned to Porter's weekly management reports and asked her why some portions of the reports seemed to be incomplete or altogether missing. Porter seemed to be unaware of these concerns. She stated that she had delegated the task of producing the weekly management reports to her senior administrative assistant and that she did not realize that her weekly management reports were so deficient. Allison said that it was the manager's responsibility to ensure that these weekly reports were complete.

Allison then expressed his concern that Porter was not progressing as well as could be expected in her new position. He asked her to explain what might be done to address the issue. Porter replied that she had been somewhat overwhelmed when she assumed her new duties and that with the complaints that had been coming in from various clients she seemed to be constantly "fighting fires" in her section. She said that this left her little time to familiarize herself with all aspects of her section's work and that it would take longer than she thought "to get up to speed" in a number of key areas. Allison suggested that she keep a log of all her activities over the next week. At the end of the week, he said that he wanted to review how she had spent her time in order to analyze her activities for the month in an effort to determine whether she might make more effective use of her time. Porter thought that this was a very good suggestion and she said that she looked forward to sitting down with Allison to do this type of activities review. Allison indicated that he wanted these activity reports submitted on a weekly basis for the next four weeks.

Allison typically spent his Friday afternoons working late to get caught up on various administrative and management tasks and to prepare for the coming week. His managers knew that if they wanted a few minutes alone with him that it was one of the best times to come by his office to speak to him. On this particular Friday, Porter happened to drop by to ask if he had received her first weekly activities report. Allison told her that he had received it but that he had not had an opportunity yet to go over it in detail. He said that he would try to do so before he left for the day. He added that if he had any comments on her activities report that he would get back to her.

Porter then started to make some small talk and the conversation turned to family and children. She asked Allison what he was planning to do with his wife because it was Valentine's Day that weekend. Allison told her that he had yet to buy anything for his wife and that he probably would get something either on the way home or the next day. Porter said that it was very important that he not forget to do so. She joked about her husband having a notoriously bad memory for those types of things. Porter then left Allison's office and returned later with a beautiful bouquet of flowers and a box of heart shaped chocolates. She said that she wanted to give these to Allison so that he could give them to his wife. Allison was taken aback by the gifts.

Porter explained that she had gone through the experience of not getting anything from her husband far too many times and wanted to ensure that Allison did not forget his wife on Valentine's Day. She said that she knew that her husband was going to forget her again this Valentine's Day and that was why she had bought the flowers and chocolates for herself. But, she said, she now wanted Allison to give them to his wife. Porter also said that she did not want to be paid anything for this gift for his wife.

Questions

1. Explain why you think that Jill Porter's gift to her supervisor, Jason Allison, was appropriate or not.

2. What are the consequences, if any, of director general Jason Allison accepting the gifts of flowers and chocolates from his manager, Jill Porter?

3. Was Jill Porter trying to gain favour with the director general, Jason Allison, by making this offer of a gift of flowers and chocolates for his wife?

4. Explain what you would do if you were in Jason Allison's position. What are his options, and what would be his most appropriate response?

5. When is it appropriate, if ever, for a person in a supervisory position to accept gifts from his subordinates?

Resource Materials

- Environment Canada
  http://www.ec.gc.ca/

- Disclosures for Public Servants, Public Sector Integrity Canada
  http://www.psic-ispc.gc.ca/doc.php?sid=10&lang=en

- Proactive Disclosure, Public Sector Integrity Canada
  http://www.psic-ispc.gc.ca/pd-cp/index.php?&lang=eng

- Values and Ethics Code for the Public Service
  http://www.tbs-sct.gc.ca/pubs_pol/hrpubs/TB_851/vec-cve_e.asp

- Conflict of Interest and Post-Employment Code for Office Holders, Government of Canada, Privy Council Office
  http://www.bcp-pco.gc.ca/index.asp?lang=eng&page=information&sub=publications&doc=code/code-conflict_e.htm

- Ontario, Office of the Conflict of Interest Commissioner
  http://www.coicommissioner.gov.on.ca/en/default.htm

The Unacceptable Performance Appraisal

Adam MacRea had been senior policy analyst with the Refugee Division of Citizenship and Immigration Canada (CIC) for the past seven years. Prior to his current position he had served in various senior capacities with the United Nations High Commissioner for Refugees (UNHCR). He had not only worked at the UNHCR offices at the United Nations in New York City, but also at the UNHCR headquarters in Geneva, Switzerland. MacRea also had extensive field experience working in a number of posts in high-risk areas in several countries in Africa and Asia, and he had first-hand experience working directly with refugees in major refugee camps operated by the UNHCR. He had also authored several books on issues dealing with asylum and refugees. Within the UNHCR, he was respected as an authority on international human rights and refugee law. MacRea had left his promising career in the UNHCR only after his children had reached the age where they were ready to start high school. Both he and his spouse wanted to ensure that their three children received the best affordable private education possible. They also wanted to ensure that their children had an opportunity to spend more time with their respective families during their children's impressionable teen years.

Although Gerry Freeman had been with CIC for five years, he was relatively new to the refugee division. In fact, he had been appointed the director of the refugee division for less than a year. Before coming to the refugee division, Freeman worked as a senior analyst in the immigration enforcement section of the immigration division. Prior to coming to CIC, Freeman had worked in the Ontario provincial government as a manager in the enforcement section of the Ontario Ministry of Citizenship and Immigration. He had served in the Ontario government for many years before he had been finally appointed as manager, a position he served for less than two years when he finally got the opportunity to apply for the senior analyst position with CIC. It was a position that he had wanted for quite some time and that paid much better than his management position in the Ontario government.

Freeman did not have an extensive background in asylum and refugee law but he did have managerial experience, which made him a strong candidate, when he eventually had the opportunity to apply for his current position. MacRea was not interested in a managerial position and he did not apply for Freeman's position when the post was advertised. Freeman was well aware that MacRea had not competed for his position as director of the refugee division.

For all intents and purposes, MacRea thought that he and Freeman got along well personally and had a very positive working relationship. At their team meetings, Freeman always treated him with courtesy and respect and seemed genuinely pleased with his contribution to the meetings. MacRea also thought that Freeman was satisfied with his assignments, which he made a point of always completing on time. Consequently, when MacRea received his annual performance appraisal he was taken aback at some of Freeman's comments. It was, in his opinion, the poorest performance appraisal that he had ever received from anyone throughout his long, illustrious career.

MacRea was also shocked to find a number of statistical inaccuracies in his performance appraisal. For instance, the performance appraisal stated that four out of the seven reports that he had been assigned were submitted well after they were due. From MacRea's personal records, he knew that he had been assigned 10 reports. Three of these reports were major reports that typically took twice as long to complete as the usually reports that were required and all of these reports dealt with complicated and technically difficult issues and problems. From his own records, he also knew that the reports had, in fact, been submitted on their due dates. Indeed, his personal records indicated that at least two of these reports had been submitted one week *before* their due dates.

The performance appraisal gave him a rating of "satisfactory" in the category of technical sophistication and analytical skills and abilities. MacRea considered this as patently unfair in light of the fact that the colleagues on his team frequently sought his advice and assistance when they were confronted with a difficult problem or were grappling with highly technical issues. His performance appraisal also gave him an overall rating of "satisfactory" with respect to his "general knowledge" in the field of asylum law.

MacRea found this to be insulting, given his educational background and years of experience in the field, and his strong publication record. Moreover, MacRea found his performance appraisal to be inconsistent with the one that he had received the previous year from Freeman's predecessor. His previous manager had rated him as "above expectations" with respect to his general knowledge and "above expectations" in terms of his technical and analytical skills and abilities. MacRea felt that, if anything, he had improved in these areas over the past year rather than staying the same or diminishing at all in these key areas. MacRea found this performance appraisal to be totally unacceptable. He carefully considered what his next step should be in responding to Freeman's inaccurate and insulting performance appraisal.

Questions

1. How should Adam MacRea respond to his unacceptable performance appraisal?

2. Explain what Adam MacRea needs to do before speaking with his manager, Gerry Freeman, about his performance appraisal?

3. What fundamental errors did Gerry Freeman make as a manager with respect to the way he presented Adam MacRea's performance appraisal?

4. What are Adam MacRea's options if Gerry Freeman does not amend his performance appraisal in a manner that he would consider to be accurate and fair?

5. How should Gerry Freeman, as a manager, respond to Adam MacRea and any other employee who does not accept his performance appraisal?

Resource Materials

- Citizenship and Immigration Canada (CIC)
  http://www.cic.gc.ca/english/index.asp

- Donald L. Kirkpatrick, *Improving Employee Performance Through Appraisal and Coaching.* Second Edition. AMACOM, 2005.
  http://books.google.ca/books?id=ufl6Sh0JfAUC&printsec=frontcover&dq=Employee+
  Performance+Apprais ls&ei=fkaXSNboF56ujgGFz6GvDA&sig=
  ACfU3U22mYHJGf2mJA3ZXe_exal-H_exKg#PPP1,M1"

The Unacceptable Performance Appraisal

- "Managing Day-to-Day Employee Performance," About.com, Human Resources
  http://humanresources.about.com/od/manageperformance/
  Managing_DaytoDay_Employee_Performance.htm

- William Gresse, "Performance Appraisal Interviewing," Ezine Articles
  http://ezinearticles.com/?Performance-Appraisal-Interviewing&id=951970

- Boston University, SPH Performance Appraisal, Exempt, October 2007.
  http://sph.bu.edu/insider/images/stories/resources/forms/performance_appraisal_exempt07.doc

The Underachiever

Helen Jones was a lawyer who had served on the Canadian Human Rights Tribunal for many years before she was appointed to serve on the Immigration and Refugee Board of Canada (IRB). She had had her own private law practice, but once she was appointed to the IRB she had to wind down her law practice and devote herself as a full-time member of the Refugee Protection Division of the IRB. Her previous experience on the Canadian Human Rights Tribunal made her a particularly valuable member of the IRB. It was not surprising then that when Jones was going through her intensive three-week new-member training program she was identified as someone who had the necessary skills to perform exceedingly well as a Member of the IRB. She had formal legal training and she was a member of the British Columbia bar, and she had many years of private practice in law. She also had many years of experience as a member of the Canadian Human Rights Tribunal, hearing and deciding cases involving violations to Canadian citizens' fundamental human rights. She was also an extremely bright and capable person who met seemingly all the requirements to serve as a member of the IRB.

Tom Clark was very pleased to have Helen Jones assigned as a member on his team. Being new to the team, he introduced her to the other members and staff and ensured that she had everything that she might need to get settled in her new job and surroundings. He also made sure that she was properly briefed on team procedures and that she would be eased into the hearing schedule.

As for all new team members, he ensured that she would be given a light hearing schedule to start with and only be assigned to cases that were identified as simple and straightforward. He also took the time to ensure that she was properly prepared for her hearings before going into the hearing room and that she could identify the pertinent issues that needed to be resolved during the course of the hearing.

Clark found that Jones had no difficulty identifying the determinative issue in her assigned claims to refugee protection. Not surprisingly, he also found that she had a firm grasp of the pertinent jurisprudence necessary to decide the issues relevant to the claims to refugee protection that she was assigned to hear. It was evident that she was thoroughly prepared, in advance, for hearing the cases that had been assigned to her.

Clark also observed a number of Jones' hearings to assess her presiding skills and to see how she performed during the course of a hearing. Again, not surprisingly, he found that she had strong presiding skills and that she handled the tribunal officers, the claimants and their counsel with courtesy and respect. He also found Jones to be very professional and businesslike in the conduct of her hearings. She had little time for counsels who tried to waste time on irrelevant issues or who tried to extend the length of a hearing needlessly. He also found Jones's written reasons for decision to be thoughtful, on point, and extremely well written. He was very pleased to have her on his Team.

Jones continued to make stead progress in her development as a new member. One of the things that Clark noted about Jones, in contrast to other members with her skill and experience, was that she was very quiet and reserved. At monthly team meetings, she rarely spoke on the issues under discussion. Nor did she wish to take the lead on any proposal or take on any other roles or tasks on the team. It was typical for new members, particularly with Jones' obvious abilities and previous experience, to want to take on additional responsibilities to prove themselves. However, this was definitely not the case for Jones. Nonetheless, she seemed to work well with both staff and members alike.

After her first three months on the team, Jones slowly began to be assigned a full schedule of hearings. Typically, full-time IRB members were assigned five or six hearings a week. She seemed to adapt well to the additional workload without any difficulties. However, after about six months with the team, Clark noticed that Jones was getting behind on her written reasons. He met with her to discuss his concern about what appeared to be an apparent delay in completing her written reasons. Clark pointed out that this was considered to be an important area in assessing a member's performance — that is, whether they could complete their written reasons for a decision in a timely manner. Jones assured him that this would not be an outstanding concern for her in the future because she was only just beginning to feel comfortable completing her written reasons. Clark was well aware that it often took new IRB members one or more years to master the different aspect of their job. He was also aware that some members never totally mastered some aspects of their job, irrespective of their professional background, previous work experience, or their desire and motivation to succeed.

A year later, Clark was reviewing the statistical reports on his team's performance. He noticed that among the 17 members on his team, Jones was one of the members with the highest number of outstanding written reasons for decision. He also noticed that she had one of the lowest number of cases completed on the team. These two statistics indicated that Jones was among the least productive members on his team. When he compared Jones' statistics to Members on other Teams he found that she was, in fact, one of the least productive members in the regional office.

Clark approached Jones to discuss why her statistics on the number of outstanding written reasons and the number of cases concluded were so low. The only explanation that she could provide was that she was getting a great deal of complicated cases that were taking much longer than expected to complete. Clark was reluctant to reduce her case load so that she could get caught up on her outstanding written reasons because this would also reduce the number of hearings that she would be able to complete. Moreover, it did not directly address her problem of not being able to do written reasons in an efficient and timely manner. Nevertheless, despite his better judgment, he decided to reduce her hearing schedule somewhat so that she could devote this additional time to completing her outstanding written reasons.

One month later, the assistant deputy chairperson (ADC) called Clark into his office and asked him what the problem was with Jones and what he was doing to correct it. Clark explained that he had met with Jones to try to find a solution for her outstanding written reasons and her low hearing completion rate. He said that so far he has had little success in dealing with these difficulties in her performance. Clark stated that he was at a loss to understand why she was having these difficulties. He said that she was a very bright person who had all the skills necessary to be a first-rate member. The ADC pointed out that Jones now had 15 written reasons over 60 days, one of the highest number of outstanding written reasons in the office. He also said the average weekly hearing completion rates on Clark's team was four hearings per week and that Jones was completing only about one-and-a-half hearings per week. He said that Clark's team was above the office average for the number of hearings completed, which stood at three hearings completed per week. He remarked that Jones was completing about half as many hearings as anyone else in the office. He also added that this was probably one of the lowest weekly hearing completion rates not only in the regional office but likely the entire country. Clark was quite surprised to hear this comment from the ADC, who was obviously very concerned with Jones' poor performance statistics.

The ADC then directed Clark to provide him with a full assessment of Jones' performance and to try to come up with a strategy for how she might improve her overall performance. He said that after he presented his report then they would have a meeting with her to try and implement the strategy.

Clark reviewed all of the scheduling and hearing reports to try to determine what, if anything, might account for Helen Jones' problem with the inordinately high number of outstanding reasons and her dismally poor hearing completion rate. Clark noticed that although most members had only one or two seized cases on their hearing schedule from week to week, Jones had as many as four or five. This meant that she was being scheduled on only one or two new hearings each week. Moreover, he found that it was taking her multiple sittings to complete a hearing. While the average member completed most hearings in one sitting that took three hours to do, Jones took, on average, three sittings to complete a hearing that took over seven hours to complete. Clark also found that many of Jones's hearings were being postponed. A pattern clearly emerged that seemed to suggest that Jones was deliberately looking for ways not to proceed with her hearings. However, none of this explained why, with so few completed hearings, she had so many outstanding written reasons.

Clark tried to come up with some reasonable explanations for these negative findings on Jones' poor performance record. Could this suggest that perhaps Jones had some type of medical problem? Was she experiencing some sort of difficulties outside the workplace that might be contributing to her poor performance? Or was Jones simply not motivated to perform well at this job? Clark certainly ruled out the possibility that she did not have the requisite skills to do the job or to perform at least at the level of an average member. Indeed, he was of the opinion that Helen Jones could perform better than most members, if she put her mind to it and was sufficiently motivated to do so.

Questions

1. What should Tom Clark put in his report to the ADC and what should he recommend as a strategy for helping to improve Helen Jones's performance?

2. Is Tom Clark, as Helen Jones's immediate manager, at fault in any way for Helen Jones's poor performance? What is his responsibility as her manager to try to ensure that she is performing well?

3. From the information provided in this case study, explain whether it is fair to say that Helen Jones is or is not an example of a classic underachiever?

4. How should the ADC and Tom Clark handle their meeting with Helen Jones?

5. What options would the ADC and Tom Clark have if Helen Jones refused to cooperate with any of their suggestions for how she might be able to improve her performance?

Resource Materials

- Immigration and Refugee Board of Canada (IRB)
  http://www.irb-cisr.gc.ca/en/index_e.htm

- Gifted and Talented Underachievers, Center for Applied Motivation Inc.
  http://www.appliedmotivation.com/gifted_and_talented_underachieve.htm

- Dealing Effectively With Under-Performance, go2
  http://www.go2hr.ca/ForbrEmployers/ManagingStaff/PerformanceManagement/
  DealingEffectivelywithUnderPerformance/tabid/410/Default.aspx

- Leo Babauta, "14 Essentials for Meeting a Deadline," The FreelanceSwitch
  http://freelanceswitch.com/freelancing-essentials/14-essential-tips-for-meeting-a-deadline/

- Employee Motivation: Theory and Practice, ACCEL-Team
  http://www.accel-team.com/motivation/index.html

The Unproductive Team

Gloria Mair, manager of the Birth Registry, was responsible for issuing a birth certificate to all those who were born in Ontario. Kevin Sargent, manager of the Death Registry, was responsible for issuing death certificates in Ontario. Betty Nosters, manager of the Marriage Registry, issued marriage certificates to couples who were duly married in Ontario, and Stephen Houston, manager of the Land Registry, was tasked for ensuring that the all land sales were properly registered in Ontario. These managers were colleagues in the Office of the Registrar General, Ministry of Government Services (MGS), and they all reported to Ben Camben, the registrar general for the province of Ontario.

One of the challenges that the Office of the Registrar General faced was to deliver these vitally important documents to the citizens of the province of Ontario as quickly as possible. Given the importance of this documentation, for identification purposes and for legal transactions, it was not surprising that the public expected to receive these documents as quickly as possible. Protracted delays were rarely, if ever, tolerated.

Whenever the registrar general, Camben, received an inquiry or complaint from those who had not yet received a birth, marriage or death certificate or had any concern about registering the sale or purchase of property he immediately referred the matter to the appropriate manager in his Office. However, whenever he received an inquiry from either the Minister of Government Services or a Member of Provincial Parliament (MPP), he was sure to have the matter dealt with directly by a member of his own staff. If it was determined that it was a matter that required his own intervention, then he would personally handle the file, but he would also call on the appropriate manager to resolve the matter and seek their advice on how to resolve the situation as quickly as possible. He did not want any matter involving the Minister of Government Services or an MPP left unattended or resolved without his direct participation in the matter.

In recent weeks, Registrar General Ben Camben was beginning to get signals from various quarters that the government was not satisfied with the response times for the issuance of these key public documents. Camben sensed that the Ontario Auditor General might select the Office of the Registrar General for its next major audit and assessment. He thought that prudence dictated that he should initiate a program to try to find simpler, quicker and more cost-effective solutions for issuing these certificates and for registering land transactions. Accordingly, Camben thought that he would raise this at his next weekly meeting with the Managers of the Office of the Registrar General.

In preparation for this meeting, Camben decided to review the current production statistics for his Office. As always, he found that the most productive unit was Stephen Houston's Land Registry team. The least productive unit was Gloria Mair's Birth Registry team, while Betty Nosters' Marriage Registry team and Kevin Sargent's Death Registry team were the next most productive units, in that order, in his office. Although there were differences in the work performed in each of the units, fundamentally, they each performed the same function and task. Accordingly, they were allocated the same level of resources, in terms of budgets, personnel, and materiel. In effect, the four units were virtually identical and administrative mirror images of each other. However, where they differed dramatically was in their production levels.

Houston's Land Registry team could process more than twice as many land registry transactions than Mair's Birth Registry team could issue birth certificates. Although it was acknowledged, generally, that processing land registry sales and purchases was much easier than processing applications for a birth certificate, this could not explain why the Land Registry team could outperform the Birth Registry team by two to one. Likewise, Nosters' Marriage Registry team and Sargent's Death Registry team were processing marriage and death certificates above the office average. Everyone knew that there was little, if any, difference whatsoever in the processing of these two types of certificates relative to the processing of birth certificates.

The stark contrast in production levels among the units was also the cause of some considerable tension and friction. Houston's Land Registry team took enormous pride in being the most productive team in the Office of the Registrar General. In addition to the general recognition and the "bragging rights" as it were, that the staff in the Land Registry unit enjoyed within the office, the unit's manager, Houston, seemed to command greater respect and appeared to wield more influence in management meetings in the office and throughout MGS.

The staff in the Marriage Registry and Death Registry teams seemed to think that the Birth Registry team was getting a "free ride." The staff in these two units seemed to attribute the marginal differences in the production level between the Land Registry unit and their own units to the functional and technical differences inherent in processing real property as opposed to people. However, this same logic could not be applied in the case of the seemingly low production levels in the Birth Registry team. To some degree, Sargent and Nosters appreciated the fact that Mair's team was a low producer because it not only lowered the overall production levels for the office but it made it that much easier for both of them to maintain their team's production levels above the office average. On the other hand, like Houston, they resented the fact that Mair seemed to be allowed to get away with such low production levels.

The disparity in production levels among the four teams also created an internal dynamic within the office that the other three managers disliked. It generated an informal demand amongst a high number of office staff, although by no means all staff in the office, to request to be transferred to the Birth Registry team. The general impression was, of course, that because the Birth Registry team was unique and "special," the staff on this Team did not have to work as hard as staff on the other teams. Consequently, some staff were always looking for opportunities to get on the Birth Registry team. The managers on the other teams resented this because it meant that they had to work harder to try to keep their best employees. It also complicated matters at management meetings when the managers were trying to negotiate hiring new staff and the transfer of staff within the office. This placed Mair in a privileged position among the managers because she always had many more people seeking to transfer to her team than she required, and she could hand-pick and choose the people that she wanted on her team.

Although the lack of productivity on the Birth Certificate team was a bane to the other managers and staff within the office, and to the Registrar General, it seemed to create a unique *esprit de corps* among the staff within the Birth Certificate team. Formally, the Office of the Registrar General, of course, sought to promote the ever-increasing quality and quantity of the delivery of key documentation to the citizens of Ontario. For instance, the MGS's annual performance targets always sought to achieve higher overall production targets within the Office of the Registrar General.

Although all units and teams within the office seemed "to pay lip service" to these noble aspirations, in reality only some unit managers and staff actually bought into or accepted these explicit objectives. Mair seemed quite accomplished at always underscoring the value of "quality" in any discussion involving production or establishing overall office production targets. She never stated, but always implied, that the Birth Certificate team qualitatively outperformed any other unit in the office by a wide margin. Since there were no reliable or agreed-upon qualitative measures on which to assess any unit's performance, Mair's assertions with respect to her unit's performance could not be proved or disproved.

Informally, the staff on the Birth Certificate team seem to take a quiet pride in "lowering the bar" on the office's overall production targets. Some staff on the Birth Certificate team saw themselves as "realists" who were injecting sanity back into the workplace. As realists, they saw themselves as protecting their own interests as "workers" who were entitled, through their collective agreement, to work at a particular pace and not at any unsanctioned management induced pace that would lead inevitably either to a premature "burn out" or even worst still "illness." Oddly enough though, it seemed that the staff on the Birth Certificate team experienced more lost time due to sick leave and serious long-term illness than any other team in the office. Informally, then, and some might say perversely, the Birth Certificate team prided itself on its overall lack of productivity and for being the undisputed Office leader in this regard.

A further complicating factor was that Mair was perceived, rightly or wrongly, as being in an unassailable position. Before she came to work in the public service, she had been a lawyer, which was not, of course, unusual in itself. However, Mair differed in that her husband, who was also a lawyer, was the deputy attorney general for the province of Ontario. Mair was broadly known in senior law circles throughout the country, and she also had an extensive network of personal contacts throughout the Ontario public service. Socially, she attended dinners and parties with high officials and, occasionally, senior cabinet ministers. Naturally, this tended to distance Mair from the other managers in the Office of the Registrar General.

One of the first things that Registrar General Camden did when Mair was appointed the manager of the Birth Certificate Registry was to meet with her to ensure her that they would not have any difficulty working together. Camden ensured that he was true to his word and always treated Mair with appropriate respect and the accord that she expected, given her social position, was her due.

It also helped, of course, that Mair was a friendly, pleasant and easygoing person. In addition, she contributed to the office in many other ways. She had an interest in professional development and contributed to the training programs that were held in the office. She also contributed by bringing a particular perspective to management meetings that came from someone with a privileged background and connections.

Another significant aspect of the Birth Certificate team was that it had a number of staff who were active in the Ontario public service union. Blair Kinney, for example, was a long-serving staff member of the Office of the Registrar General who had been active in the Ontario public service union since he had joined the public service 15 years earlier. He had held various positions within the local union, including unit steward.

Kinney described himself as a "high-profile union" activist. He was a senior union official in the MGS. Many considered Kinney to be quite militant in support of the Ontario public service union and worker rights. As a union official and activist, he always seemed to see things from a decidedly union perspective. He was bright and articulate and he was never shy about voicing his opinion on any matter in the workplace. Kinney was known for being an efficient worker but it was also widely known that he would not do anything beyond what was required of him within the terms of the current collective agreement. Further, it was also accepted generally that no unit that Kinney would be assigned to work on would ever lead the office in production. Although this was never expressed explicitly it was obvious to anyone who was the least bit conscious of labour–management relations and trade union politics that this was a matter of principle for any union activist.

Registrar General Camden was, of course, aware of the internal dynamics within each of the units in his office. He also appreciated that it would be extremely difficult, if not impossible, to try to persuade the Birth Certificate team to consider taking on the task of trying to find simpler, quicker and more cost-effective ways to process birth certificates. He knew that as the self-professed contrarian and anti-establishment unit in the office, the Birth Certificate team would immediately oppose or actively work against any initiatives that he proposed in this regard. By the very same token, Camden knew that he would get, most likely, the immediate support of the Land Registry team and its manager, Houston, for any proposed initiative. Camden also knew that getting the support of the other two managers, Sargent and Nosters, and the staff on their teams, the Marriage and the Death Registries, was far more problematic and, therefore, less predictable. After all, Camden knew that it was the managers and staff on these two teams that would likely have to bear the brunt of any work increase within the office.

Questions

1. Explain what you would advise Registrar General Ben Camden to do to get his proposed initiative accepted by the managers and staff in his office.

2. What factor or factors would you say are the keys to explaining the apparent low productivity on the Birth Certificate team?

3. Explain why you agree or disagree with the statement that Gloria Mair is in an "unassailable position."

4. Based on the information presented in this case study, justify who you think is the best manager in the Office of the Registrar General of Ontario and why. Be sure to outline the criteria that you have used in making your selection.

5. What lessons in public management and administrative reform does this case study highlight?

Resource Materials

- Ontario Ministry of Government Services (MGS)
  http://www.gov.on.ca/mgs/en/Home/STEL01_039054.html

- Jim Clemmer, "A Coach's Playbook for Workplace Teams," *Expert Magazine*, Management, February 4, 2006.
  http://www.expertmagazine.com/artman/publish/article_811.shtml

- Al Williams and Samuel Lankford, "Evaluating Esprit de corps: Jobs that have low motivating potential are often the result of poor job design — Research Update," BNET
  http://findarticles.com/p/articles/mi_m1145/is_1_38/ai_97393815

- Jocelyn S. Davis and John H. Cable, RA PMP, "Positive Workplace: Enhancing Individual and Team Productivity," allPM.com, The Project Manager's Homepage, November 8, 2006
  http://allpm.com/print.php?sid=1634

- Performance Management for Teams, teamtechnology.co.uk
  http://www.teamtechnology.co.uk/tb-tpm.html

The Unreliable
Executive

Geoffrey Stark had just been retained to conduct a special project for the International Law Practitioners Association (ILPA). The ILPA was the largest international professional association in the world devoted exclusively to promoting international law and the legal counsel who practised in this specialized area of the law. The ILPA was managed on a day-to-day basis by its executive officers: the president, vice-president, treasurer, secretary and the immediate past president of the association. The governing council of the association met only on a quarterly basis and with 25 members was far too unwieldy to run the association on a daily basis. However, it was understood that any important decisions would, in fact, have to be decided by the ILPA council.

Stark was tasked with writing a review of the accomplishments of the ILPA over the past decade. The review was intended to assist the Association with not only recording its past activities and achievements but also with the plans for its future development as a professional association.

It was also agreed that Stark would work under the direction of the ILPA president, Murray Papin, who was keenly interested in this special project.

Papin saw this review of the ILPA over the past decade as a very important step in the ongoing development of the ILPA and as a tool to use in its fundraising efforts. The ILPA was not a well-endowed association and had to rely primarily on its membership fees to maintain its secretariat, its operations and various programs.

Part of this review project entailed doing interviews with a number of key ILPA members and other outside groups. Stark worked diligently contacting ILPA members and arranging interview dates and times and then calling them to conduct interviews.

For these interviews, Stark had devised a series of common questions to ask each of the ILPA members and outside groups he interviewed. He transcribed all the responses that he received from each of the respondents and then he analyzed their answers to determine a pattern. He incorporated these findings in his study and review of the ILPA's activities over the past decade.

Early in the process of conducting his research and interviews, Stark was invited to an ILPA executive meeting. He had prepared a preliminary draft of the ILPA activities review report that he had circulated to the ILPA executive officers for their review and comment. Papin happened to be on a business trip at the time and could participate in the meeting only by telephone. Most of the meeting dealt with a number of administrative issues that the ILPA was currently engaged in. At the conclusion of this meeting, Papin, the President of the ILPA, had to conclude his telephone call and attend to other matters. The remaining ILPA executive officers then held their own informal meeting and questioned Stark at length. The person who asked the most questions on the preliminary draft ILPA activities review report during this informal meeting was Carol Sinclair, ILPA vice-president. She was particularly annoyed with Stark because he refused to state specifically who had said what during his interviews with ILPA members and other groups.

One of the conditions for these interviews with ILPA members and outside groups was that all those persons who were interviewed would remain anonymous. As a minimum, no one who participated in the survey would have any remarks attributed to them in any papers or reports. In fact, Stark had told all the respondents that their responses during the interview would remain anonymous. He stated that he would never attribute their remarks to anyone without first obtaining their express permission to do so. Accordingly, Stark thought that it was inappropriate for Sinclair to even ask him to reveal who said what in his interviews. He knew that what she was asking him to do was to break his commitment to those whom he had interviewed.

Sinclair and the other ILPA executive officers thought that the preliminary draft ILPA activities review report was far too critical of the association and implied that the preliminary draft put the ILPA executive officers in a very poor light. They directed Stark to rework or remove entire sections of his preliminary draft ILPA activities review report.

Stark found that his informal meeting with the other ILPA executive officers did not go well. It appeared that the ILPA executive officers were not "in sync" with President Papin on the ILPA activities review report. Prior to the ILPA executive officers meeting, Stark had discussed the preliminary draft with Papin, who told him it was a solid piece of work.

In fact, Stark, as required, had worked closely with Papin on the preliminary draft. He had sent Papin drafts of the ILPA activities review report and had spoken with him, at length by both telephone and face to face, discussing the draft report in great detail. Any suggestions or changes that Papin made were incorporated in the draft activities review report. Stark knew that Papin was satisfied with the ILPA draft activities review report. However, it seemed that the other ILPA executive officers were not of the same mind. The immediate past-president of the ILPA, Hugh Graham, was particularly outspoken in his negative comments on the preliminary draft ILPA activities review report.

Stark noticed that Sinclair and Graham were united in their outspoken negative commentary against the draft report. Stark took down all of their concerns and suggested changes. He was quite conscious of the fact that his ILPA activities review report would be accepted only if it had the approval of a majority of the members of the ILPA executive and council. He knew that if it did not have their approval, it would not be supported by the majority of the members of the ILPA council and, hence, it would not be adopted by the ILPA.

In his next discussion with Papin, Stark told him that the other ILPA executive officers were not satisfied with the direction of the preliminary draft ILPA activities review report and that they recommended that it undergo a number of major changes.

Papin was really surprised when he heard this information. He stated that he did not think that the report was too negative at all. He pointed out that the preliminary draft ILPA activities review did report the genuine negative comments of ILPA members and outside groups. In this sense, Papin said, the preliminary draft ILPA activities review report was accurate. He pointed out that the other ILPA executive officers wanted the report to be entirely positive, irrespective of what others might think about the ILPA.

Stark continued to work on the draft ILPA activities review report. He finished the interviews with all those who were identified as potential respondents both within the ILPA and with outside groups. Stark also incorporated nearly all the changes that were suggested by the other ILPA executive officers. When he finished the full new draft of the ILPA activities review report he first sent it to Papin. The ILPA president, again, gave him a number of detailed changes. When Stark completed all of Papin's suggested changes, he then sent this revised text to all of the ILPA executive officers. Papin told Stark that he thought that the completed draft was a solid piece of work. He said that he was impressed with its breadth of coverage and its in-depth analysis of the various ILPA activities.

Stark did not get this same positive response from the other ILPA executive officers. Again, Sinclair was outspoken in her criticisms of the draft report. The basis of her criticism, once again, was that the draft was far too negative. Similarly, Graham said that the new draft should be an item on the next ILPA executive and council meeting. There was general agreement that this should be the major item for discussion at the next meeting.

The views of the draft were again divided at the subsequent ILPA executive and council meeting. The ILPA president had the support of a number of council members and the ILPA vice-president and immediate past-president had what appeared to be an equal number opposed to the current draft of the ILPA activities review report in its current form. In fact, Sinclair had come to this meeting well prepared. She had a detailed critique of the draft printed and circulated to everyone at the meeting. She fought very hard to have the report revised. Not everyone who was opposed to the draft report necessarily agreed with Sinclair's suggested alterations or amendments. Nevertheless, a consensus emerged when Sinclair stated that she would be prepared to try and rework the draft in a manner that she thought would be appropriate and then present it for the council's review and consideration. She stated that she would work closely with Stark to rework the report in a manner that would be acceptable to the entire ILPA executive and council. Everyone found this to be an acceptable compromise on how to address this apparent impasse and move on to resolving the issue.

After the meeting, Sinclair had an informal chat with Stark and told him that she would have something available for him to look at within seven to 10 days. She said that she did not think that she would need more than a day or two to rework his draft ILPA activities review report.

Several days later, Stark tried to contact Sinclair to see whether he could provide her with any assistance in reworking the draft ILPA activities review report. However, he did not get any reply from her. One week later, Stark tried to reach Sinclair, both by telephone and by email, and was again unable to reach her. He learned subsequently that she was not feeling well. A full two weeks passed and Stark was still unable to contact Sinclair. It was more than evident that she was simply not returning his emails or telephone calls. Stark then apprised Papin about Sinclair's lack of response to his efforts to contact her and to try to work with her on the preparation of a reworked draft ILPA activities review report.

Three weeks passed and Stark still had not heard from Sinclair. It was more than evident that the ILPA vice-president had no intention of working with Stark to revise the draft ILPA activities review report. Stark contacted Papin about this situation and advised him that, in his opinion, Sinclair probably had no intention of reworking the draft ILPA activities review report as she had committed to at the ILPA executive and council meeting. Papin, agreed and they both considered what they should do next.

Questions

1. What do you think Geoffrey Stark and Murray Papin should do in this situation?

2. Explain why you think Carol Sinclair has or has not adopted an effective strategy to deal with her objections to the draft ILPA activities review report.

3. What, if anything, has Geoffrey Stark done wrong in the manner that he has undertaken this special project? Was there any way that he could have avoided this open division in the ILPA executive and council?

4. Justify what you think ought to be done in this situation that would serve the best interests of the ILPA as a whole.

5. What issues in international public administration and management, if any, are exemplified by this case study?

Resource Materials

- International Non-Governmental Organizations (INGOs), Canadian International Development Agency (CIDA)
  http://www.acdi-cida.gc.ca/CIDAWEB/acdicida.nsf/En/REN-218124529-NZB

- Challenges to the Action of International Non-governmental Organizations, *laetus in praesens*
  http://www.laetusinpraesens.org/docs/ingo.php

- Andrew E. Rice, "Relationships between International Non-governmental Organizations and the United Nations," Transnational Associations, 47, 5, 1995, pp. 254–265.
  http://www.uia.org/uiadocs/unngos.htm

- International Non Governmental Organizations' Accountability Charter, December 20, 2005
  http://www.consumersinternational.org/Shared_ASP_Files/UploadedFiles/78C36DEE-66C5-41E7-B887-9310B6E8A24C_INGOAccountabilityCharter.pdf

Troublemaker

Howard Stone had served on the Ontario Parole and Earned Release Board (OPERB) for six years. Prior to his appointment on the OPERB, he had worked for the Ministry of the Attorney General in the Ontario Government. Howard Stone had worked his way up the Ontario civil service the hard way. He had entered the civil service after completing one year of college and after some 25 years of service in various positions before he managed to get an appointment on OPERB.

Stone was not known for his sharp analytical mind or his sensitivity to participants in OPERB hearings. On the contrary, he was seen as a rather weak member who seemed to rely heavily on others for his work. One of his major deficiencies was in his writing skills. He not only took forever to complete his written decisions but when they were completed they were invariably of minimal quality. His grasp and understanding of the law was tenuous at best. It seemed that even though Howard Stone liked the status and the salary that came with the position of being a member of OPERB, he did not really enjoy the work. More specifically, the job requirements for the position of member did not suit his skills or strengthens. In fact, he found doing the work of a member on OPERB to be a real struggle.

When he was first appointed to OPERB, he was surprised with the workload that members were expected to do. He never expected to have to sit on so many hearings or to do so much reading and case preparation. The demands of the position of member consumed much more of his time than he had anticipated. His expectations were that he would have to sit on only one or two parole hearings a week and that most of the work required for the member position would be done by OPERB staff.

Stone found himself working harder than he had ever worked in any other previous civil service position that he had held in the Ontario government. Nonetheless, he had thoroughly enjoyed his first few months at OPERB when he was given the standard orientation and training program for new members. But when he found himself scheduled on a full caseload of parole hearings he realized that the job was going to be a real challenge. Although he assumed that the work would get easier over time, as he gained more experience, this did not prove to be the case. Gradually, he fell further and further behind in his work, the job became more demanding and stressful and, as a result, ever more frustrating and that much more difficult.

Over his years on the OPERB, Stone began to develop a reputation for being a "loose cannon." No one knew when he was going to go off or, in fact, explode. For example, something might arise during the course of a parole hearing that would lead to a complaint being filed against Howard Stone for what he said or what he did during the parole hearing. Consequently, Howard Stone's file was replete with complaints that had been filed against him by inmates and their counsels.

Stone was also known for being argumentative with both staff and colleagues. He often displayed a surly temperament and personality. In fact, it appeared, to many people at the OPERB that he enjoyed controversy and conflict. Indeed, Stone seemed to be much more adept at getting embroiled in some sort of minor tiff with a colleague or staff member than completing his work.

Stone worked in the Southwest Service Sector Office of the OPERB. He reported to senior board member, Stanley Benson. Benson and Stone had been appointed to the board at the same time and had completed their training together. However, the two had not really worked together until Benson had been designated a senior member of OPERB, some six months earlier. During that time, Benson got to know Stone fairly well. Benson thought that the truism that managers have to spend 80 percent of their time dealing with two or three of their most troublesome staff members certainly seemed to hold true for Stone, who appeared to be getting himself in some sort of difficulty at least once each week.

On Monday morning at 10:00 a.m., Janine Naylor, OPERB member, came into Benson's office. She was very upset and told Benson that she did not want to work with Stone again and asked him never to assign her to another parole hearing with Stone. She stated that Stone had caused a crisis in the parole hearing by using inappropriate language with an inmate. Further, she said that she found him very difficult to work with. She added that she thought that Stone had a flawed understanding of how to do "risk assessments" on inmates. She said that this had become clearly evident to her after she had wasted nearly two hours going over, in great detail, the merits on one their joint cases.

Naylor was clearly emotionally distraught. She had found her experience sitting in the parole hearing with Stone to be both disturbing and nerve wracking. She said that she would not be surprised if the inmate's counsel filed a complaint against Howard Stone and possibly herself for his conduct at the parole hearing. Janine Naylor wanted to make it very clear that she was not responsible for what had taken place at the hearing and that she wanted to ensure that she did not have to bear the brunt of another of Stone's "meltdowns" in a parole hearing. She stated that she did not want to be the subject of an investigation by either the Ontario Ombudsman or the Ontario Human Rights Commission.

Benson tried to calm Naylor down. He asked her to explain what had happened at the parole hearing. She stated that Stone was chairing the parole hearing when he got into an argument with the inmate and accused him of lying. The inmate asked him if he was calling him a liar and Stone replied that the inmate was not only a liar but that he thought he was "beyond rehabilitation." The hearing then degenerated into a shouting match and had to be adjourned.

Naylor stated that Stone had told her prior to the hearing that he had seen this type of criminal many times before and thought that parole was simply out of the question for this type of person as far as he was concerned. She said that Stone had made up his mind in the case without even allowing the inmate an opportunity to speak. She said that he had not gone into the hearing with an open mind prepared to hear the inmate's testimony. She stated that as far as Stone was concerned, everything that the inmate had to say was untrue and not even worth considering. Naylor said that Stone was clearly biased against the inmate before the hearing even commenced.

Naylor stated that Stone did not seem to understand the basic principles of fundamental justice and fairness in a proceeding. Irrespective of what Stone might have thought of this inmate, the person had a right to be heard and to be given a fair hearing before any decision was rendered in his application for parole. Naylor declared that she could not understand how Stone could have been a Member of OPERB for six years without understanding these basic principles.

Benson thanked Naylor for sharing this information with him and stated that they would just have to wait and see whether there would be any complaints filed against either Stone or herself. However, in the interim he said that he would have to speak to Stone about this parole hearing.

Shortly after his meeting with Naylor, Benson went to Stone's office. He found that Stone was not there and left a note on his telephone asking Stone to call him because he wanted to discuss a parole hearing.

Several hours later Benson heard shouting outside his office and down the hall. When he went outside his office to see what was going on, he saw Stone engaged in a loud conversation with a number of staff. When Benson approached the group he heard Stone say that he resented the comments that he had heard coming from one of the two staff. The person stated that he needed to get some files from Stone's office for an upcoming parole hearing. The person said that he had a right to go into his office to get these files and that he resented Stone's tone of voice and his overbearing attitude. Benson intervened and asked what was the matter. Stone replied that the staff members had come into his office and ordered him to turn over two files. The two staff members denied that they ordered Benson to turn over any files. On the contrary, they insisted that Stone had immediately begun to challenge them as to why they wanted the parole hearing files. Things had deteriorated from there they said. They noted that they had still not been able to obtain the files. Benson then told the two staff to go into Stone's office to get the files that they needed.

Benson then told Stone that he needed to speak with him as soon as possible. Stone replied that he could see him in his office in 15 minutes.

While Benson waited for Stone to come to his office, it occurred to him that every time Stone was under pressure or was confronted with a situation that he knew he could not handle, something would always happen. Arguments would inevitably ensue and the resulting conflict that arose regarding the incident would take precedence over the task at hand. Indeed, the controversy that Stone instigated would become the focus of everyone's attention and everyone would forget about the matter at hand and the work that they were doing or that was supposed to get done. Benson realized that controversy and conflict were Stone's method of dealing with his inadequacies and his inabilities to do his job effectively.

Questions

1. If you were Stanley Benson, how would you handle your meeting with Howard Stone?

2. Do you think that Stanley Benson has come up with a plausible explanation for why Howard Stone always seems to be in some kind of trouble at the board?

3. Explain what you think Stanley Benson, as manager, should do with Howard Stone with respect to the incident that allegedly took place in the parole hearing with Janine Naylor?

4. What strategies, if any, are available to Stanley Benson for effectively managing Howard Stone?

5. What lessons in public personnel and human resources management and administration are exemplified by this case study?

Resource Materials

- Ontario Parole and Earned Release Board (OPERB)
  http://www.operb.gov.on.ca/english/home.html

- OPERB — Standards of Professional Conduct
  http://www.operb.gov.on.ca/english/conduct/standards.html

- Nartreb del Alcazar, "Reconsidering the Peter Principle"
  http://www.davidalbeck.com/writings/peterp2.html

- Du Markowitz LLP, Labour and Employment Lawyers, "Incompetence: The Underdog Case Against Termination for Cause"
  http://www.wrongfullydismissed.com/incompetence.html

- Carter McNamara, "Basics of Conflict Management," Free Management Library
  http://www.managementhelp.org/intrpsnl/basics.htm

- Resolving Workplace Problems
  http://www.spot.pcc.edu/~rjacobs/career/resolving_workplace_problems.htm

- Dr. Tony Fiore, "Resolving Workplace Conflict: 4 Ways to a Win-Win Solution"
  http://www.businessknowhow.com/manage/resolve.htm

- Ontario Ombudsman
  http://www.ombudsman.on.ca/en/media/ombudsman-in-the-news.aspx

The Part-Time
Employee

Jill Dempster had worked for the Canada Industrial Relations Board (CIRB) in the Canadian government as a labour relations officer for close to 12 years. When she had started her employment with the CIRB she was a full-time employee. However, after she finished her first maternity leave she had decided that it would be better for her, and her family, if she changed her employment status from full-time to part-time. Jill Dempster found that working five days a week was just too stressful and demanding, given her responsibilities as a mother. She decided that if she worked part-time, two days a week, it would not cause an inordinate strain on her or on her family. The loss of income was not a concern since her husband earned a substantial income.

Dempster's husband was a lawyer who worked in a large prestigious law firm and earned a six-figure salary. Consequently, she lived a comfortable upper-middle class lifestyle. Her family could afford to live in a large home in an affluent neighbourhood and take annual expensive family vacations. She enjoyed the status of being a professional's spouse while at the same time having the independence of her own part-time career as a labour relations officer at the CIRB. She also enjoyed the financial benefits of a good part-time salary and partial benefits, including a government pension plan.

Dempster also enjoyed not having to come in to work for more than two days a week. As a part-time labour relations officer, she knew that she could be assigned no more than four cases per week. Since she was a part-time employee she also knew that she would likely be assigned only cases that were simple and straightforward. Moreover, as a part-time employee she appreciated that she would never be asked to take on any additional responsibilities or be considered for promotion. This suited her perfectly because she had no desire to assume any management duties or be promoted to a more senior position. Indeed, Dempster studiously avoided any possibility of having her responsibilities or workload increased in any way.

Ralph Wagner was Dempster's immediate supervisor at the CIRB. Wagner was a long-time employee with the CIRB and he had first met Dempster when she was still working full-time as a labour relations officer. Wagner knew Dempster was considered to be a bright and able labour relations officer. In fact, at that time, she had enjoyed the reputation of being amongst the best labour relations officers at the board.

When Wagner was promoted to his current manager's position at the CIRB, he found that Dempster was one of the staff in his unit. By this time, Dempster was already working as a part-time labour relations officer. During his first six months as the new manager of the unit, Wagner was busy learning as much as he could about his staff and the routines and responsibilities of his new management position. After he became more comfortable as manager of the unit, he began to notice what he considered to be disconcerting aspects of Dempster's work habits and attitude.

This first came to his notice when he could not help but overhear Dempster engaged in rather loud conversations with her close friends and colleagues at the CIRB. These disruptive conversations seemed to go on for unbearably long periods of time. In some instances, the loud "give and take" gab sessions would last for over an hour. Initially, Wagner did not think that this was too unusual, since employees often had such open conversations in their work areas with colleagues and friends. More often than not these conversations would also include some aspect of work, whether it was dealing with a particular file or some aspect of their job functions. However, what was distinctly noticeable about Dempster's workplace protracted conversations was how often they took place and the length of these discussions. It also became evident, after some time, that these discussions had little if anything to do with work-related issues. Given the frequency and pattern of these loud discussions, it clearly signaled that Dempster appeared to have either far too much free time on her hands or that she was not attending to her work. Furthermore, the conversations seemed to distract and irritate the staff that were in her immediate area.

The second thing that Wagner noticed about Dempster was that she always left work by 3:00 p.m. each day. Her justification for doing so was that she needed to get away from work at this time in order to pick up her children from daycare and school. These types of flexible work arrangements were typical of other staff with young families at the CIRB. Staff who worked under these flexible time arrangements were expected to get to the office by 7:00 a.m. or make up their work hours by taking less time for lunch or not taking their scheduled breaks. Typically, this would make up the lost hours resulting from their early departure from work. However, over time, Wagner had observed that Dempster rarely, if ever, came to the office before 8:00 a.m. and she often left well before 3:00 p.m. It was not unusual to see Dempster slip out of the office at around 2:30 p.m. on her assigned workdays. Wagner also noticed that Dempster never seemed to cut any time from her one-hour lunch or morning and afternoon breaks.

The third thing that Wagner noticed about Dempster was that she seemed to have one of the lowest production rates of anyone in the office. When Wagner first saw Dempster's statistics on the number of unfair labour practices (ULP) complaints investigated or board hearings concluded he thought that there was some sort of error. However, when he double-checked the figures and had confirmed the accuracy of the statistical reports he had received, he was quite shocked at how little Dempster, actually, seemed to be doing in terms of contributing to his unit's overall productivity.

The fourth thing that Wagner noticed about Dempster was that she was always assigned workdays whenever the unit had a meeting or professional development activity, each month. Of course, this contributed to Dempster's low production rate, but, at the same time, he noticed that she would frequently leave these meetings and training sessions early. Although this was not atypical for some staff, given other pressing priorities or deadlines that they had to meet, Dempster, a part-time employee who was never assigned such projects, also appeared to be taking advantage of this grace arrangement but without the need for it.

The fifth thing that Wagner noticed about Dempster's work habits was that when he did his occasional office "walkabout" or when he went to talk to a particular employee regarding a ULP complaint or hearing and he happened to walk past Dempster's office, he would often see her playing card games, such as solitaire, on her computer. Wagner thought that it was evident from Dempster's attitude and demeanor that she did not care who saw her doing this at the office. Again, Wagner came to the conclusion that this either signalled that Dempster was bored with her job because she had too little to do or that she just did not want to attend to her work duties.

Another thing that Wagner noticed about Dempster was that she occasionally had clashes with other members of the unit. For example, on one recent occasion two of his administrative staff, who had appeared visibly upset, had come into his office one day complaining about Dempster and how they were treated by her. The staff members had stated that Dempster had accused them of not doing their work properly and had used foul language in their presence. When he approached Dempster the next time she came to work, the following week after the alleged incident, she brushed it off as a misunderstanding on the part of the two employees. Since the two staff members of the unit did not file an official complaint, the matter was quietly dropped and conveniently forgotten in the interest of maintaining a harmonious work environment within the unit. However, it also clearly demonstrated to Wagner that Dempster was not above "stirring the pot" to maintain her interests and position within the CIRB. It also explained, at least to some degree, why administrative staff within the unit kept a "safe distance" in their dealings with Dempster.

The final thing that Wagner observed was Dempster's haughty and arrogant attitude, particularly, toward the administrative staff. As a labour relations officer, she enjoyed a certain stature in the CIRB hierarchy. Nonetheless, she seemed to exude an air of superiority and considered herself as intellectually superior to those whom she worked with at the CIRB. Wagner suspected that this had something to do with her husband's prominent position as a successful lawyer and the social status that she enjoyed as a consequence. But it could just as well have stemmed from her personality. Her swagger and condescension probably explained why she was often involved in conflicts with other staff.

Wagner came to appreciate that most of the staff, including the other labour relations officers, within his Unit were conscious of what they perceived to be Dempster's "privileged situation" and that it was having a noticeable affect on the unit's morale. What troubled Wagner most was that he had a part-time employee who clearly seemed to be taking advantage of her position and who was not contributing in any noticeable way to the office's overall productivity and was, at times, disrupting and upsetting the workplace.

Questions

1. Justify what you would consider to be the most difficult and troubling aspects of Jill Dempster's work performance.

2. Outline a strategy for how you would address Jill Dempster's performance issues if you were in Ralph Wagner's position, as the manager of this CIRB unit.

3. Explain whether Jill Dempster's performance issues, in your view, may stem, at least in part, from her status as a part-time employee. Are part-time employees inherently harder to manage than full-time employees?

4. Identify a number of the systemic issues that are raised in this case study that make it inherently difficult for public sector managers to address individual staff performance issues.

5. Are there sufficient grounds for Ralph Wagner to impose any disciplinary measures against Jill Dempster? If so, what disciplinary measures ought to be imposed and how should they be applied?

Resource Materials

- Canadian Industrial Relations Board (CIRB)
  http://www.cirb-ccri.gc.ca/index_eng.asp

- The Business Research Lab, "Flexible Work Hours"
  http://www.busreslab.com/policies/goodpol3.htm

- Directgov, "Flexible work and work-life balance: an introduction"
  http://www.direct.gov.uk/en/Employment/Employees/WorkingHoursAndTimeOff/DG_10029491

- University of Minnesota, Office of Human Resources, "Dealing With Performance Problems"
  http://www1.umn.edu/ohr/toolkit/performance/problems/index.html

- Carter McNamara, "Employee Performance Management," Free Management Library
  http://www.managementhelp.org/emp_perf/emp_perf.htm

The Arrogant Manager

John Brewer was the regional director of the Toronto office of Environment Canada (EC). He was responsible for a staff of over 400 people and had six managers who reported directly to him, including managers responsible for administrative support services, research and development, human resources, environmental programs, environmental assessment, and environmental regulations and enforcement. The Toronto regional office of EC was considered by the corporate headquarters in Ottawa to be one of the best-run regional offices in the country. Brewer's main function as the regional director seemed to be to monitor all the activities in the regional office and to ensure that it was meeting its financial and production commitments to Ottawa. As the main liaison officer between the Toronto regional office and the EC corporate headquarters in Ottawa, he was in frequent communications with senior management there, including the deputy minister of the environment, whenever the need arose. It was not unusual for Brewer to have to travel to meetings in Ottawa for senior management and other regional directors from across the country.

Brewer seemed to have a great sense of humour. He liked to look on the humorous side of life and loved to hear, as well as tell, humorous anecdotes and jokes. It seemed that he was happiest when he was with a group of people and everyone was laughing and having a good time. He was often seen with a smile on his face as he walked around the office. His friendly personality and ever-present smile led, inevitably, to people in the office calling him John "Smiling" Brewer or simply "Smiley." The nickname Smiley was used discreetly and it seemed never in Brewer's presence, although it was widely known that this was his nickname. It was generally assumed that Brewer was aware that he had been given this moniker by staff members more as a form of endearment than derision. Generally, management and staff members in the Toronto regional office found Brewer to be a friendly, pleasant and an open person. He did not appear either to take his job or himself too seriously, which was seen as a good thing.

Brewer had a rather interesting background. Although he had worked in Toronto with the federal government for most of his working career, most of his family, including, his parents and siblings, lived in Alberta. He was proud of his Western roots and heritage and he frequently made trips back to Edmonton, where he was raised, and to where his parents, in fact, still resided.

The Brewer family was fairly well known in Edmonton and throughout the rest of Alberta. Brewer's grandfather was a well-known politician in Alberta who was eventually appointed as lieutenant governor of the province. Consequently, given his family background, Brewer was not only interested in, but, also quite familiar with politics and political life, particularly in Alberta and the rest of Western Canada.

With the end of the fiscal year not far off, Brewer, knew that he could expect to hear soon from senior management at the corporate headquarters in Ottawa on the lower than expected overall production figures for the Toronto regional office, which were a great personal disappointment to Brewer. He had fully expected that by this point in the fiscal year the production figures for the Toronto regional office would be above their assigned targets. Brewer knew that if the Toronto regional office did not meet or exceed its production targets for the fiscal year, then he would not earn his annual bonus. He had earned a sizeable bonus in each of the last three years and had grown to depend on the bonus as a nice supplement to his regional director's salary.

In an effort to shore up the production figures for the fiscal year, Brewer and his senior managers decided it would be helpful if a meeting was held for all the staff in the regional office. It was agreed that the meeting would provide an opportunity to try to motivate the staff to increase their productivity in an effort to improve substantially the regional office's work output before the end of the fiscal year. Accordingly, all staff were advised that an important office-wide meeting would be held to discuss a number of pertinent regional office issues, including, the regional office's overall productivity. A full morning was set aside for the meeting to give the senior managers and Brewer an opportunity to meet with the staff to discuss a number of issues, including present workload levels and output.

On the day of the office-wide staff meeting, the regional director, as usual, had a broad smile on his face when he came into work that morning. He was seen joking with his managers during their morning meeting in his office to go over the final preparations for the staff meeting.

Brewer decided that he would greet the regional office staff as they entered the meeting room, exchanging a few friendly pleasantries, a hand-shake and his trademark smile. Occasionally, he would exchange jokes with people and laughter could be heard from all those who were around him. It was hard for some people to take Brewer, seriously, given his light-hearted humorous nature.

When the meeting commenced, Brewer started the proceedings with a long, rambling speech that included a PowerPoint presentation with colour charts and graphs that showed that the regional office's production had dropped from the previous year and that its productivity was below year-to-date targets for the current fiscal year. The comparative production statistics with the other regional offices was just as glum. Brewer tried to keep his presentation interesting and light despite the disappointing statistics. He mentioned that the EC corporate headquarters in Ottawa were not pleased with the regional office's effort for the current fiscal year.

These remarks upset a number of the staff, who thought that Ottawa's meddling in Toronto regional office affairs was uncalled for and that this was another example of the EC's senior management making its typical un-reasonable production demands. Once again, this seemed to demonstrate, to at least some staff, that the EC's corporate headquarters had little or no real knowledge or understanding of the situation in the Toronto regional office. Brewer was repeatedly asked why corporate headquarters was not willing to provide the regional office with more resources if it was not pleased with its production figures for the year.

Brewer had responded to about half a dozen questions after his presentation when, out of the blue, he stated, albeit in a joking manner, that he wanted everyone to roll up their sleeves and work hard, not only to make the production targets that were set for this fiscal year but to exceed those targets. He then added, in a rather cavalier manner, that he wanted every-one to do this so that he could get his fiscal year-end performance bonus. When Brewer was saying these words he had a "big grin" on his face. When he had finished he gave out one of his patented laughs. Unfortu-nately, very few people joined him in laughter and it was evident that most people thought his remarks were not the least bit humorous.

After the meeting, many of the staff in the office could not believe what they had just heard. All of the staff were saying that they could not believe that Brewer had asked them all to work harder so that he could earn his fiscal year end performance bonus. A number of staff stated that they found the regional director's comments to be not only inappropri-ate but offensive. Many of the newer staff were surprised by his comments, for several reasons. First, they were surprised to hear that the regional director was eligible to receive a manager's performance bonus and, secondly, they were shocked that anyone would come straight out and ask them to work harder so that he or she could get a monetary award for their efforts.

The intent of the office-wide staff meeting seemed to backfire. The morale in the Toronto regional office immediately began to drop. A number of the public service union representatives considered Brewer's remarks to be completely out of line. In their view, the staff in the Toronto regional office were working exceedingly hard and it was unconscionable that the regional director would make such an arrogant and selfish demand of the office staff. Some union representatives even contemplated filing a complaint against Brewer for his inappropriate remarks that seemed to smack of the days when the factory owners' sent their foremen around the plant trying to squeeze every ounce of effort out of the workers.

There were some staff who thought that Brewer was just being his usual humorous and jovial self. They said that he had tried to make a joke to relieve the tension from the meeting and his own stressful situation vis-à-vis senior management in Ottawa. Although his joke was a mistake, his remarks were not intended to be callous or self-serving. A number of managers in the Toronto regional office also came to his defence stating that the office-wide staff meeting was not Brewer's idea but had come out of one of the weekly regional office management meetings. They said the meeting had been intended to fully inform the staff on the challenges confronting the regional office with respect to its lower than expected production figures for the fiscal year.

Brewer appeared to be oblivious to this whole situation and to the furor his remarks had caused among the staff in the Toronto regional office. His trademark smile never seemed to leave his face when he was seen walking around the office.

Matters seemed to come to a head, however, during a computer training session that was held several weeks later. The computer training session was for managers and staff on how to use the Internet to locate specific sources of information. Brewer attended one of these computer training sessions. As the instructor was demonstrating how to use various search engines, Brewer's computer seemed to act up. Rather than going to websites that the instructor had directed, when Brewer entered the URLs he ended up at a pornographic website. When this occurred Brewer could not stop himself from laughing. However, a number of people who were seated next to him did not find this to be a laughing matter. The two female staff members sitting next to him thought that Brewer was trying to be humorous or funny at their expense. For some reason, it also took quite a while before Brewer, with the assistance of the instructor, was able to close his computer so that the pornographic images no longer appeared on his computer screen. Following this incident, it took the instructor several minutes before he was able to resume the training class.

After the computer class, a number of the staff brought the so-called computer incident to the attention of their union representatives. The chief shop stewards then brought the matter up with the most senior union officials at the Toronto regional office. After some deliberation, it was decided that a letter of complaint would be sent to Brewer's superiors at the EC's corporate headquarters, complaining about the offensive pornographic images that appeared on his computer screen during the training session.

Several weeks after the letter was sent to EC's corporate headquarters a copy of the letter was printed in the political scandal and satirical magazine, *Frank*. Apparently, someone who had a copy of the letter leaked it to *Frank* magazine. This was a cause of some embarrassment not only to Brewer, but to the EC's corporate headquarters in Ottawa, given that the matter of the union's formal complaint had yet to be resolved.

Questions

1. Justify why you think John Brewer is or is not an "arrogant" manager.

2. What fundamental error(s) did Regional Director John Brewer make at the office-wide staff meeting that was intended to motivate staff and to address the issues confronting the Toronto regional office's overall productivity?

3. What role, if any, do you think declining office morale may have had on the union's decision to file a formal letter of complaint against John Brewer?

4. Were there valid grounds for the union to file a complaint against John Brewer over the computer training incident?

5. What advice would you give Regional Director John Brewer on how to handle the leaked letter of complaint regarding the computer training incident that was printed in *Frank* magazine?

Resource Materials

- Environment Canada (EC)
  http://www.ec.gc.ca/default.asp?lang=En&n=12345678-1&xml=5830C36B-1773-4E3E-AF8C-B21F54633E0A

- Treasury Board of Canada Secretariat, Guidelines on the Grievance Procedure (Draft)
  http://www.tbs-sct.gc.ca/pubs_pol/hrpubs/TBM_11B/ggp-ldpg02_e.asp

- *Public Service Labour Relations Act* (2003)
  http://laws.justice.gc.ca/en/P-33.3/

- CUPE Local 500, "Stewards"
  http://www.cupe500.mb.ca/stewards.htm

- Humour in the Workplace, John Hoare, "Enjoy Work with Humour in the Workplace," healthandgoodness.com
  http://www.healthandgoodness.com/ManagingLife/humour_at_work.htm

- Canadian Human Rights Commission, "Anti-Harassment Policies for the Workplace: An Employer's Guide"
  http://www.chrc-ccdp.ca/publications/anti_harassment_toc-en.asp

Meeting Weekly Production Targets

Alice Hines, a coordinating member (CM) in the Refugee Protection Division of the Immigration and Refugee Board of Canada (IRB), the largest quasi-judicial tribunal in the Government of Canada, is responsible for managing a team of 10 members of the IRB. The principal task of members of the IRB is to decide whether a claimant for refugee protection is either a "Convention refugee" or a "person in need of protection."[1] Persons who are determined to be Convention refugees or persons in need of protection can apply for permanent residence in Canada and, eventually, for Canadian citizenship, to Citizenship and Immigration Canada (CIC). Persons who are determined not to be either a Convention refugee or a person in need of protection can be removed from Canada.

Alice Hines is one of six coordinating members or member managers in the IRB's central regional office in Toronto. Each coordinating member in the

---

[1] For an explanation of the refugee determination system in Canada and the legal definition of who qualifies to be a "Convention refugee" and/or a "person in need of protection" see the Immigration and Refugee Board of Canada website at http://www.irb-cisr.gc.ca/en/index_e.htm.

central regional office has responsibility for a team of about 10 to 12 IRB members. A staff of permanent civil servants consisting of file clerks, file processing officers, members' secretaries and tribunal officers, supports each of the six teams. An Operational Service Manager (OSM) manages the civil service staff on each team. The OSM and the CM are jointly responsible for ensuring that the team of adjudicators, who are governor-in-council appointments, and the civil servants, work together as a coordinated team. There are about 25 to 30 people in each of the six teams in the central regional office.

The six teams are responsible for a particular geographic region of the world. Teams have responsibility for processing and hearing refugee claims from states in their area of regional geographic specialization. In fact, the six teams are identified by their geographic area of specialization and, hence, are referred to as the Americas Team, Europe Team, Commonwealth of Independent States, including the Russian Federation Team, the Middle East Team, Africa Team, and the South East Asia and Pacific Team. In theory, each of the six teams are assigned an equivalent case load of refugee claims that must be scheduled, heard and concluded. They are also assigned equivalent resources, that is, staff and material, in order to complete a certain number of refugee claims over the course of the fiscal year. Hence, each team is allocated a specific budget and, with this budget, is expected to conclude a certain number of refugee claims over the course of a year.

Alice Hines was the CM for the South East Asia and Pacific Team and her OSM was Judith Barnes. They enjoyed a good working relationship and their team was considered one of the more productive, that is, being able to meet its overall annual targets for the number of refugee hearings concluded in the central regional office. However, this did not necessarily mean that all team members, whether member or civil servant, were equally highly productive. Some members had outstanding production numbers, in terms of the number of hearings concluded, whereas others did not. Likewise, some civil servants were considered more productive and efficient than others. One of the management challenges that the CM and OSM faced was to try to ensure that everyone on their team performed at their best and were able to contribute their fair share to the overall productivity of the team as a whole.

Phil Collins, assistant deputy chairperson (ADC), was the senior ranking adjudicator or member manager at the central regional office of the IRB. He was not only responsible for directing and managing the six CMs in the central region, but he was also responsible, through the CMs, for each of the IRB members in his region. In an effort to try to increase the central regional office's overall productivity, Collins introduced a new system of monitoring individual member's weekly productivity in terms of the number of hearings heard and concluded. Collins created a reporting form that each member was required to complete and submit to his office each week. His staff then used these self-reporting forms to compile a weekly productivity report for each member in the central regional office.

The weekly productivity report was a week-to-week and month-to-month cumulative report that showed how many refugee hearings each member had concluded over each week in the year. The weekly productivity report also offered a number of other relevant statistics. It included the average number of refugee hearings that the member had concluded year-to-date and the average number of refugee hearings that were concluded by all of the members on the team.

The weekly productivity report sought to measure, in terms of the number of hearings concluded, how productive each IRB member was relative to the average hearings concluded for all the other members of their team. The report was intended specifically to inform each member how productive they were relative to their team's average. However, it also provided the ADC, Collins, with weekly statistics on the productivity of each IRB member and each team in the central regional office. The ADC shared these statistics with each of his CMs. Consequently, each CM not only received the weekly productivity report for each of their members but also the average weekly productivity reports for each of the other teams in the central regional office. All the CMs knew where their team stood relative to each of the other teams in the region.

When this system was first introduced by Collins, it was not welcomed universally by either the IRB members or the CMs. The reasons for opposing this weekly productivity reporting system varied widely from complaints that it increased the administrative burden on IRB members to the new reporting system was fundamentally flawed and unfair. Some IRB members complained that they were already overburdened with work and, therefore, should not have to spend more of their valuable time having to fill in additional forms. It was also noted that these statistics were probably readily available through other means. There were already a number of different record-keeping systems and reporting mechanisms and, consequently, the new weekly productivity reporting system for IRB members was a waste of their valuable time and everyone else's administrative energy and time. There were also concerns regarding the confidentiality of these statistics. Although the information gathered for the weekly productivity report was intended to be a private matter of the individual member, their CM and the ADC, members complained that the information in these weekly reports was available to all staff in the regional office. Still others argued that since the staff had an important role to play to ensure that hearings were completed, it was patently unfair to place the onus on concluding hearings exclusively on the members. Moreover, no other staff in the regional office were required to complete weekly reporting forms on the number of files they processed or the number of administrative tasks they performed on a weekly basis. Therefore, members should not be expected to do so nor should members be saddled with the burden of bearing all of the responsibility for concluding hearings when they were merely one element, albeit a critical one, in the process of hearing and concluding refugee claims.

The counterarguments for these various points were that IRB members had to become more conscious of how many hearings they actually were completing each week and the new weekly reporting system would force them to review how many refugee hearings they actually managed to complete each week. The new system also afford them an opportunity to see whether they were completing their refugee hearings above or below the average for all of the other members on their team. It was also pointed out that the administrative burden argument was exaggerated because it took only a few minutes each day to complete the form. Collins was fond of noting that lawyers had to keep a daily log of the hours that they had spent on a client's file and that this system was really no different. He argued that since many members were lawyers who had been in private practice before they were appointed to the IRB, they would be use to this type of record-keeping system and would understand its value.

Other IRB members saw the new weekly productivity reporting system as fundamentally flawed because not all refugee claims or hearings were the same. For instance, some refugee claims could be completed quickly because they had a limited number of issues that needed to be addressed in the hearing. The refugee claim was simple and straightforward and, therefore, could be done quickly. However, other refugee claims were much more complicated because they had to address a wide variety of issues and, consequently, took much more time to conclude. For example, refugee claims and hearings where the Minister intervened under Article 1F of the *1951 Convention*, exclusion, that is, for those refugee claimants where there was serious reasons for considering that they had committed a crime against peace, war crime or crime against humanity, are inherently more difficult cases not only procedurally but also on the basis of the legal issues that have to be addressed. These types of refugee claims and hearings are, by definition, much more complicated than the usual type of refugee claim or hearing and, accordingly, take much more time to conclude. Completing four ordinary refugee hearings, it was argued, might be equivalent to completing one ministerial intervention case. Hence, the weekly productivity reports were fundamentally flawed and unfair because they did not distinguish between the different types of refugee claims or hearings that IRB members were responsible for hearing and completing.

Those who opposed the new weekly productivity reporting system also argued that it did not take into consideration the peculiarities of each refugee claim or hearing. The maxim that every refugee case had to be decided on its own merits underscored the unique nature of each and every claim for refugee protection. Further, no matter how well a member prepared for a refugee hearing in advance, no one could predict what could happen during the course of the refugee hearing itself — for example, unanticipated issues might be raised during the course of the refugee claimant's testimony; the refugee claimant might complain about the quality of interpretation; the counsel representing the refugee claimant might raise repeated objections; the counsel could request an adjournment once the hearing was commenced; the refugee claimant might decide to dismiss their counsel in the midst of their refugee hearing; and so on. All of these examples, and others, could lead to a refugee hearing not proceeding immediately to a conclusion. The IRB member could spend hours preparing for a refugee hearing and, despite spending hours hearing the refugee claimant's testimony or working hard at dealing with counsel's objections, the refugee hearing still might not conclude. Accordingly, it was argued that the new weekly productivity reporting system was unable to account for the time and effort that an IRB member actually expended in preparing for and trying to hear a refugee claim to its conclusion but, through no fault of their own, can not be concluded.

The argument presented against these complaints and protests opposing the new weekly reporting system was that the more complicated types of cases — that is, ministerial interventions and the unusual protracted refugee claims and hearings — were really the exceptions rather than the norms. Further, these types of refugee cases tended, over time, to be fairly evenly distributed among members; therefore, over the course of a fiscal year these factors should be balanced out or equalized across teams and among all the IRB members in the central regional office. Hence, although the new weekly productivity reporting system might not be perfect in every way, it was far from being fundamentally flawed or unfair as the opponents claimed.

Over the ensuing weeks, the new weekly productivity reporting system gradually became part of the IRB members' weekly routine. However, there were still strong pockets of resistance to the weekly productivity reports, particularly among those members who had low refugee hearing completion averages that fell well below their team's average or below the central regional office weekly average completion rate.

Like the other five CMs, Hines had some members on her team who had better than average weekly refugee hearing completion rates and some members who had below-average weekly refugee hearing completion rates. Two of these members had consistently poor weekly refugee hearing completion rates. Despite the fact that her team's completion rate was above the central regional office average, she was concerned that these two members were not putting their best efforts forward in trying to improve their performance and increase their weekly refugee hearing completion average. Hines was convinced that if these members could improve their averages then the other members of her team would not have to work as hard and that, in addition, there would be greater team harmony and morale as a consequence.

Hines considered a number of strategies for how she could try and improve her two colleagues' weekly refugee hearing completion rates. One of the things that she noted was that both of these members had a high postponement and adjournment rate. In other words, many of their refugee hearings were being postponed before the hearing commenced or failed to conclude because once the hearing commenced the refugee hearing adjourned and a new hearing date had to be set to conclude the matter. A detailed look at the two members' hearing schedules revealed that many of the hearings that these members were scheduled on in any given week were refugee hearings that were either postponed or adjourned. Consequently, these two members were actually being scheduled on fewer new hearings than other members on the team.

Hines also noticed that these two members were behind on completing their reasons for their decisions. Not only were these members requiring multiple sittings or hearing dates to conclude their refugee hearings, but once they had been concluded it was taking them longer to issue their reasons for the decision in these refugee claims than the other Members on her team. After reviewing these statistics, Hines concluded that these two members were perhaps among the least productive in the entire central regional office.

Armed with these statistics, Hines went to see ADC Collins to seek his advice on how she could best handle this situation with these two members on her team. She knew that Collins had access to the same statistics as she did and was probably aware of the situation on her team.

Questions

1. Did CM Alice Hines do the right thing in first seeking the advice of her ADM, Phil Collins, regarding the low weekly refugee hearing completion averages for the two colleagues on her team?

2. Critically assess whether the weekly productivity report is not only sound conceptually but a useful management tool. Justify why you think that ADM Phil Collins decided to proceed with this new weekly productivity reporting system.

3. What advice would you give CM Alice Hines on how she ought to deal with her two member colleagues and their below average weekly refugee hearing completion rates?

4. What pressure, if any, can CM Alice Hines impose on her two member colleagues if her best efforts do not result in any improvement in her two colleagues' weekly refugee hearing completion rates?

5. What role or impact can the permanent civil service staff have on IRB member's weekly refugee hearing completion rates?

Resource Materials

- Immigration and Refugee Board of Canada (IRB)
  http://www.irb-cisr.gc.ca/en/index_e.htm

- Citizenship and Immigration Canada (CIC)
  http://www.cic.gc.ca/english/index.asp

- Definitions of Productivity
  http://www.npccmauritius.com/definition/
  http://stats.oecd.org/glossary/detail.asp?ID=2167

- Construction Innovation Forum, Nova Award Nomination, Weekly Job Productivity Report
  http://www.cif.org/nominations/nom_152.html

- Employee Productivity
  http://employee-resource.com/s/employee_productivity

The New Computer Software Purchase

The decision to purchase a new computer system for the Canadian Industrial Relations Board (CIRB) was certainly not made in haste. An expenditure of $15 million had taken over one year to finalize and was driven by the necessity of replacing an existing computer system that was not only antiquated, but also in constant need of repair. The decision was also buttressed by the need to ensure that all of the work of the CIRB was adhering to statutory and regulatory requirements and procedures and that all of its work was being properly documented, stored and archived.

Unfortunately, several years before this current round of upgrading its computer system, the CIRB had gone through the rather embarrassing experience of trying to update its existing main board-wide computer program. After spending several years developing a new computer system, with a reputable software design company that cost some $5 million, the CIRB had had to abandon the project. The growing cost overruns and the fact that the computer program under development was many years away from being close to being even ready for testing or a pilot application in one of the CIRB's regional offices had led to the decision that it was better to cut its losses rather than continue to pursue a project with no end in sight. The CIRB claimed that it had learned a great deal from this sobering experience in computer systems design.

The purchase of a new computer system required the effort of the entire board but, most importantly, the concentrated efforts of a number of units within the CIRB. The principal organizational units involved were the Corporate Planning and Operational Information Systems; Information Technology, Telecommunication and Security Services; Information Management; and, Materiel Management and Administration Services.[1] The Corporate Planning and Operational Information System was charged with the chief responsibility for this initiative. However, the chairperson of the CIRB and the chairperson's office also had a special interest in this project as well.

The supervisor of the Case Management Secretariat, George Perry, was sceptical when he, and a number of other Supervisors at the CIRB, were called in to meet with the senior outside consultants on the new computer system. The consultants held a full morning briefing outlining the broader plans and objectives for the new computer system planning team and discussing the CIRB's present computer system requirements as well as the anticipated future requirements. Perry saw the meeting as little more than an information session and a needs assessment, from the perspective of the managers, of their computer system requirements.

Perry detected a great deal of scepticism with the current effort at trying to develop a new computer system for the CIRB. He recognized that the existing computer system would eventually have to be replaced but he was not confident that the senior management at the CIRB had the skill or abilities to bring this about. After all, there had been various attempts under different chairpersons at the CIRB to implement a new computer system, but even though each of these efforts had been launched with great fanfare and promise, in the end, they had managed to achieve very little except a huge expenditure of public funds that went to computer software design firms and information technology consultants.

The CIRB started its current effort with a grand two-day meeting in Ottawa of all of the key managers and personnel who were in any way engaged in this project as a way of outlining the vision of the new computer system purchase. The Chairperson, the Executive Director, General Council, and the Chief of Corporate Planning and Operational Information Systems, all made the case for why the current computer system was inadequate and how the ongoing costs of trying to maintain the current computer system were a drain on CIRB's financial resources. A great deal was also said about the carefully planned efforts to ensure that the new computer system acquisition would be an open and consultative exercise that would involve not only management, but as many staff as possible in the early planning stages of the new computer systems design. The objective was to design a

---

[1] See the CIRB website "Organizational Chart" found at http://www.cirb-ccri.gc.ca/about-apropos/cirborg.pdf.

computer system that would not only meet the needs of the CIRB currently, but also over the long term. The new computer system design would need to incorporate a capacity to expand and grow with the CIRB as it evolved and developed over time. The meeting further emphasized that the new computer system that was being purchased was a pre-existing computer program that had been in use by various quasi-judicial agencies both at the provincial level in Canada and in a number of states in the United States. It would be modified for use at the CIRB, but it was, essentially, a computer system that was already fully developed and currently in use in a number of jurisdictions in North America. Hence, rather than being an entirely new computer system that was being developed from "scratch," it was instead a fully developed and tested computer system that could be purchased "off the shelf," as it were. This did not imply that it would not need to be modified and adapted to suit the needs and requirements of the CIRB or tested prior to full implementation. Nonetheless, the advantage of this new computer system over previous efforts at adopting a new computer system for the CIRB was that this computer system was not only fully developed and proven, but it was also supported by a large computer software company with experience putting it into service with a number of different quasi-judicial agencies in Canada as well as the United States.

Perry was very pleased to hear that the CIRB had modified its approach of how to deal with the new computer system purchase by, at least, acquiring a product that was available "off the shelf" with the necessary technical support to ensure it could be implemented fully within the board. He was also impressed with how the two-day Ottawa meeting was organized and presented. For much of the meeting, the managers and staff were broken up into various working groups that "brainstormed" a number of key issues and concerns related to implementing a new computer system for the CIRB. The brainstorming and consultation sessions were useful in raising a number of issues and concerns regarding the current computer system and how these could be avoided or addressed through the board's new computer system. The information within each of the working groups was captured on various handouts, forms, and flip charts, and then gathered for review and analysis by the Chief of Corporate Planning and Operational Information Systems.

Over the course of the next year, the external consultants and the staff from the computer firm that was selling the new computer system to the CIRB held meetings with management across the country regarding the implementation of the new computer system. Keeping management and staff informed with the progress in the modification and development of the new computer system was considered an essential component of the implementation of the new computer system at the CIRB. Staff were also very much part of this process as well. For instance, a number of senior staff at all levels and regions within the CIRB were selected to go to the corporate headquarters in Ottawa for special training sessions on the new computer program.

A detailed implementation plan was also announced that outlined the "roll out" of the new computer system for the CIRB. Since everyone at the board would have to use the new computer system for their work this meant that they would need to get not only the basic introductory training on the computer system but, then, the necessary specialized training required for their particular task or function within the organization.

The training for the new computer program would take place in stages over the course of a full year. The detailed training plan called for the introductory training to be conducted in each of the four regional offices (Atlantic, Quebec, Ontario, and western regional office) as well as the corporate headquarters in Ottawa. This involved half-day training sessions, either morning or afternoon, for no more than a dozen employees with two instructors who would provide the employees with a hands-on demonstration and practice on the fundamentals of the new computer system. Since everyone at the CIRB would be using the new computer system, everyone needed to be scheduled for the basic introductory training session.

The intermediate training sessions were also planned for each organizational unit within the CIRB. For instance, the Financial Services unit and the Human Resources unit had their own specialized functional tasks and sub-programs within the new computer system, and the staff within each of these units would need to become familiar with how to use their respective sub-programs within the new computer system. These intermediate training sessions, again, would be organized to be held with no more than a dozen staff at one training session. These sessions were scheduled with two instructors and were for a full-day. Again, the training sessions were planned to be highly interactive with staff having an opportunity to undertake a variety of different routine functional tasks using the new computer system. However, in addition to this, staff members would also be introduced to a number of new procedures that they would not be familiar with, which were planned to enhance the efficiency of their unit's operations. The implementation of the new computer system provided an opportunity to change work patterns and procedures that were designed to achieve greater efficiencies in the way that units worked at the CIRB and, hence, the overall the operations of the board itself.

The advanced training sessions would, again, be based on specialized unit training; however, they would be intended primarily as a review and follow-up session to see how staff members were applying the new computer system and whether they were utilizing their specific sub-programs as intended. Again, this training session would be held with two instructors and no more than 12 staff from the same unit at any one time. This ensured that each employee would be able to get the individual attention that he or she needed during the training sessions, and it also allowed the instructors to observe how employees were using the new computer system and whether they were having difficulties with the new computer system that ought to be modified or changed.

These training sessions also provided a useful means for the new computer system company staff to "tweak" and "fine-tune" the new computer system to meet the needs of CIRB staff. Some of the best ideas actually came from the staff members themselves. The training, therefore, was not only essential for preparing the staff to use the new computer system, but also for the proper adaptation and implementation of the new computer system.

Perry, as the supervisor of the Case Management Secretariat, was responsible for managing 20 employees. He knew that his unit would lose at least two-and-a-half days of training for the implementation of the new computer system. However, he also knew that senior management would not be modifying their workload expectations despite the fact that the new computer system meant that staff would need training time as well as an extended adjustment period to familiarize themselves with the new system. Perry estimated that it would take about six months for everyone to get fully comfortable with the new computer system, provided there were no glitches and everything worked according to plan. He knew that there would be an inevitable increase in the number of errors because of the adjustment period required for staff.

There was a further complicating factor in terms of staff workload. The CIRB wisely decided that the old computer system would not be phased out or abandoned immediately. It would be maintained after the official launch of the new computer system as the back-up computer system, not only in the event that there were any serious problems with the new computer system, but also to catch any inadvertent errors. The plan was to maintain the old computer system for at least the first six months after the launch of the new computer system. If everything worked properly, then the old computer system could then be gradually phased out. What this meant was that staff had to do double entries on the old as well as the new computer systems, which would, in effect, increase the workload of each staff member. Increasing the workload in this manner would decrease staff productivity for at least six months. Again, senior management was not prepared to decrease its productivity demands during the implementation phase of the new computer system.

Perry also foresaw other difficulties that would result from the implementation of the new computer system. These stemmed directly from the new computer system's enhanced capacity to perform new functions that the old computer system was not capable of doing. These became particularly apparent in a special meeting that Perry was invited to attend with senior management and where another supervisor, Edward Stevenson, gave a detailed PowerPoint presentation on a number of the new enhanced capabilities of the computer system. Stevenson was one of the supervisors who were on the CIRB New Computer Implementation Committee. This national committee had been meeting in Ottawa for the past year, working out the various plans and details on the appropriate implementation of the new computer system at the board.

One of the core functions of the CIRB in its efforts to promote effective industrial relations in Canada was to investigate complaints of unfair labour practices. A large segment of the CIRB's work was to hold hearings dealing with complaints of unfair labour practices. Scheduling these hearings with the complainants and their counsel is a time-consuming process. Stevenson outlined that one of the new capabilities of the new computer system was to include the counsels' schedules into the board's master hearing schedule. In other words, the new computer system could actually not only keep track of the CIRB's members' hearing schedules, but also those of legal counsel. Through this means, the CIRB would be able to automate the way that it scheduled its hearings in order to maximize the number of hearings it could schedule with counsels who appeared before the board and its board members. Stevenson made the point it could also be a way of keeping track of counsels who were known for double-booking themselves and for having notoriously high postponement and adjournment rates. Stevenson also noted that one of the real values of the new computer system was that it could allow counsels to schedule their own hearings with the CIRB via computer as opposed to using a staff scheduling officer.

Perry stated that this might work for the high-volume counsels, that is, those labour lawyers who primarily practised before the CIRB, but not all the counsels, who also practiced before other Boards and who also did appeal work at the Federal Court of Canada. He noted that since most labour lawyers did appeal work there might be occasions when counsels would be required, legitimately, to appear before the Federal Court and, consequently, have to request that their hearings be postponed. He also said that he had some concerns about how effective a scheduling system could be if it was controlled by counsel. Perry also expressed concern about the degree of latitude that counsels would have in scheduling their own hearings. For example, he asked whether counsel could book with the member of his or her own choice. He stated that he had serious concerns about counsel determining who would hear their cases. This was, he emphasized, the prerogative of the CIRB and not of counsels and the complainants. There was the further difficulty, he noted, of scheduling members' vacation and sick leave or time off for training and professional development. Much of this was not determined months in advance, but it was usually done with only several weeks notice and in some circumstances virtually at the last moment.

Stevenson acknowledged that these were legitimate concerns and that the new computer system hearing schedule subprogram was still undergoing further refinements. However, he did note that there were preliminary plans to test this new online computer scheduling protocol in Montreal in the Quebec regional office. These would test and monitor how the online scheduling protocol operated before adjusting and modifying this new computer system scheduling subprogram and before introducing it across all the regional offices at the board.

Perry thought that this was typical of the way in which new innovations or routines were introduced at the CIRB. He also thought that the new computer system would alter many existing routine procedures. These changes would not only take time to work out but could potentially be quite disruptive to the productive operations of not only his own secretariat, but to other units at the CIRB. Again, he came to the conclusion that the new computer system would not only be costly in terms of the expenditure of public funds but also in terms of the CIRB's overall productivity.

Questions

1. Outline the key challenges confronting the CIRB as it attempts to successfully implement its new computer system.

2. Is the training program described in the case study a reasonable approach for helping to ensure that the implementation of the new computer system will run smoothly?

3. What do you anticipate will be some of George Perry's major difficulties in trying to implement the new computer system in his own unit, the Case Management Secretariat, at the CIRB?

4. What does this case study reveal about the acquisition and implementation of new computer systems within government departments and agencies and the public sector in general?

5. What strategies or approaches can George Perry adopt to protect his unit from the inevitable blows and challenges that his unit will face having to implement the CIRB's new computer system?

Resource Material

*   Canadian Industrial Relations Board (CIRB)
    http://www.cirb-ccri.gc.ca/index_eng.asp

*   Public Works and Government Services Canada, SARC, Software Acquisition Reference Centre, Appendix D: Procurement Guidelines
    http://software.pwgsc.gc.ca//general/opappd-e.cfm

*   Public Works and Government Services Canada, SARC, Software Acquisition Reference Centre, Software Resource Centre Initiative, Frequently Asked Questions
    http://software.pwgsc.gc.ca//resource_centre/faq-e.cfm

*   Public Works and Government Services Canada, Computer Acquisition Guide (CAG), Terms and Conditions — Mass Storage — MNSO (SAN)
    http://computer.pwgsc.gc.ca/index.cfm?fuseaction=storage.sannas_terms&lang=e

*   Lindsay Russell, "10 Things to Consider When Making a New Computer Purchase," *Technology,* December 26, 2007.
    http://www.associatedcontent.com/article/170048/10_things_to_consider_before_making.html?cat=15

*   Irene Zeitler, "A Costly Lesson in IT Acquisition," Australia FindLaw, June 2003.
    http://www.findlaw.com.au/article/9034.htm

*   Michael M. Gorman, "A New Paradigm of Successful Acquisitions of New Information Systems," *The Data Information Administration Newsletter,* July 1, 2000,
    http://www.tdan.com/view-articles/4868

Filing a Complaint
with the Law Society
of Upper Canada

The Competition Tribunal was established under the federal *Competition Act* in 1986. The Competition Tribunal is an adjudicative body that functions independently of any governmental department and hears and decides applications made under Parts VII, 1, Deceptive Marketing Practices, and VIII, Restrictive Trade Practices, of the *Competition Act*. The Competition Tribunal is composed of not more that six judicial members and not more than eight lay members.[1] Three member panels, which consist of a judge and usually two lay members of the tribunal, hear matters that fall under Part VIII of the *Competition Act*. Cases that fall under Part VII, 1, of the *Competition Act* are heard by a single judicial member of the tribunal. Decisions of the Competition Tribunal can be appealed to the Federal Court of Appeal.

---

[1] Competition Tribunal, About Us, http://www.ct-tc.gc.ca/english/View.asp?x=213. [Last accessed on January 3, 2009]

Mathew Caine, an Ontario legal counsel who specialized in corporate law and cases heard by the Competition Tribunal, had built, over the years, a reputation of being a difficult counsel to work with. This was the way that Caine was viewed not only with the administrative staff of the Competition Tribunal but also its judicial and lay members. He was particularly troublesome with the staff of the Competition Tribunal, whom he treated with disdain.

Caine was known especially for his radical antics in the hearing room where, from time-to-time, he would raise the most outlandish motions bordering on contempt. These motions could only be interpreted as intending to incite either confusion and/or a sharp emotional response from the judicial and lay members who were hearing the case. He was also known for the letters that he wrote occasionally to whomever was the minister of Industry Canada at the time, irrespective of their political affiliation. These letters purported to identify problematic areas of the Competition Tribunal's practices or procedures. At times his letters would even question whether the Competition Tribunal was making decisions that were, fundamentally, in the public interest. Caine's letters to the minister of Industry Canada were always copied to the chairperson of the Competition Tribunal. More often than not, the Industry Canada minister's office would contact the Tribunal requesting that they provide a possible draft response to Caine's letters.

From time to time, Caine would also send letters to the newspapers on specific issues of concern regarding the Competition Tribunal. Sometimes these letters would be printed in the "letters to the editor" portion of the newspaper and would prompt a response from the minister of Industry Canada or the chairperson of the Competition Tribunal. In this way, Caine was able to cultivate and maintain a public profile as someone with expertise and knowledge in this particular policy sphere and who was not afraid to speak his mind on a broad range of issues. It also seemed calculated to attract new clients for his practice.

Caine would argue frequently with Competition Tribunal staff. On one occasion, he claimed that he sent materials to the tribunal about an upcoming case and that the Tribunal staff had misplaced these documents. On other occasions, he accused staff of not scheduling his clients' cases in a timely fashion and lambasted them for refusing to schedule his hearings on dates and times to accommodate his availability and work schedule. At times, this could flare up into shouting matches with staff about their competence. As a consequence, staff members did not like dealing directly with Caine because they feared his emotional outbursts and considered him to be deliberately abusive in an effort to cover his own shortcomings as a counsel.

By the same token, Caine was accused by the Tribunal staff of deliberately overbooking himself and then requesting that his hearing dates be postponed. In fact, he did have one of the highest postponement and adjournment rates of any of the legal counsels who appeared before the Competition Tribunal. In his defence, Caine stated that he also did a great deal of appeal work before the Federal Court of Appeal and that he was obligated to appear there whenever he was called upon. However, not everyone accepted his rationale for his inordinately high rate of postponed and adjourned cases before the Competition Tribunal.

Over the years, the senior managers at the Competition Tribunal had tried to raise their concerns with Caine on an informal basis. As one of the tribunal's high-volume counsel — that is, he handled a large number of cases that were heard by the tribunal — changing his unacceptable behaviours and attitude would go some way in improving the working relations between the tribunal and Caine and, therefore, the tribunal's overall operations. It would also assist in improving the Competition Tribunal's hearing completion rate. The informal methods used to try to address the tribunal's concerns with Caine had a measurable impact for a few weeks, but it was not long before Caine returned to his usual pattern of behaviour at the tribunal.

None of these interventions seemed to have an appreciable impact on Caine's clients or on the demand for his services as a counsel of choice before the Competition Tribunal. In fact, to the uninitiated or to those unfamiliar with the *Competition Act* and the workings of the Competition Tribunal, Caine may have appeared to be a tough, no nonsense legal counsel who was prepared to fight whole heartedly for his clients' vis-à-vis the other parties in the matter, but also vis-à-vis the administrative bureaucracy at the Competition Tribunal.

Jeanette Rachon, the Competition Tribunal's general counsel, supported by the other senior managers and administrators at the tribunal, reached the conclusion that they could no longer tolerate Caine's behaviour and the nature of his practice before the tribunal. Consequently, it was determined that the Competition Tribunal would file a complaint against Caine with the Law Society of Upper Canada.

Under the *Rules of Professional Conduct,* Rule 4.01, The Lawyer as Advocate, states, in part, as follows:

> 4.01 (1) When acting as an advocate, a lawyer shall represent the client resolutely and honourably within the limits of the law while treating the tribunal with candour, fairness, courtesy, and respect.

> 4.01 (2) When acting as an advocate, a lawyer shall not ... (e) knowingly attempt to deceive a tribunal or influence the course of justice by offering false evidence, misstating facts or law, presenting or relying upon a false or deceptive affidavit, suppressing what ought to be disclosed, or otherwise assisting in any fraud, crime, or illegal conduct, (f) knowingly misstate the contents of a document, the testimony of a witness, the substance of an argument, or the provisions of a statute or like authority,

> 4.01 (6) A lawyer shall be courteous, civil, and act in good faith to the tribunal and with all persons with whom the lawyer has dealings in the course of litigation.[2]

---

[2] The Law Society of Upper Canada, *Rules of Professional Conduct*, Rule 4, Relationship to the Administration of Justice, http://www.lsuc.on.ca/regulation/a/profconduct/rule4/. [Last accessed on January 4, 2009.]

Rachon was of the view that Caine was in breach of the *Rules of Professional Conduct* of the Law Society of Upper Canada and that he should be the subject of a complaint to the Law Society for his conduct before the Competition Tribunal.[3]

The legal branch of the Competition Tribunal had, in fact, prepared the following documentation in support of its complaint to the Law Society of Upper Canada regarding Caine's practice before the tribunal. The first was a document that outlined the average postponement and adjournment rates of high volume counsel who had appeared before the Competition Tribunal over the last two fiscal years compared to Caine's average postponement and adjournment rate. Caine's postponement and adjournment rates were substantially higher than the average of those of other high volume counsel who appeared before the Tribunal — in fact, Caine's postponement and adjournment rate exceeded the average of other high-volume counsel, over this same period, by about 30 percent. In addition, it was noted that there were some 20 examples where Caine's hearings had gone down or postponed because he had been either unable to appear for a scheduled hearing or because his clients failed to appear for various reasons. In some of these instances, the tribunal alleged that Caine failed to appear before the Competition Tribunal because he had deliberately double booked himself. The tribunal alleged that Caine had scheduled himself on more than one hearing at the same time fully knowing that he would not be able to proceed with one or other of these cases.

The legal branch had also gathered affidavits from a number of staff at the Competition Tribunal that documented instances where they found Caine had used profanity or was attempting to "bully" them into scheduling hearings or falsely accusing them of misplacing documentation that he alleged to have sent to the tribunal. The tribunal also included copies of two letters that it had sent to Caine in the last two years. The first letter outlined its concerns about Caine's conduct vis-à-vis his interaction with staff and his proclivity for introducing motions in hearings that could only be described as obtuse. The second letter, dated some 10 months after the first, referred to the first letter and noted that he had failed to appreciably alter his behaviour vis-à-vis staff or his conduct in the hearing room. The second letter also went further in raising the issue that the tribunal was concerned about Caine's high postponement and adjournment rate and requested that he endeavour to try to reduce the postponement and adjournment rate for his hearings as quickly as possible.

Caine was incensed when he received notice that the Law Society of Upper Canada had received a copy of the Competition Tribunal's formal complaint regarding the nature of his practice before the tribunal. He not only immediately appreciated the possible consequences of this complaint to the Law Society, but to his livelihood and his professional standing. After carefully reading the copy of the Competition Tribunal's formal complaint,

---

[3] The Law Society of Upper Canada, Complaint Form Information Sheet, http://www.lsuc.on.ca/media/helpform.pdf. [Last accessed on January 4, 2009.]

he saw it as deliberately seeking to present him as someone who was engaged in "conduct unbecoming a barrister and solicitor." He was well aware that *Rules of Professional Conduct* defined this in the following way:

> Conduct unbecoming a barrister or solicitor" means conduct, including conduct in a lawyer's personal or private capacity, that tends to bring discredit upon the legal profession including, for example, (a) committing a criminal act that reflects adversely on the lawyer's honesty, trustworthiness, or fitness as a lawyer, (b) taking improper advantage of the youth, inexperience, lack of education, unsophistication, ill health, or unbusinesslike habits of another, or (c) engaging in conduct involving dishonesty or conduct which undermines the administration of justice.[4]

Caine took his time in drafting his reply to the Competition Tribunal's formal complaint to the Law Society of Upper Canada. He knew that it would have to be carefully worded in an effort to try to persuade the Law Society of Upper Canada not to proceed with an investigation and, therefore, avoid a disciplinary hearing.

Caine also knew that he would have to devote a great deal of attention and effort to this formal complaint and possibly even seek the advice of expert legal counsel in this field of law. This would be not only potentially very expensive but also enervating. It would take him away from his busy practice and, as a consequence, have an impact on his own earnings, both his revenue earnings but also, more significantly, his expenditures.

Caine also knew that he would have to request a meeting with Rachon to discuss the Competition Tribunal's formal complaint and to try to find out why they had decided to proceed with such a measure without first advising him of their intention to do so.

Questions

1. Was the Competition Tribunal justified in bringing the formal complaint against Mathew Caine to the Law Society of Upper Canada? What other action(s) could it have taken to deal with his unacceptable behaviour and conduct?

2. If you were advising counsel Mathew Caine, what would you advise him to include in his response to the Competition Tribunal's formal complaint to the Law Society of Upper Canada?

3. Should Jeanette Rachon agree to meet with Mathew Caine? If so, explain why she should meet with him and when the meeting should be arranged. If not, explain why she should not be meeting with him.

---

[4] The Law Society of Upper Canada, *Rules of Professional Code,* Rule 1: Citation and Interpretation, 1.02, Definitions, http://www.lsuc.on.ca/regulation/a/profconduct/rule1/. [Last accessed on January 4, 2009.]

4. Administrative tribunals have to work with legal counsel and other stakeholders in order to ensure that they have good working relationships with those who appear before them as well as to maintain a positive public persona. However, administrative tribunals also have to address the problems of dealing with difficult situations with those whom they often work most closely with on an ongoing basis. What does this case study reveal about how adjudicative administrative tribunals can deal with some of these challenges?

5. How could the Competition Tribunal have avoided resorting to the measure of filing a formal complaint with the Law Society of Upper Canada in this instance? After all, Mathew Caine is an experienced high volume counsel who has practised at the tribunal for years.

Resource Materials

- Competition Tribunal
  http://www.ct-tc.gc.ca/Home.asp

- Industry Canada
  http://www.ic.gc.ca/eic/site/ic1.nsf/eng/home

- Competition Bureau
  http://www.competitionbureau.gc.ca/eic/site/cb-bc.nsf/eng/home

- The Law Society of Upper Canada
  http://www.lsuc.on.ca/index_en.html

- Rules of Professional Conduct
  http://www.lsuc.on.ca/regulation/a/profconduct/

- Federal Court of Appeal
  http://www.fca-caf.gc.ca/index_e.shtml

Reply to All

The Canadian Intellectual Properties Office (CIPO) is a special operating agency within Industry Canada. Its primary functions are to provide intellectual property (IP) rights and to administer the following statutes: the *Patent Act*, the *Trade-marks Act*, the *Industrial Design Act*, the *Integrated Circuit Topography Act*, and parts of the *Copyright Act*.[1]

The CIPO's role in the Government of Canada is to promote "the effective use of IP information and the IP system to further innovation, invention and creativity for the benefit of Canadians and Canadian businesses."[2]

The CIPO is comprised of nine distinct organizational units, which include the following: the Client Services Centre; Information Branch; Patent Branch; Patent Appeal Board (PAB); Trade-marks Branch; Trade-marks Opposition Board (TMOB); Copyright Office; Industrial Designs and Topographies; and, Corporate Strategies and Services.

The Copyright Office has authority under the *Copyright Act* to register copyrights that have been duly submitted and applied for. Randolf Woodworth, the Registrar of Copyrights, who also serves as the director of the Copyright

---

[1] Industry Canada, Department Structure, Canadian Intellectual Properties Office (CIPO), http://www.cipo.ic.gc.ca/eic/site/ic1.nsf/eng/h_00258.html. (Last accessed March 22, 2009.)

[2] Ibid.

Office, is responsible for a staff of 43 officials, at various levels and positions within the Copyright Office. Woodworth reports to Catherine Binders, the Canadian Intellectual Property Office Commissioner of patents, registrar of trade-marks, and Chief Executive Officer (CEO) of the CIPO.

One of the challenges facing the Copyright Office is the growing backlog of applications for copyright registration. A copyright "is the exclusive right to copy a creative work or to allow someone else to do so. It includes the sole right to publish, produce or reproduce, to perform in public, to communicate a work to the public by telecommunication, to translate a work, and in some cases, to rent the work."[3] Copyrights apply to all original literary, dramatic, musical and artistic works. Copyrights do not protect themes, ideas, most titles, names, catch phrases or short-word combinations that do not have substance.[4]

"Facts, ideas and news are all considered part of the public domain, that is, they are everyone's property."[5] Generally, copyrights are held by the creators of the work and registration is the official acknowledgement of a copyright claim.

In an effort to try to address the growing backlog of copyright registrations, Woodworth, the copyright registrar, emphasized the importance of addressing the escalating backlog of copyright registration applications with his staff. To this end, he held several general meetings to motivate staff to increase the number of copyright registration applications that were being processed each month. He also tried to elicit ideas from his staff on how to improve the office workflow and the way in which applications for a copyright registration actually were being reviewed, examined, verified, authenticated and approved. Woodworth was looking for ways that the copyright registration applications process could be simplified, streamlined and, possibly, automated so that the amount of time that it took for a staff member to process an application was actually being reduced.

Woodworth already had two all-staff copyright office meetings when Binders, the commissioner of patents and his immediate supervisor at the CIPO, called him in to see her. Binders stated that she was concerned about the continuing growing backlog of copyright registrations applications. In fact, she had made this point on several occasions at the CIPO senior management biweekly meetings that she chaired. Woodworth's response to Binders' concerns at the senior management biweekly meetings had been to initiate the round of all-staff meetings to look for ways to try to address the growing backlog of applications for copyright registration.

When Binders asked Woodworth what he was doing to address this concern, he stated that he was meeting with staff to try to find ways to

---

[3] Canadian Intellectual Properties Office (CIPO), Frequently Asked Questions, http://www.cipo.ic.gc.ca/eic/site/cipointernet-internetopic.nsf/eng/wr00090.html [Last accessed March 22, 2009.]

[4] A Guide to Copyrights: Copyright Protection, Canadian Intellectual Property Office. "When Copyright Does Not Apply," http://www.cipo.ic.gc.ca/eic/site/cipointernet-internetopic.nsf/eng/wr00506.html#no1.

[5] Ibid.

reduce the amount of time it was taking to process a copyright registration. In addition, he noted, he was trying to motivate his staff so that they would finalize more copyright registrations each month. Binders said that Woodworth should give this task his particular attention and priority to ensure that the backlog of applications for copyright registration was being reduced as quickly as possible.

One month later, when Binders saw that there had been little progress in dealing with the growing backlog of copyright registration applications, she called Woodworth into her office for another meeting to discuss this pressing situation and how it ought to be addressed. At this meeting, Binders stated that she wanted a list of all of the staff members in the Copyright Office who were directly responsible for processing copyright registrations. She further specified that this list of copyright office staff members should also include the number of copyright registrations that each staff member had processed, broken down on a monthly basis, over the past year. She further specified that she wanted to know what the monthly copyright registrations processing average was for the entire Copyright Office and for each of these staff members. She said that the monthly copyright registration application processing averages would be used as a basis of comparison for each staff member's performance, on a month-to-month basis, over the past year. She told Woodworth that she wanted these figures on her desk in the next two days and that on the following day she would meet with him to discuss his statistical reports.

When Woodworth and Binders met again three days later, he presented, as requested, the list of Copyright Office staff members and their monthly and annual copyright registrations processing statistics over the past year. The statistical report was somewhat surprising to both Woodworth and Binders. Binders asked Woodworth whether he was confident that the figures in the staff statistical report were accurate. Woodworth replied that he had had the figures doubled checked to confirm their accuracy.

What the staff statistical report indicated was that there was a wide discrepancy in the number of copyright registration applications that were being processed by staff in the Copyright Office. Some staff were averaging a monthly copyright registration application completion average of 90 copyright registrations each month, or about three copyright registrations each day, while other staff were averaging only about 30 copyright registrations per month, or only one copyright registration per day. In fact, there were several staff in the Copyright Office who were processing fewer than one copyright registration each day.

Binders asked Woodworth why he thought there was such a wide discretancy in copyright registration processing among his staff. Woodworth stated that he was aware that some staff were much more efficient at processing copyright applications than others. However, he said that he had to admit that he was quite surprised to see such a wide variation between the highest and lowest producers. He explained that he could have identified his high and low performing staff, prior to the preparation of the staff statistical report, but, he stated, he had no idea how wide the discrepancy was between how much work the top performers in his office were doing relative to how little work appeared to be done, or at least accomplished, by other office staff.

Binders stated that the staff statistical report was quite troubling because it identified a serious problem of workload inequity within the copyright office. She noted that the staff in Woodworth's copyright office were all making about the same in salary and benefits, yet there was an enormous gulf between the performance of staff within his unit. Moreover, she stated that with a growing backlog in copyright registrations at that time, the tremendous discrepancy in the copyright registration processing rates amongst staff was intolerable.

Binders further noted that this was, in fact, a growing area of concern within Industry Canada, as a whole, and that a number of applicants who had been waiting for some time to register a copyright for their creative work were starting to complain to the Minister of Industry Canada regarding the protracted delay. Worse still, some of these same applicants were now complaining to the opposition MPs and there was now a growing expectation that the minister might have to answer questions regarding the delay in processing copyright registration applications during question period in the House of Commons and, then, later in media scrums outside the House of Commons. The minister's staff had already brought these concerns to the attention of the deputy minister, who, in turn, had brought this to the attention of Binders, in her capacity as the CEO of CIPO, and told her "to deal with the matter as quickly as possible." In fact, she said that the deputy minister had stated, in no uncertain terms, that he did not want to have the minister's staff raising this matter with him again.

Binders suggested that one way to help address the mounting backlog of copyright registration applications was to decrease the processing time for registering a copyright. This should, she noted, almost immediately increase the productivity of the Copyright Office staff and it should make it easier, in particular, for those staff who were completing, on average, the lowest copyright registrations per month. Binders also emphasized that it was clear that it was no longer acceptable, if it ever was, for some staff members in Woodworth's office to be processing only one copyright registration or less, on average per day, or 30 or less, on average per month. Binders said that it was evident that these staff members would have to increase the number of copyright registrations applications that they were completing each day.

Binders noted that this would not only benefit the Copyright Office and the CIPO, not to mention the department, as a whole, but it would also be much fairer for all of the staff in the copyright office. She emphasized that the wide discrepancy in productivity among the staff in the unit could not be sustained. She said that the staff who were averaging 90 copyright registrations per month were doing three times more work than those who were managing to complete only 30 each month. She said that this was unconscionable and had to be corrected as soon as possible.

Woodworth replied that he would start with the least productive staff in his office and then work his way up the list of staff until he had completed all of the staff who were averaging one copyright registration or less per day. He said that the two least productive staff members in the Copyright Office were Elisa Benson and Stanley Fennel. He told Binders that he would meet with these two staff members right away and try to work out a method to improve their copyright registration application processing times and their average daily completion rates.

The following day Woodworth sent an email message to all the staff in the Copyright Office, indicating that senior management in Industry Canada, along with himself, were very concerned about the growing backlog and the lengthy processing times for copyright registration applications and that he would be meeting with all staff members on an individual basis to get their comments, ideas and suggestions on how to improve the overall operations of the copyright office. He said that there was some urgency in addressing the matter, so he would immediately start meeting staff members individually.

Later that same day, he set up a meeting with Benson to discuss the growing backlog of copyright registration applications and the lengthy processing times for completing copyright registrations in the Copyright Office. In the meeting with Benson, he shared the statistics that he had that showed that Benson was *one* of the lowest producers, if not *the* lowest producer, of copyright registration applications. Further, he noted that there were other staff in the office that were producing three times as many copyright registration applications as she was. He also underscored the point that things would have to change and that overall office productivity would have to be increased and the time that it took to process a copyright registration application would have to be decreased.

Woodworth then asked Benson what she thought she could do to help resolve this situation. Benson said that she appreciated the predicament that the Copyright Office was in, but she said that she was already working as hard as she could. Woodworth said that he wanted Benson to see if she could process at least two copyright registrations each day. She said that if she increased her pace then this would lead inevitably to more errors on her part and more complaints from the applicants. Benson said that she always prided herself on the quality of her work and not necessarily the quantity. She noted, afterall, what was the point of trying to process two or three copyright registration applications a day if they are not being done properly and accurately? Woodworth replied that he had statistics that showed that staff who were processing on average three copyright registration applications per day had the same error rate as those staff who were only producing one or fewer copyright registration application per day. In fact, he noted that the application processing statistics that he had for her showed that her error rate was amongst the highest in the copyright office, despite the fact she averaged less than one copyright registration per day.

This disclosure not only embarrassed Benson, when she heard this from Woodworth, but it also upset her to the point that she said that she could not continue with the meeting any longer and needed some time to reflect on what he had just told her. Woodworth then stated that he would send her an email following up on their meeting and that he would outline some suggestions for how she might be able to improve her overall productivity.

Immediately following this meeting, Woodworth drafted an email to Benson, outlining what had transpired during their meeting. He made a point of noting that she was currently not only one of the lowest producing staff members in the Copyright Office, but that she also had one of the highest error rates in the office. He also described, in some detail, what he thought she could do to improve the average number of copyright registration applications she was completing each month, while at the same time reducing her overall error rate.

While Woodworth was composing and typing this email, he was being interrupted with the usual office routine of telephone calls and his administrative assistant coming into his office to ask him to sign routine documents and correspondence and to attend to other administrative matters. Among all of this activity and distractions, when it came time for Woodworth to send his email to Benson, instead of clicking on the "Reply" button, he inadvertently clicked on the "Reply to All" button instead. By doing so, he sent the email message that was intended for Benson only to all of the staff in the copyright office. Shortly after Woodworth sent out the email he realized his mistake and tried to retrieve the email message that was sent in error to everyone in the Copyright Office. Although he did manage to recall the email, it was too late, because the email message had already been opened and read by a number of staff in the office.

Woodworth realized immediately he had blundered and that confidential information regarding the nature of his meeting with Benson had been disclosed to a number of staff in the Copyright Office. Worse still, he realized that all the staff in the office knew that he was meeting with them, principally, to review their individual productivity and performance and not to discuss, necessarily, their ideas for how the office could address the growing backlog of copyright registration applications.

Questions

1. What fundamental errors, if any, did Randolf Woodworth make as a manager in his meetings with Catherine Binders and with Elisa Benson?

2. What are the likely consequences that Randolf Woodworth will face, given his blunder of sending a private and confidential email to all the staff in the Copyright Office?

3. If you were in Randolf Woodworth's predicament, how would you handle this situation in order to minimize the negative consequences of sending out the private and confidential email to all the staff in the office, while at the same time, trying to address the problems confronting the growing backlog of applications for copyright registration and the growing processing times for these applications?

4. How should Elisa Benson respond to this inadvertent breach in her privacy by the Copyright Registrar and Copyright Office Director Randolf Woodworth?

5. This case study exemplifies a number of adages of management and administration, including Murphy's Law, "If anything can go wrong, it will," Hanlon's Razor, "Never attribute to malice that which can be adequately explained by stupidity," and the Planning Fallacy, "The tendency to underestimate the task completion times." Which one of these management adages, or any others, is most applicable to this case study and why?

Resource Material

- Industry Canada
  http://www.cipo.ic.gc.ca/eic/site/ic1.nsf/eng/home

- Canadian Intellectual Property Office (CIPO)
  http://www.cipo.ic.gc.ca/eic/site/cipointernet-internetopic.nsf/eng/home

- Office of the Privacy Commissioner of Canada
  http://www.privcom.gc.ca/aboutUs/index_e.asp

- Privacy Breaches
  http://www.privcom.gc.ca/resource/pb-avp/pb-avp_intro_e.asp

- Privacy Quiz
  http://www.privcom.gc.ca/quiz/index_e.asp

- Constraints to Productive Management in the Public Sector 1983 Report of the Auditor General of Canada
  http://209.71.218.213/internet/English/parl_oag_198311_02_e_3367.html

References

Baetz M. C. and Beamish, P.W. (1987) *Strategic Management: Canadian Cases*. Illinois: Irwin.

Barker, Paul. (2008) *Public Administration in Canada, Brief Edition*. Toronto: Nelson, a division of Thomson Canada Limited.

Barraket, J. (2005) "Teaching Research Methods Using a Student-centred Approach? Critical Reflections on Practice," in *Journal of University Teaching and Learning in Practice* Vol 2 (2), 65–74.

Beckman, M. D.; Kurtz, D. L.; Boone, L. E. (1987) *Foundations of Marketing, 4th Edition*. Toronto: Holt, Rinehart and Winston.

Bigg, John (1996) "Enhancing Teaching Through Constructive Alignment," Higher Education, Vol. 32, pp. 347–364.

Bittner, Marie. (1990) "The IRAC Method of Case Study Analysis: A Legal Model for the Social Studies," *The Social Studies*, Vol. 81, No.: 5, (September/October), 228.

Borins, Sanford F. (1990) "Simulation, the case method, and case studies: their role in public management teaching and research," *Canadian Public Administration*, 33:2 (Summer), 214-228.

Bourgault, Jacques and Savoie, Donald J. (2000) "Managing at the Top," in B. Guy Peters and Donald J. Savoie (Eds.) *Governance in the Twenty-first Century: Revitalizing the Public Service*, Montreal & Kingston: McGill-Queen's University Press.

Brady James E. and Allen, Theodore T. (2002) "Case Study Based Instruction of DOE and SPC," *The American Statistician*, Vol. 56, No.: 4 (November).

Brewer, Ernest W. (1997) *13 Proven Ways to Get Your Message Across: The Essential Reference for Teachers, Trainers, Presenters, and Speakers*. Thousand Oaks, California, Corwin Press Inc.

Brookfield, S. (1987) *Developing Critical Thinkers*. San Francisco, CA, Jossey-Bass.

____. (1995) *Becoming a Critically Reflective Teacher*. San Francisco, CA, Jossey-Bass.

Brown-John, C. Lloyd. (1997) "Book Review: Public Management and Administration: Case-Study Resource Book, by Petrus Brynard and Kallic Erasmus, van Schaik, Pretoria, 1995, 229p," *Public Administration and Development*, 17:5 (December), 546.

Camill, Philip. (2006) "Case Studies Add Value to a Diverse Teaching Portfolio in Science Courses," *Journal of College Science Teaching*, Vol. 36, No.: 2 (October), p. 31.

Cameron, Beverley J. (1999) *Active Learning*, Green Guide No. 2, Society for Teaching and Learning in Higher Education, Halifax: Dalhousie University Bookstore.

Chamany, Katayoun.(2006) "Science and Social Justice: Making the Case for Case Studies," *Journal of College Science Teaching*, Vol. 36, No.: 2, pp. 54-59

Chetkovich, Carol and Kirp, David L. (2001) "Cases and controversies: How novitiates are trained to be masters of the public policy universe," *Journal of Policy Analysis and Management*, Vol. 20, No.: 2, (Spring).

Clark, Tom. (2008) *The Global Refugee Regime: Charity, Management and Human Rights*. Second Edition. Victoria, B.C.: Trafford Publishing.

Cline, Paul C. and Graham, P. Tony. (1977) "The Case Study Method: An Inquiry Approach for Law-Related Education," *The Social Studies*, Vol. 68, No.: 1, (Jan./Feb.), p. 20.

References

Dooley, A. R. and Skinner, W. (1997) "Casing casemethod methods," *The Academy of Management Review,* Vol. 2, No.: 2, pp. 277

Dopson, Sue. (2003) "The potential of the case study method for organisational analysis," *Policy & Politics,* Vol. 31, No.: 2, pp. 217-226.

Dunn, Christopher, Ed. (2002) *The Handbook of Canadian Public Administration*, Oxford: Oxford University Press.

Dunne, David and Brooks, Kim. (2004) *Teaching With Cases*, Green Guide No. 5, Society for Teaching and Higher Education, Halifax, Nova Scotia: Dalhousie University Bookstore.

Evans, J. M., Janisch, H.N., Mullan, David J., (1995) *Administrative Law: Cases, Text, and Materials*, Fourth Edition. Toronto: Emond Montgomery Publications Limited.

Garrison, D. R. (1997) "Self-directed learning: toward a comprehensive model," *Adult Education Quarterly*, 48(1), pp. 18–34.

____. (1992) "Critical thinking and self-directed learning in adult education: an analysis of responsibility and control issues," *Adult Education Quarterly*, 42, pp. 136–148.

Garvin, D. A. (2003) "Making the Case: Professional Education in the World of Practice," *Harvard Magazine*, 106, (September-October): 1-15.

Goodwin-Gill, Guy and McAdam, Jane., (2007) *The Refugee in International Law*, Third Edition. Oxford: Oxford University Press.

Halpin, G., Halpin, G., Good, J., Raju, P.K. & Sankar, C. (2000) "Creative methods to evaluate case study instruction: Can problem-solving skills be measured?" paper presented at the meeting of the American Educational Research Association (AERA), New Orleans, LA, 24 April.

Hathaway, James C. (1991) *The Law of Refugee Status*. Toronto: Butterworths.

Hoffman, Randy, Jurkowski, Diane, MacKinnon, Victor, Nicholson, Janice, Simeon, James C. Eds. (1998) *Public Administration: Canadian Materials*, Third Edition. Toronto: Captus Press Inc.

Hoffman, Randy G., MacKinnon, Victor S., Nicholson, Janice E., Simeon, James C., Eds. (1993) *Public Administration: Canadian Materials. Second Edition*, Toronto: Captus Press, Inc.

____. (1998) *Public Administration: Canadian Materials. Third Edition*, Toronto: Captus Press Inc.

Hoffman, Randy. and Rueper, Fred., Eds., (1991) *Organizational Behaviour: Canadian Cases and Exercises*. North York, Ontario: Captus Press, McGraw-Hill Ryerson Limited, 1991.

Howard, W. Gary. (2006) "Socrates and Technology a New Millennium Conversation," *International Journal of Instructional Media*, 33 (2), (Spring), p. 197.

Hutchings, Pat. (1993) *Using Cases To Improve College Teaching: A Guide to More Reflective Practice.* Washington, D.C.: American Association of Higher Education.

Inwood, Gregory J. (2009) *Understanding Canadian Public Administration: An Introduction to Theory and Practice*. Third Edition. Toronto: Pearson Education Canada.

Irby, David M. (1994) "Three Exemplary Models of Case-Based Teaching," *Academic Medicine,* Vol. 69, No.: 12, (December).

Johnson, David. (2006) *Thinking Government: Public Sector Management in Canada*. Second Edition. Peterborough, Ontario: Broadview Press, Ltd.

Johnson J. and Purvis, J. (1987) "Case Studies: An Alternative Learning/Teaching Method in Nursing," *Journal of Nursing Education,* 26, pp. 118-120.

Jones, Martin and Baglay, Sasha. (2007) *Refugee Law*. Toronto: Irwin Law Inc.

Kernaghan, Kenneth. (1977) *Canadian Cases in Public Administration* Toronto: Methuen Publications.

Kerber, Carolin. (2001) "Learning experientially through case studies? A conceptual analysis," *Teaching in Higher Education, 6 (2).*

Knoop, R. (1984) *Case Studies in Education.* St Catharines, Ont., Praise Publishing.

Lee Yong S. (1983) "Public Management and Case Study Methods," *Teaching Political Science,* Vol. 11, No.: 1, (Fall).

Maltby, Hendrika J. and Andrusyszyn, Mary Anne. (1990) "The case study approach of teaching decision-making to post-diploma nurses," *Nurse Education Today* 10.

Marquis I. B. and Huston, C. J. (1987) *Management Decision Making for Nurses: 101 Case Studies.* Philadelphia: Lippincott.

Merseth, Katherine K. (1994) "Cases, Case Methods, and the Professional Development of Educators," *ERIC Digests*, ED401272, ERIC Clearinghouse on Teaching and Teacher Education, Washington, D.C., pp. 1-2.

Michaelsen, Larry K., Bauman Knight, Arletta, Dee Fink, L., Eds., (2002) *Team-Based Learning: A Transformative Use of Small Groups in College Teaching,* Sterling, VA: Stylus Publishing, LLC.

Monro, Joyce Huth. (1987) "Mastering the Case Method," *Innovations in Education and Training International*, Vol. 34, No.: 2, (May).

Mullan, David. (2001) *Administrative Law*. Toronto: Irwin Law Inc.

Newton, Janice., Ginsburg, Jerry., Rehner, Jan., Rogers, Pat., Sbrizzi, Susan., and Spencer, John., Eds. (2001) *Voices from the Classroom: Reflections on Teaching and Learning in Higher Education.* Toronto: Centre for Support of Teaching, York University, and Garamond Press.

Pross, A. Paul, (1990) "Assessing Public Administration Education in Canada," *Canadian Public Administration* Vol. 33, Issue 4 (Winter), pp. 618–632.

Ruggiero, Josephine A. (2002) "'Ah Ha' Learning: Using Cases and Case Studies to Teach Sociological Insights and Skills," *Sociological Practice: A Journal of Clinical and Applied Sociology,* Vol. 4, No. 2, (June), p. 115.

Shulman, L. S. (1992) "Toward a Pedagogy of Cases," in J. H. Shulman, ed., *Case Methods in Teacher Education,* pp. 1-30, New York: Teachers College Press.

Spiro, R. J. et al. (1987) "Knowledge Acquisition for Application: Cognitive Flexibility and Transfer in Complex Content Domains," in B. C. Britton, and S. Glynn, Eds. *Executive Control Processes.* pp. 177-200. Hillsdale, New Jersey: Erlbaum.

Watson, C. E. (1975) "The case-study method and learning effectiveness," *College Student Journal* 9(2), pp. 109-116.

Wilcox, Susan., Knapper, Christopher., Weisberg, Mark. (1997) *Teaching More Students:* Assessing More Students, Instructional Development Centre, Queen's University at Kingston, Canada.